Fourth Grade

Everyday Mathematics®

Math Masters

The University of Chicago School Mathematics Project

A Division of The McGraw·Hill Companies

Columbus, Ohio
Chicago, Illinois

UCSMP Elementary Materials Component

Max Bell, Director

Authors

Max Bell
John Bretzlauf
Amy Dillard
Robert Hartfield
Andy Isaacs
James McBride, Director

Kathleen Pitvorec
Peter Saecker
Robert Balfanz*
William Carroll*
Sheila Sconiers*

Technical Art

Diana Barrie

*First Edition only

Photo Credits

Phil Martin/Photography; National Aeronautics and Space Administration, p. 278
Cover: Bill Burningham/Photography; Photo Collage: Herman Adler Design Group

 This material is based upon work supported by the National Science Foundation under Grant No. ESI-9252984. Any opinions, findings, and conclusions or recommendations expressed in this material are those of the authors and do not necessarily reflect the views of the National Science Foundation.

www.sra4kids.com

SRA/McGraw-Hill

A Division of The McGraw-Hill Companies

Send all inquiries to:
SRA/McGraw-Hill
P.O. Box 812960
Chicago, IL 60681

Printed in the United States of America.

ISBN 1-57039-909-3

3 4 5 6 7 8 9 QPD 07 06 05 04 03 02 01

Contents

Teaching Masters

Unit 3

Unit 4

Unit 5

Unit 6

Assessment Masters

Calculator Masters

Game Masters

Touch and Match It Quadrangles

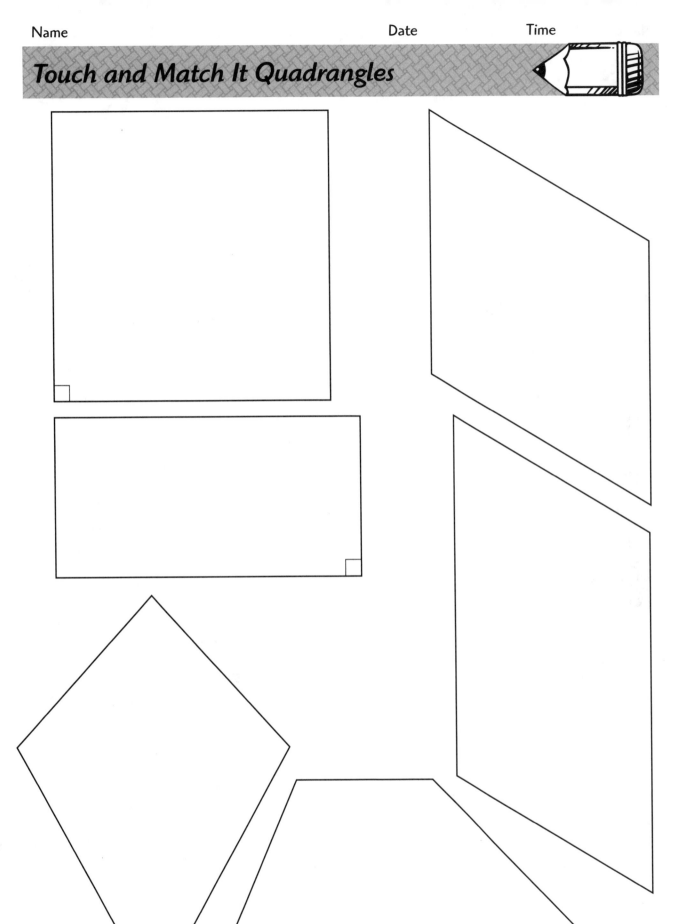

Math Message 1.4

Name _____

Date _____

True or false? Write T or F.

Every dog is

_____ a mammal

_____ an animal

_____ a cat

_____ a poodle

_____ a Saint Bernard

_____ a living thing

_____ a four-legged creature

Name _____

Date _____

True or false? Write T or F.

Every dog is

_____ a mammal

_____ an animal

_____ a cat

_____ a poodle

_____ a Saint Bernard

_____ a living thing

_____ a four-legged creature

Name _____

Date _____

True or false? Write T or F.

Every dog is

_____ a mammal

_____ an animal

_____ a cat

_____ a poodle

_____ a Saint Bernard

_____ a living thing

_____ a four-legged creature

Name _____

Date _____

True or false? Write T or F.

Every dog is

_____ a mammal

_____ an animal

_____ a cat

_____ a poodle

_____ a Saint Bernard

_____ a living thing

_____ a four-legged creature

Timed Test 1: Addition and Subtraction Facts

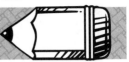

4 + 1 = _____   9 + 9 = _____   6 − 4 = _____   12 − 4 = _____

6 + 3 = _____   8 + 7 = _____   5 − 2 = _____   16 − 8 = _____

3 + 0 = _____   6 + 9 = _____   6 − 3 = _____   13 − 9 = _____

4 + 4 = _____   5 + 8 = _____   7 − 1 = _____   12 − 7 = _____

6 + 2 = _____   9 + 3 = _____   11 − 2 = _____   14 − 6 = _____

3 + 4 = _____   7 + 7 = _____   12 − 6 = _____   11 − 4 = _____

8 + 2 = _____   5 + 6 = _____   8 − 0 = _____   15 − 6 = _____

3 + 5 = _____   7 + 9 = _____   11 − 3 = _____   17 − 9 = _____

2 + 2 = _____   6 + 7 = _____   10 − 6 = _____   15 − 8 = _____

1 + 9 = _____   9 + 5 = _____   9 − 3 = _____   13 − 7 = _____

5 + 4 = _____   8 + 6 = _____   7 − 5 = _____   14 − 9 = _____

2 + 5 = _____   4 + 7 = _____   8 − 7 = _____   18 − 9 = _____

2 + 7 = _____   9 + 8 = _____   10 − 3 = _____   13 − 5 = _____

Use with Lesson 1.5.

+, − Fact Triangles 1

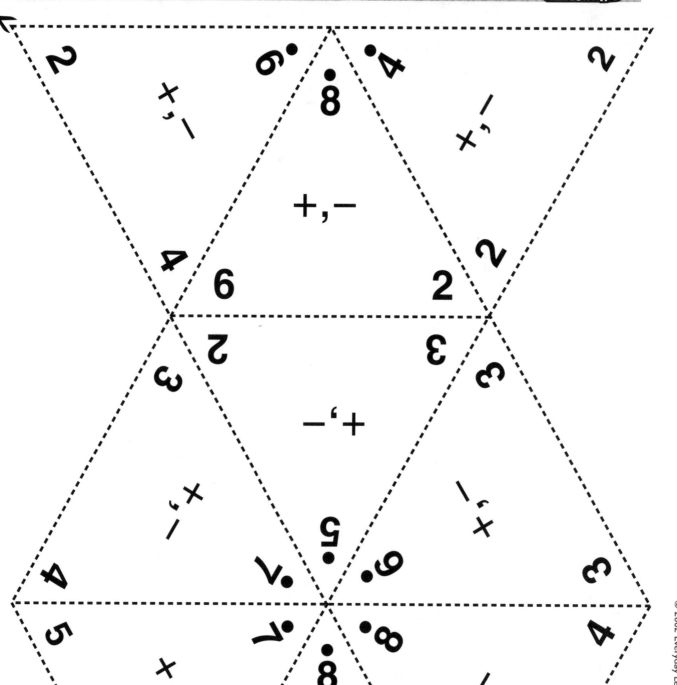

4

Use with Lesson 1.5.

+,− Fact Triangles 2

5
+,−
10 6 · · 9
9 ·
+,−
3
+,−
4
5
5
6
7
4
3 2
+,−
+,−
8
11 · 11 ·
9 ·
+,−
7
8
10 · 10 ·
10 ·
+,−
4
+,−
+,−
2 7
3 6

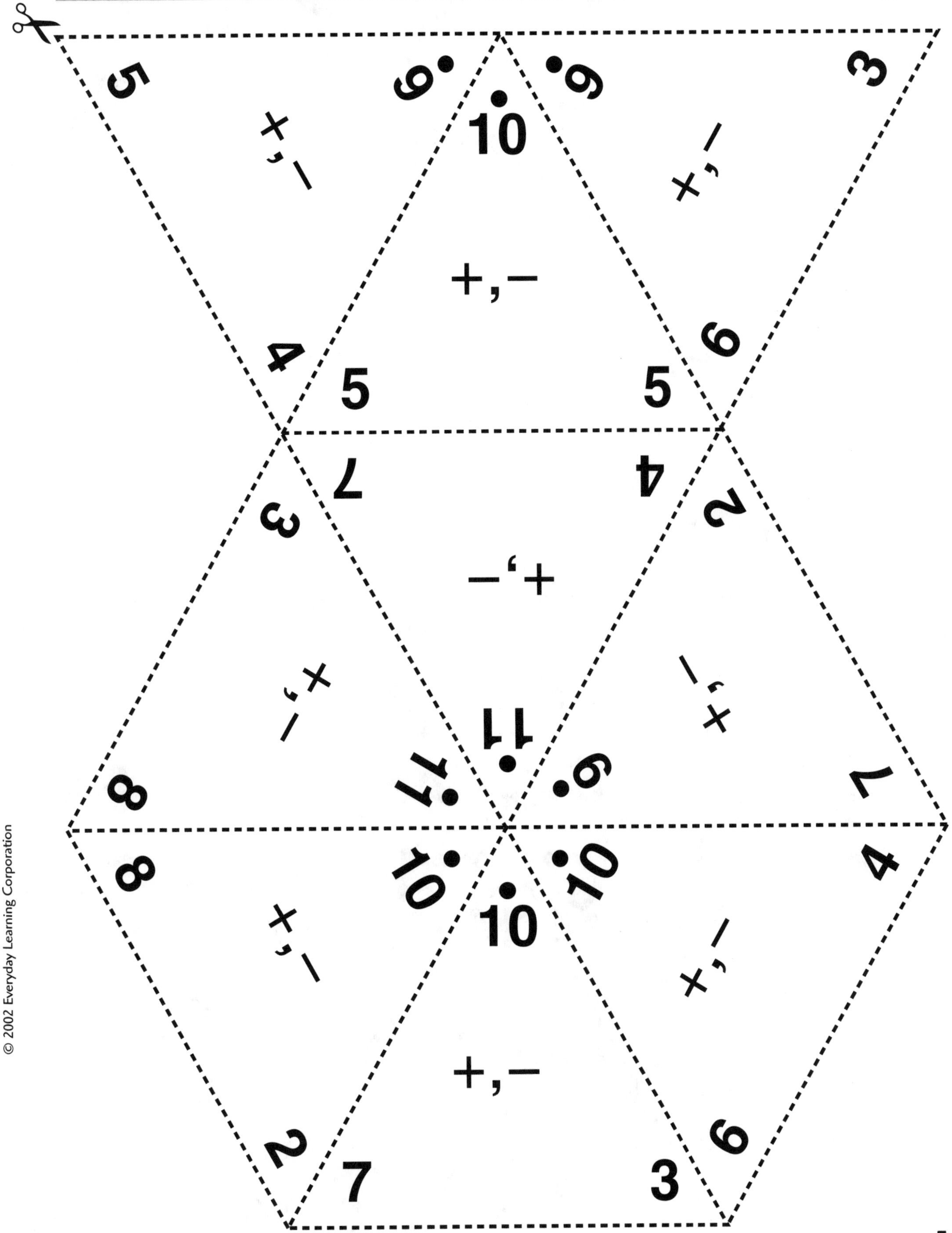

+, – Fact Triangles 3

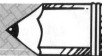

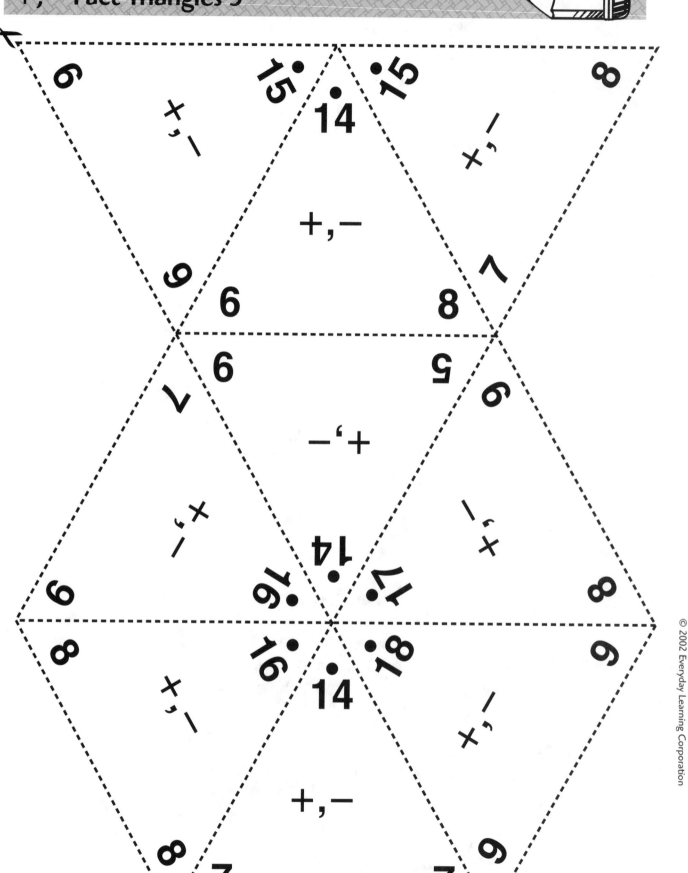

Use with Lesson 1.5.

+, − Fact Triangles 4

6   12   •11 12•   5

+, −

+, −   +, −

+, −

6   7
2   9

9   5

6   6

9

−, +

+, −   +, −

7   13•   •11 13•   4

5   13• •12   8

+, −   12

+, −   +, −

8   3   9   4

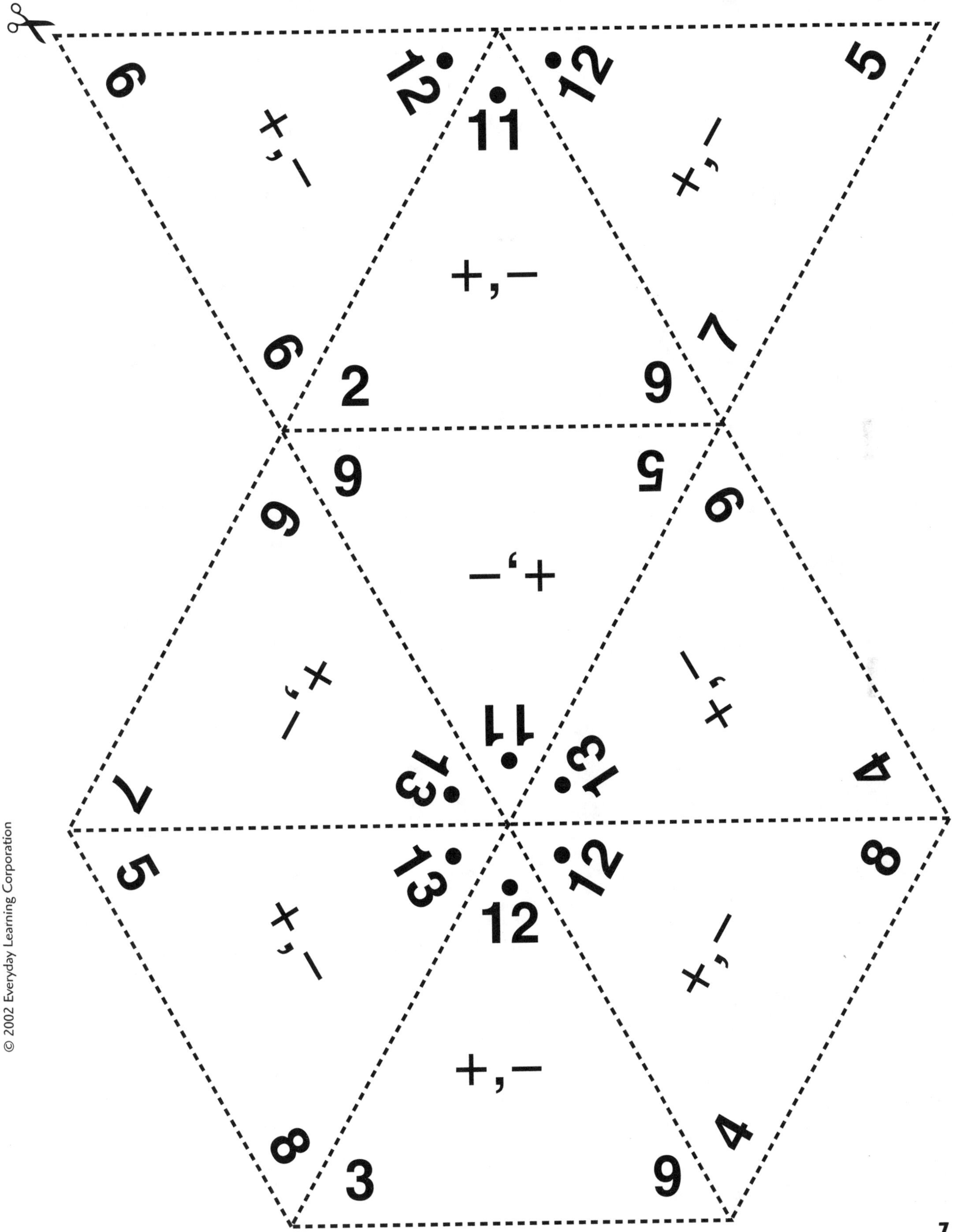

What Is a Kite?

These are kites.

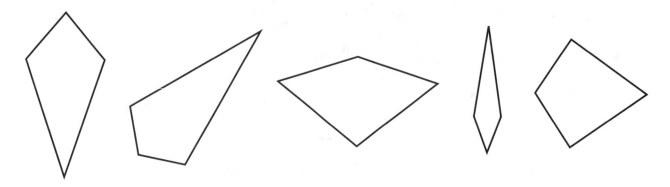

These are not kites.

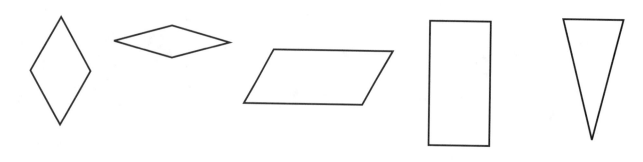

If you had to explain what a kite is, what would you say?

_____

_____

_____

_____

_____

_____

Use with Lesson 1.5.

What Is a Rhombus?

These are rhombuses.

 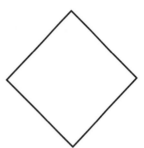 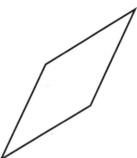 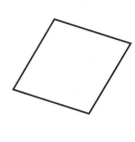

These are not rhombuses.

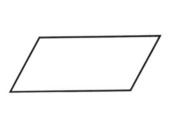  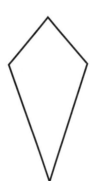  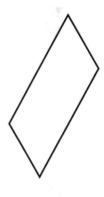

If you had to explain what a rhombus is, what would you say?

_____

_____

_____

_____

_____

_____

_____

Tangent Circles

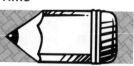

> Two circles that "barely touch" (touch at just one point) are said to be **tangent** to each other.

On a separate sheet of paper, draw two same-size circles that are tangent to each other. Then draw a third, same-size circle that is tangent to each of the other two circles.

Here's one way.

1. Draw a circle. Afterward, do not change the opening of the compass.

2. Use a straightedge to draw a line segment from the center of the circle. Make the segment at least twice as long as the radius of the circle.

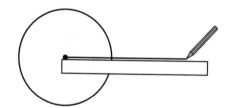

3. On this segment, mark a point that is outside of the circle. Make the distance from the circle to the point equal to the radius of the circle. Use your compass.

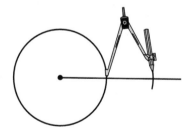

4. Draw a second circle, using the point you marked for the center of the circle.

Directions continue on *Math Masters,* page 11.

© 2002 Everyday Learning Corporation

Use with Lesson 1.7.

Tangent Circles (cont.)

5. Open the compass so that the anchor is on the center of one circle and the pencil point is on the center of the other circle.

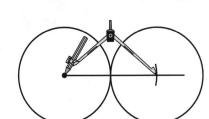

6. Swing the compass and make a mark (an arc) above the two circles.

7. Move the anchor to the center of the other circle and make an arc through the first arc.

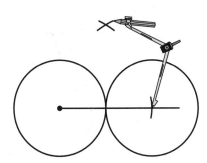

8. Close the compass to the original opening (the radius of the original circles).

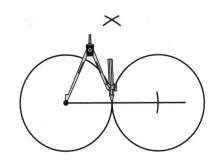

9. Put the anchor on the point where the two arcs intersect. Draw a third circle.

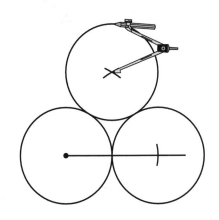

Creating 6-Point Designs

1. This 6-pointed star is called a **hexagram.** Use your compass and straightedge to construct a hexagram on a separate sheet of paper.

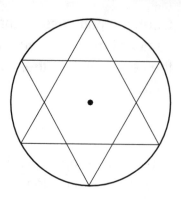

2. Construct a large hexagram on a separate sheet of paper. Draw a second hexagram inside the first, and then a third hexagram inside the second. Make a hexagram design by coloring your construction.

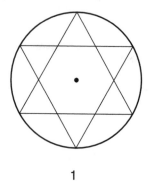 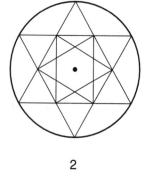 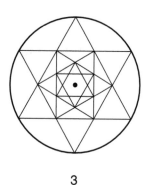 

      1   2   3   sample design

3. Construct the hexagram pattern several more times. Color each one in a different way to create a new design.

4. Construct the following pattern several times on separate sheets of paper. Color each one in a different way.

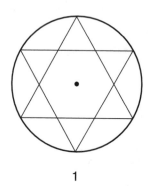 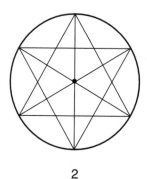 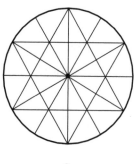

      1   2   3

5. Create and color your own 6-point designs on separate sheets of paper.

Using a Compass

1. Use a compass to draw a circle in the space below. Divide the circle into 6 equal parts.

  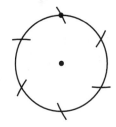

2. Construct an equilateral triangle inscribed in the circle.

Use with Lesson 1.8.

How to Construct a Kite

Follow the steps to construct a kite in the space below.

Step 1 Draw points *A* and *B*. (*See sample below.*)

Step 2 Set your compass opening so that it is a little more than half the distance between *A* and *B.* Place the point of the compass on point *A* and draw an arc. *Without changing the compass opening,* place the point of the compass on point *B* and draw a second arc that intersects the first arc. Label the point where the two arcs meet point *C.*

Step 3 Change your compass opening. Set it so that it is almost the full distance between point *A* and point *B* (about $\frac{4}{5}$ of the width). Repeat Step 2 as shown in the picture, and label the new point of intersection point *D.*

Step 4 With your straightedge, connect the 4 points to form a quadrangle.

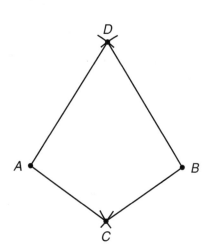

Timed Test 2: Addition and Subtraction Facts

4 + 5 = _____	8 + 8 = _____	7 − 2 = _____	13 − 6 = _____
0 + 8 = _____	7 + 6 = _____	6 − 5 = _____	12 − 5 = _____
7 + 2 = _____	5 + 9 = _____	10 − 7 = _____	14 − 8 = _____
1 + 4 = _____	6 + 8 = _____	6 − 2 = _____	11 − 7 = _____
5 + 2 = _____	7 + 8 = _____	5 − 3 = _____	15 − 9 = _____
5 + 3 = _____	9 + 6 = _____	6 − 3 = _____	14 − 5 = _____
2 + 2 = _____	9 + 7 = _____	11 − 8 = _____	18 − 9 = _____
7 + 1 = _____	7 + 4 = _____	10 − 4 = _____	13 − 8 = _____
3 + 6 = _____	8 + 9 = _____	9 − 6 = _____	17 − 8 = _____
4 + 3 = _____	8 + 5 = _____	4 − 1 = _____	15 − 7 = _____
2 + 8 = _____	3 + 9 = _____	11 − 9 = _____	12 − 8 = _____
4 + 4 = _____	7 + 7 = _____	12 − 6 = _____	16 − 8 = _____
2 + 6 = _____	6 + 5 = _____	9 − 0 = _____	13 − 4 = _____

Use with Lesson 1.9.

7-Digit Place-Value Mat

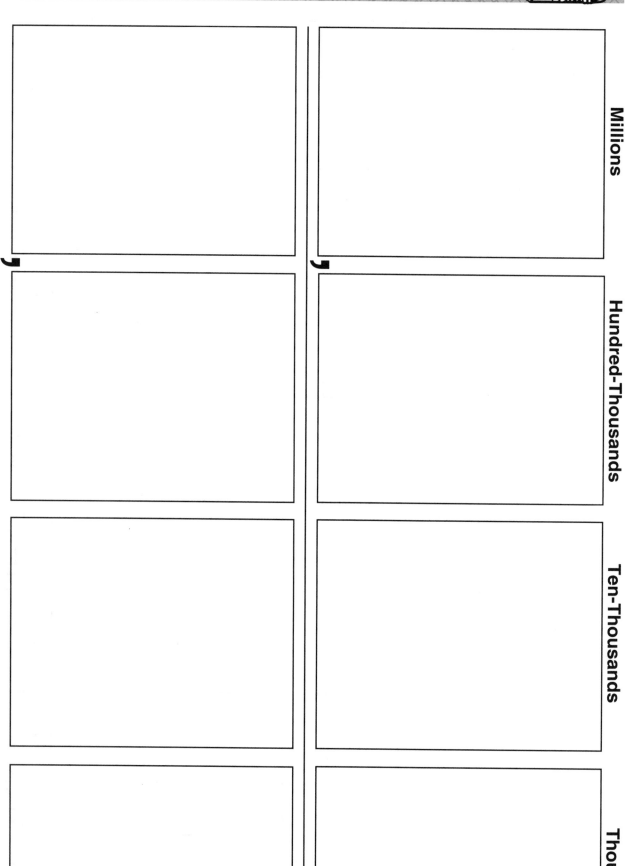

Millions

Hundred-Thousands

Ten-Thousands

Thous|

Timed Test 2: Addition and Subtraction Facts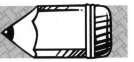

4 + 5 = _____	8 + 8 = _____	7 − 2 = _____	13 − 6 = _____
0 + 8 = _____	7 + 6 = _____	6 − 5 = _____	12 − 5 = _____
7 + 2 = _____	5 + 9 = _____	10 − 7 = _____	14 − 8 = _____
1 + 4 = _____	6 + 8 = _____	6 − 2 = _____	11 − 7 = _____
5 + 2 = _____	7 + 8 = _____	5 − 3 = _____	15 − 9 = _____
5 + 3 = _____	9 + 6 = _____	6 − 3 = _____	14 − 5 = _____
2 + 2 = _____	9 + 7 = _____	11 − 8 = _____	18 − 9 = _____
7 + 1 = _____	7 + 4 = _____	10 − 4 = _____	13 − 8 = _____
3 + 6 = _____	8 + 9 = _____	9 − 6 = _____	17 − 8 = _____
4 + 3 = _____	8 + 5 = _____	4 − 1 = _____	15 − 7 = _____
2 + 8 = _____	3 + 9 = _____	11 − 9 = _____	12 − 8 = _____
4 + 4 = _____	7 + 7 = _____	12 − 6 = _____	16 − 8 = _____
2 + 6 = _____	6 + 5 = _____	9 − 0 = _____	13 − 4 = _____

Name-Collection Boxes

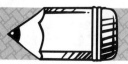

Name _____

Date _____

Name _____

Date _____

Name _____

Date _____

Name _____

Date _____

Use with Lesson 2.2.

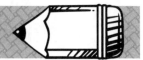

Place-Value Chart

Number	Hundred-Millions	Ten-Millions	Millions	Hundred-Thousands	Ten-Thousands	Thousands	Hundreds	Tens	Ones
	100M	10M	M	100K	10K	K	H	T	O

7-Digit Place-Value Mat

Millions

Hundred-Thousands

Ten-Thousands

Thous

Use with Lesson 2.4.

7-Digit Place-Value Mat (cont.)

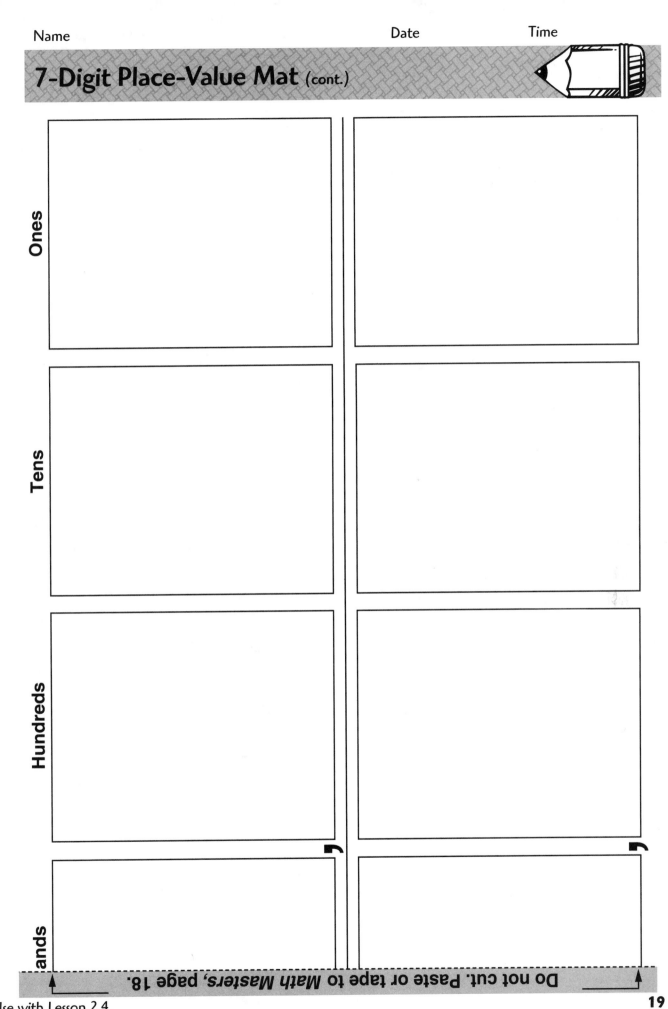

Do not cut. Paste or tape to *Math Masters*, page 18.

Use with Lesson 2.4.

Grid Paper (1 cm)

Use with Lesson 2.7.

Computation Grids

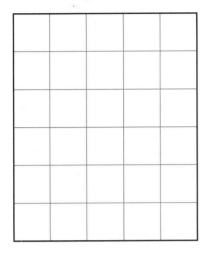
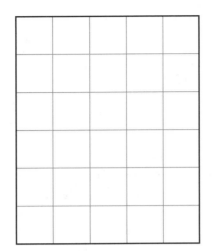
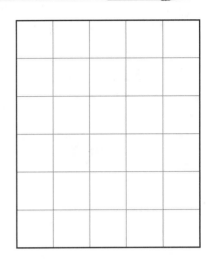

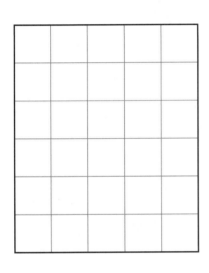
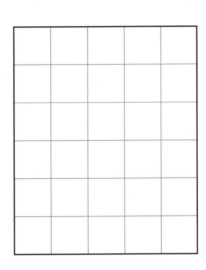
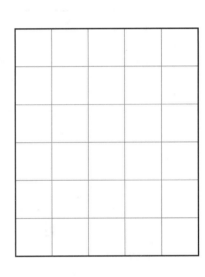

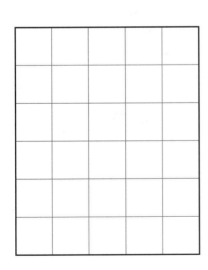
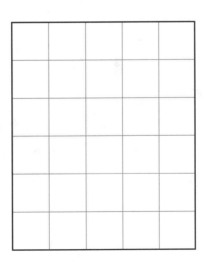
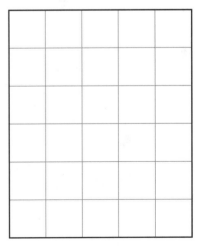

Use with Lesson 2.7.

Measuring and Drawing Line Segments

Measure the following line segments to the nearest $\frac{1}{2}$ centimeter:

1. _____

_____ cm

2. _____

_____ cm

3. _____

_____ cm

4. _____

_____ cm

Draw line segments having the following lengths:

5. 8 centimeters

6. 3.5 centimeters

7. 46 millimeters

8. 29 millimeters

Use with Lesson 2.8.

My Addition Strategy

1. Solve the problem below. Show your work.

2. Tell how you solved this problem.

_____

_____

_____

_____

_____

_____

_____

_____

Use with Lesson 2.10.

My Subtraction Strategy

1. Solve the problem below. Show your work.

2. Tell how you solved this problem.

_____

_____

_____

_____

_____

_____

_____

_____

Use with Lesson 2.10.

Multiplication/Division Facts Table

*,/	1	2	3	4	5	6	7	8	9	10
1	1	2	3	4	5	6	7	8	9	10
2	2	4	6	8	10	12	14	16	18	20
3	3	6	9	12	15	18	21	24	27	30
4	4	8	12	16	20	24	28	32	36	40
5	5	10	15	20	25	30	35	40	45	50
6	6	12	18	24	30	36	42	48	54	60
7	7	14	21	28	35	42	49	56	63	70
8	8	16	24	32	40	48	56	64	72	80
9	9	18	27	36	45	54	63	72	81	90
10	10	20	30	40	50	60	70	80	90	100

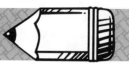

*, / Fact Triangle

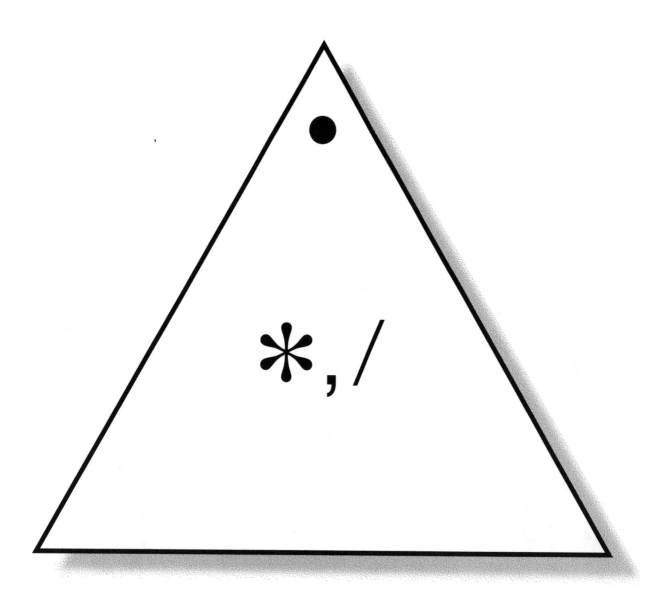

Use with Lesson 3.1.

50-Facts Test 1

7 * 7 = _____	9 * 8 = _____	5 * 8 = _____	5 * 7 = _____
5 * 6 = _____	4 * 7 = _____	5 * 3 = _____	5 * 2 = _____
3 * 8 = _____	2 * 0 = _____	7 * 8 = _____	9 * 4 = _____
7 * 9 = _____	4 * 9 = _____	6 * 4 = _____	6 * 9 = _____
0 * 4 = _____	1 * 0 = _____	3 * 9 = _____	8 * 9 = _____
6 * 6 = _____	2 * 7 = _____	7 * 6 = _____	7 * 3 = _____
4 * 5 = _____	8 * 4 = _____	5 * 5 = _____	5 * 4 = _____
3 * 5 = _____	8 * 2 = _____	9 * 9 = _____	9 * 7 = _____
9 * 5 = _____	2 * 6 = _____	7 * 2 = _____	9 * 6 = _____
4 * 1 = _____	4 * 8 = _____	2 * 9 = _____	8 * 7 = _____
2 * 4 = _____	8 * 6 = _____	4 * 4 = _____	7 * 5 = _____
5 * 9 = _____	6 * 5 = _____	8 * 8 = _____	3 * 3 = _____
4 * 3 = _____	6 * 3 = _____		

1-Minute Score: $\dfrac{\text{_____}}{50} = \dfrac{\text{_____}}{100} =$ _____ %

3-Minute Score: $\dfrac{\text{_____}}{50} = \dfrac{\text{_____}}{100} =$ _____ %

Use with Lesson 3.2.

50-Facts Test 2

6 * 6 = _____   4 * 7 = _____   8 * 3 = _____   7 * 7 = _____

5 * 0 = _____   4 * 2 = _____   6 * 5 = _____   6 * 9 = _____

4 * 4 = _____   5 * 8 = _____   5 * 5 = _____   4 * 6 = _____

6 * 3 = _____   5 * 9 = _____   9 * 8 = _____   3 * 6 = _____

8 * 7 = _____   2 * 5 = _____   8 * 2 = _____   9 * 5 = _____

2 * 7 = _____   8 * 8 = _____   7 * 8 = _____   9 * 9 = _____

4 * 9 = _____   4 * 8 = _____   8 * 6 = _____   8 * 5 = _____

5 * 3 = _____   6 * 8 = _____   9 * 7 = _____   7 * 6 = _____

8 * 1 = _____   7 * 3 = _____   3 * 3 = _____   5 * 4 = _____

3 * 8 = _____   9 * 6 = _____   7 * 5 = _____   3 * 7 = _____

7 * 9 = _____   7 * 4 = _____   9 * 4 = _____   9 * 2 = _____

6 * 7 = _____   4 * 3 = _____   4 * 5 = _____   8 * 9 = _____

3 * 5 = _____   9 * 3 = _____

1-Minute Score: _____ = _____ = _____ %
                       50   100

3-Minute Score: _____ = _____ = _____ %
                       50   100

50-Facts Test 3

2 * 0 = _____	6 * 9 = _____	4 * 6 = _____	9 * 2 = _____
3 * 3 = _____	7 * 6 = _____	9 * 3 = _____	7 * 9 = _____
5 * 7 = _____	6 * 5 = _____	5 * 6 = _____	5 * 9 = _____
5 * 5 = _____	8 * 6 = _____	3 * 7 = _____	9 * 4 = _____
4 * 8 = _____	7 * 2 = _____	9 * 5 = _____	4 * 5 = _____
4 * 4 = _____	2 * 6 = _____	9 * 9 = _____	6 * 8 = _____
3 * 9 = _____	9 * 7 = _____	8 * 5 = _____	6 * 3 = _____
2 * 4 = _____	6 * 7 = _____	2 * 3 = _____	3 * 8 = _____
9 * 6 = _____	1 * 1 = _____	7 * 7 = _____	4 * 7 = _____
8 * 7 = _____	8 * 4 = _____	7 * 5 = _____	5 * 4 = _____
9 * 8 = _____	8 * 8 = _____	6 * 4 = _____	6 * 6 = _____
3 * 5 = _____	8 * 9 = _____	7 * 8 = _____	3 * 6 = _____
3 * 4 = _____	8 * 3 = _____		

1-Minute Score: $\dfrac{\rule{2cm}{0.4pt}}{50}$ = $\dfrac{\rule{2cm}{0.4pt}}{100}$ = _____ %

3-Minute Score: $\dfrac{\rule{2cm}{0.4pt}}{50}$ = $\dfrac{\rule{2cm}{0.4pt}}{100}$ = _____ %

Use with Lesson 3.2.

50-Facts Test 4

4 * 8 = _____	7 * 5 = _____	9 * 9 = _____	7 * 6 = _____
3 * 7 = _____	5 * 7 = _____	4 * 9 = _____	3 * 4 = _____
6 * 6 = _____	5 * 8 = _____	8 * 5 = _____	4 * 5 = _____
8 * 3 = _____	1 * 3 = _____	6 * 8 = _____	8 * 8 = _____
6 * 9 = _____	7 * 9 = _____	4 * 4 = _____	9 * 4 = _____
2 * 4 = _____	9 * 8 = _____	7 * 4 = _____	9 * 6 = _____
4 * 6 = _____	2 * 8 = _____	8 * 9 = _____	7 * 3 = _____
7 * 0 = _____	5 * 5 = _____	9 * 7 = _____	2 * 9 = _____
9 * 3 = _____	3 * 1 = _____	1 * 1 = _____	6 * 4 = _____
6 * 7 = _____	8 * 6 = _____	5 * 9 = _____	3 * 6 = _____
2 * 5 = _____	1 * 0 = _____	5 * 6 = _____	6 * 2 = _____
4 * 3 = _____	3 * 5 = _____	7 * 7 = _____	8 * 7 = _____
4 * 7 = _____	7 * 2 = _____		

1-Minute Score: _____ = _____ = _____ %
                 50   100

3-Minute Score: _____ = _____ = _____ %
                 50   100

Class 50-Facts Test Scores

Write the date on the bottom line. Make a dot above each date to record each student's one-minute score.

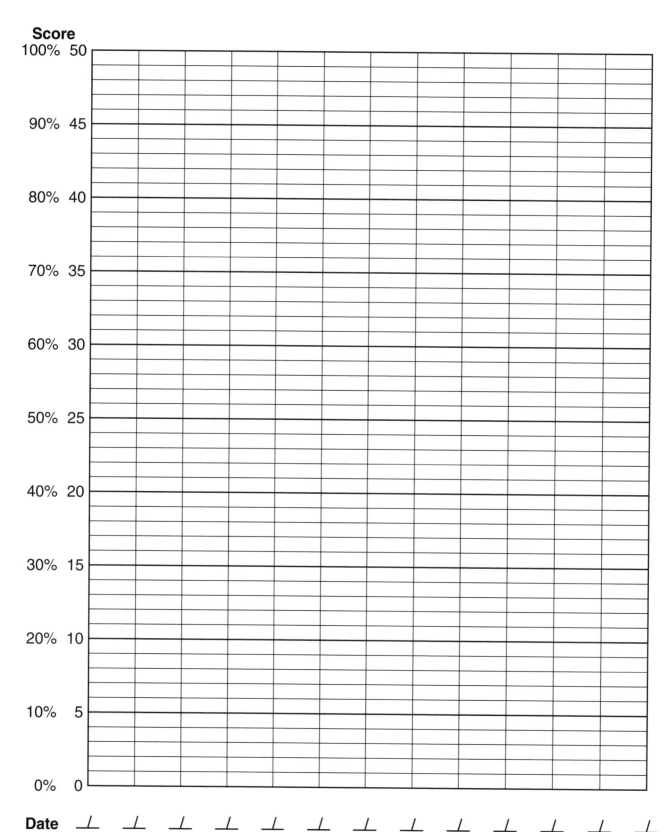

Use with Lesson 3.3.

Class 50-Facts Test Scores (cont.)

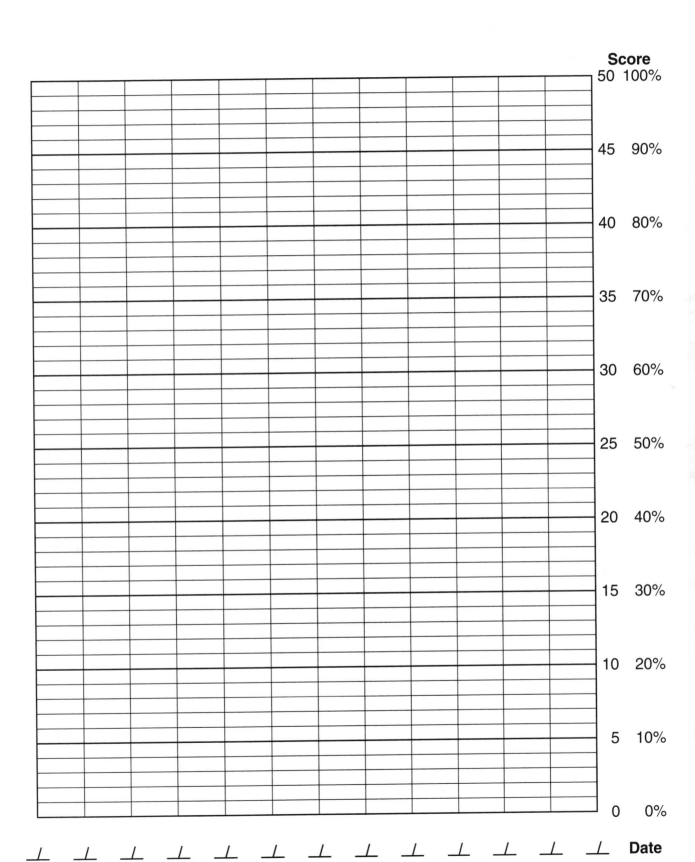

Score

Score	Percent
50	100%
45	90%
40	80%
35	70%
30	60%
25	50%
20	40%
15	30%
10	20%
5	10%
0	0%

Date

Use with Lesson 3.3.

35

My Country Notes

A. Facts about the country

_____ is located in _____.
       name of country   name of continent

1. It is bordered by _____
                               countries, bodies of water

_____.

2. Population: _____   Area: _____ square miles

3. Languages spoken: _____

_____

4. Monetary unit: _____

5. Exchange rate (optional): 1 _____ = _____

B. Facts about the capital of the country

_____   Population: _____
        name of capital

1. When it is noon in my hometown, it is _____ in _____.
                                 time (A.M. or P.M.?)   name of capital

2. In _____, the average temperature in
            month

_____ is about _____ °F.
    name of capital

3. What kinds of clothes should I pack for my visit to this capital? Why?

_____

_____

_____

_____

My Country Notes (cont.)

4. Turn to the Route Map found on journal pages 180 and 181.
Draw a line from the last city you visited to the capital of this country.

5. If your class is using the Route Log, take journal page 179 or *Math Masters,*
page 38 and record the information.

6. Can you find any facts on pages 246–249 in your *Student Reference Book*
that apply to this country? For example, is one of the 10 tallest mountains in
the world located in this country? List all the facts you can find.

_____

_____

_____

_____

_____

C. My impressions about the country

Do you know anyone who has visited or lived in this country? If so, ask
that person for an interview. Read about the country's customs and about
interesting places to visit there. Use encyclopedias, travel books, the travel
section of a newspaper, or library books. Try to get brochures from a travel
agent. Then describe below some interesting things you have learned about
this country.

_____

_____

_____

_____

_____

_____

_____

_____

_____

© 2002 Everyday Learning Corporation

My Route Log

Date	Country	Capital	Air distance from last capital	Total distance traveled so far
	1 U.S.A.	Washington, D.C.	■■■■■	
	2 Egypt	Cairo		
	3			
	4			
	5			
	6			
	7			
	8			
	9			
	10			
	11			
	12			
	13			
	14			
	15			
	16			
	17			
	18			
	19			
	20			

Use with Lesson 3.5.

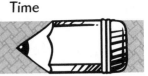

A Guide for Solving Number Stories

1. Understand the problem.

- Read the problem. Can you retell it in your own words?

- What do you know?

- What do you want to find out?

- Can you estimate what the answer might be?

- Can you draw a picture?

- Can you write a number model?

- Can you draw a diagram?

2. Plan what to do.

- Is the problem like one you have solved before?

- Is there a pattern you can use?

- Can you use arithmetic to find the answer?

- Can you use counters, base-10 blocks, or some other tool?

- Can you make a table?

- Can you guess the answer and check to see if you're right?

3. Carry out the plan.

- After you decide what to do, then do it. Be careful.

- Make a written record of what you do.

4. Look back.

- Does your answer make sense?

- Does your answer agree with other people's answers?

- Estimate the answer. Does your answer agree with your estimate?

- Can you write a number model for the problem?

- Can you solve the problem in another way?

Situation Diagrams

Total	
Part	**Part**

Total	
Part	**Part**

Total	
Part	**Part**

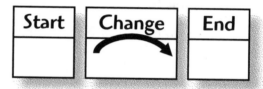

Quantity	
Quantity	**Difference**

Quantity	
Quantity	**Difference**

The Great Pyramid and the Gateway Arch

Great Pyramid of Giza

Gateway Arch

The Great Pyramid of Giza is perhaps the greatest structure ever built by humans. It stands in the desert near Cairo, Egypt. Completed about 2580 B.C., it was the tomb of Pharaoh (king) Khufu. It is estimated that 100,000 workers labored over 20 years to build the Great Pyramid. It contains more than 2 million stone blocks with an average weight of around $2\frac{1}{2}$ tons each.

Originally, the Great Pyramid was about 147 meters tall. Over the years, stones were removed from its surface, reducing its height by about 9 meters. The Great Pyramid was the tallest structure in the world for 44 centuries, until the Eiffel Tower was built in Paris in 1889.

Today, the tallest monument in the United States is the Gateway Arch, or Jefferson National Expansion Memorial, in St. Louis, Missouri. The Gateway Arch was completed in 1965 and is about 192 meters tall.

1. How much taller is the Gateway Arch than the Great Pyramid?

About _____ meters

2. Use data from the essay above to write your own problem. Ask a partner to solve it.

_____

_____

_____

_____

_____

Baseball Multiplication Playing Mat

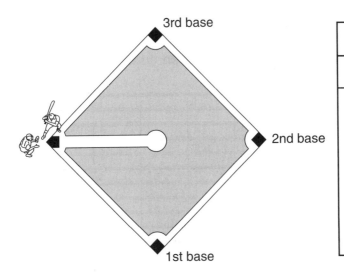

3rd base

2nd base

1st base

Hitting Table	
1-to-6 Facts	
1 to 9	Out
10 to 19	Single (1 base)
20 to 29	Double (2 bases)
30 to 35	Triple (3 bases)
36	Home Run (4 bases)

Inning		1	2	3	Total
Team 1	Outs				
	Runs				
Team 2	Outs				
	Runs				

Inning		1	2	3	Total
Team 1	Outs				
	Runs				
Team 2	Outs				
	Runs				

Inning		1	2	3	Total
Team 1	Outs				
	Runs				
Team 2	Outs				
	Runs				

Inning		1	2	3	Total
Team 1	Outs				
	Runs				
Team 2	Outs				
	Runs				

Broken Calculator

Broken Key:

To Solve:

Use with Lesson 3.10.

Broken Calculator Record Sheet

Broken Key:

To Solve:

Broken Key:

To Solve:

Broken Key:

To Solve:

Broken Key:

To Solve:

Broken Key:

To Solve:

Broken Key:

To Solve:

Logic Problems

Math Message

1. There are three children in the Smith family: Sara, Sam, and Sue.
   Use the following clues to find each child's age:

   • Each of the two younger children is half as old as the next older child.

   • The oldest is 16.

   • Sara is not the oldest.

   • Sara is twice as old as Sam.

   What is the age of each person?

   Sara _____ Sam _____ Sue _____

---

2. **a.** DeeAnn, Eric, Brooke, and Kelsey all have a favorite sport. Each one likes a different sport. Their favorite sports are basketball, swimming, golf, and tennis.

   • DeeAnn doesn't like water.

   • Both Eric and Brooke like to hit a ball.

   • Eric doesn't like to play on a playing field that has lines on it.

   What is each person's favorite sport?

   DeeAnn _____ Eric _____

   Brooke _____ Kelsey _____

   b. Write an explanation of how your group found the answers.

   _____

   _____

   _____

   _____

   _____

Use with Lesson 3.11.

Logic Problems (cont.)

3. Raoul, Martha, Kwan, and Karen like to draw. One of them likes working with colored markers best, another with watercolor paints, another with colored chalk, and another with colored pencils.

• Raoul does not like to work with paintbrushes.

• Martha likes to sharpen her drawing tools.

• Kwan and Karen do not like dust.

• Karen sometimes gets bristles in her artwork.

Find out what each child likes best. Use the logic grid to help you.

	Colored markers	Watercolor paints	Colored chalk	Colored pencils
Raoul				
Martha				
Kwan				
Karen				

Raoul _____   Martha _____

Kwan _____   Karen _____

Logic Problems (cont.)

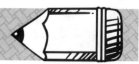

4. Sam, Don, Darla, Jon, and Sara all have a favorite kind of cookie. They each like a different kind best.

- Sam and Jon do not like peanut butter.

- Don has never tried sugar cookies and neither has Sara.

- Darla does not like raisins.

- Jon doesn't like sugar cookies.

- Darla and Jon do not like chocolate.

- Sara does like chocolate.

- Don likes cinnamon.

What kind of cookie does each like best? Use the logic grid to help you.

	Peanut butter	Sugar	Cinnamon	Oatmeal raisin	Chocolate
Sam					
Don					
Darla					
Jon					
Sara					

Sam _____ Don _____

Darla _____ Jon _____

Sara _____

Use with Lesson 3.11.

Logic Grids

Writing and Solving Number Stories

Make up number stories using some of the information below. Then solve them.

1. Maria was born July 9, 1985.

Her brother Tyrone was born in June 1988.

Her dad was 32 when she was born.

Her older sister is 4 years older than she is.

Number story:

_____

_____

_____

_____

Number model: _____

Answer: _____
                                          (unit)

2. Allison earns $5.00 per hour babysitting.

Tysha earns $4.50 per hour babysitting.

Allison earned $50.00 last week.

Tysha babysat for 6 hours last week.

Number story:

_____

_____

_____

_____

Number model: _____

Answer: _____
                                          (unit)

Use with Lesson 3.12.

10-Centimeter Grids

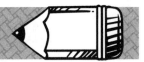

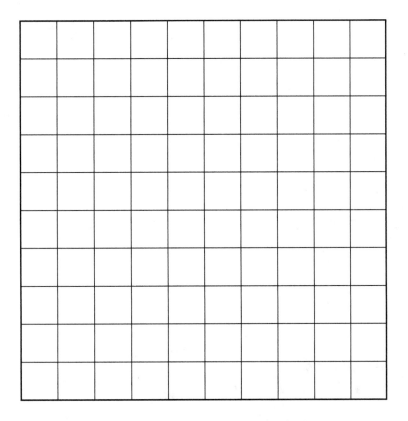

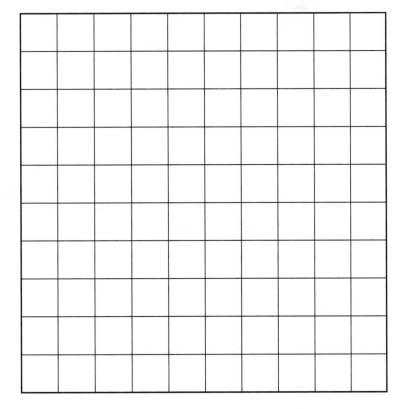

Place Value with Decimals

Part A

Anthony made a list of facts, but he forgot to use decimal points.
Rewrite each number with the decimal point in the right place.

1. It costs $33 to mail a 1-ounce letter. $_____._____

2. Linford Christie ran the 100-meter
dash in 996 seconds in the 1992 Olympics.   _____._____ seconds

3. In the same Olympics, Jan Zelezny
threw the javelin 294166 feet.   _____._____ feet

4. Valentina Yegorova ran the marathon in
2 hours, 32 minutes, and 41 seconds.
She ran a distance of 413 kilometers.   _____._____ kilometers

5. In 1993, the winner of the Indianapolis
500 car race was Emerson Fittipaldi.
His average speed was 157207 miles per hour.   _____._____ miles per hour

Part B

Use decimals. Write 3 numbers that are between the following:

6. $5 and $6 $_____._____ $_____._____ $_____._____

7. 4 centimeters and
5 centimeters   _____._____ cm   _____._____ cm   _____._____ cm

8. 21 seconds and
22 seconds   _____._____ sec   _____._____ sec   _____._____ sec

9. 8 dimes and 9 dimes $_____._____ $_____._____ $_____._____

10. 2.15 meters and
2.17 meters   _____._____ m   _____._____ m   _____._____ m

11. 0.8 meter and 0.9 meter   _____._____ m   _____._____ m   _____._____ m

Number Top–It Mat (2-place decimals)

Ones

 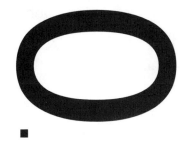

■   ■

Tenths

Hundredths

Will I Run Out of Gas?

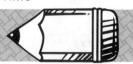

You are driving with your family from Denver, Colorado, to Des Moines, Iowa.
You know the following:

- Your car's gasoline tank holds about 12.1 gallons.

- Your car uses about 1 gallon of gasoline for every 30 miles on the highway.

- You start your trip with a full tank.

Here is a map of the route you follow.

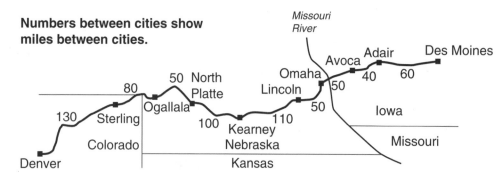

1. About how many gallons of gasoline would
your car use traveling from Denver to Sterling?   About _____ gallons

2. When you get to Ogallala, you would expect your gas tank to be

   a. almost empty.   **b.** about $\frac{1}{4}$ full.   **c.** about $\frac{1}{2}$ full.   **d.** about $\frac{3}{4}$ full.

3. Is it OK to wait until you get to Kearney to buy more gas? _____

   Explain.

   _____

   _____

   _____

4. You decide to stop at North Platte to buy more
gasoline. If you buy 7.6 gallons, about how
many gallons are there in your tank now?   About _____ gallons

5. Could you get to Des Moines from North Platte without running
out of gas if you filled your gasoline tank just one more time? _____

   If so, where would you stop? _____

Finding a Car's Gasoline Mileage

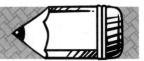

The average number of miles a car can go on 1 gallon of gasoline is called the car's gasoline **mileage.** Find out your family car's gasoline mileage. Here is what you do:

1. **First fill-up:** The next time your family goes to the gas station, ask the person pumping the gas to get a full tank. Record the number of miles shown on the odometer. (See **Mileage Record** below.)

2. **Second fill-up:** When it's time to buy gas again, ask the person at the pump to fill the tank up again. The gasoline pump will show the number of gallons it took to fill the tank. Record the number of gallons. Also, record the number of miles on the odometer.

3. Figure out how many miles were driven between the first and second fill-ups.

4. Find the average number of miles the car can go on 1 gallon of gasoline (the mileage). Use a calculator to help you find the answer. (*Hint:* Suppose your car traveled 100 miles between fill-ups and you needed 5 gallons to fill it up after driving 100 miles. On average, how many miles did your car travel on 1 gallon of gasoline? How did you find the answer?)

Mileage Record

Odometer reading on first fill-up: ____.____ miles

Odometer reading on second fill-up: ____.____ miles

Number of miles driven between fill-ups: ____.____ miles

Number of gallons used between fill-ups: ____.____ gallons

Mileage: _____ miles per gallon

Miles per Gallon

Most vehicles get better gasoline mileage on a highway than in the city. A car that travels 35 miles on a single gallon of gasoline on an interstate highway may travel only 25 miles on a gallon in stop–and–go city driving.

Cold weather can also make a difference. Most cars get better mileage in the summer than in the winter.

Whole-Number Addition and Subtraction

Use your favorite addition and subtraction methods to solve the problems.
Record your work on another sheet of paper.

1. $48 + 79 =$ _____

2. $296 + 514 =$ _____

3. $937 + 652 =$ _____

4. _____ $= 392 + 75$

5. _____ $= 1,156 + 555$

6. $23 + 45 + 12 =$ _____

7. $98 - 57 =$ _____

8. _____ $= 122 - 82$

9. _____ $= 900 - 632$

10. _____ $= 512 - 239$

11. $822 - 468 =$ _____

12. $706 - 459 =$ _____

© 2002 Everyday Learning Corporation

Name   Date   Time

Whole-Number Addition and Subtraction

Use your favorite addition and subtraction methods to solve the problems.
Record your work on another sheet of paper.

1. $48 + 79 =$ _____

2. $296 + 514 =$ _____

3. $937 + 652 =$ _____

4. _____ $= 392 + 75$

5. _____ $= 1,156 + 555$

6. $23 + 45 + 12 =$ _____

7. $98 - 57 =$ _____

8. _____ $= 122 - 82$

9. _____ $= 900 - 632$

10. _____ $= 512 - 239$

11. $822 - 468 =$ _____

12. $706 - 459 =$ _____

© 2002 Everyday Learning Corporation

A Hiking Trail

The Batona Trail is a hiking trail in Southern New Jersey. The Batona Hiking Club measured the trail very carefully and found that it is about 47.60 kilometers long.

The trail crosses several roads, so it can be reached by car at a number of places.

Carpenter Spring is at the north end of the trail. Washington Road, near Batsto, is at the trail's south end.

Go to *Math Masters,* page 56.

Map of Batona Trail

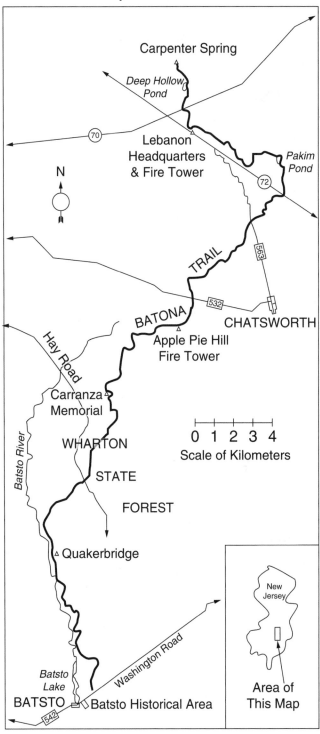

Source: Batona Hiking Club of Philadelphia

© 2002 Everyday Learning Corporation

Name   Date   Time

A Hiking Trail (cont.)

The following table shows distances from several points of interest on the trail to the north and south ends of the trail. Fill in the missing distances.

Batona Trail		
Point of Interest	**Distance from Carpenter Spring (km)**	**Distance from Washington Road (km)**
Carpenter Spring	0	47.60
Deep Hollow Pond	1.91	45.69
Route 70	3.37	
Lebanon Headquarters	4.66	
Pakim Pond	9.91	
Route 72	12.10	
Route 563		33.56
Route 532	19.53	
Apple Pie Hill Fire Tower	21.31	
Carranza Memorial		19.80
Hay Road	33.05	
Quakerbridge	37.92	9.68
Washington Road	47.60	0

How can you check your answers?

_____

_____

_____

_____

© 2002 Everyday Learning Corporation

Use with Lesson 4.5.

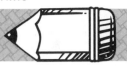

Items to Purchase

light bulbs 4-pack **$1.09** 	VCR tape **$3.25** 	tissues **$0.73** 
transparent tape **$0.84** 	batteries **$3.59** 	toothpaste **$1.39**
ballpoint pen **$0.39** 	tennis balls can of 3 **$2.59** 	paperback book **$2.99** 

Use with Lesson 4.5.

$1 and $10 Bills

Number Top–It Mat (3-place decimals)

Ones

Tenths

Hundredths

Thousandths

Use with Lesson 4.6.

59

Name _____ Date _____ Time _____

Pole Vault Measurements

The table below shows the 10 highest outdoor pole vaults.

1. Convert between meters and centimeters to complete the table.

Athlete	Country	Year	Height (m)	Height (cm)
Sergey Bubka	Ukraine	1994	6.14	
Okkert Brits	SA	1995	6.03	
Igor Trandenkov	Russia	1996		601
Rodion Gataullin	USSR	1989		600
Lawrence Johnson	United States	1996	5.98	
Scott Huffman	United States	1994	5.97	
Joe Dial	United States	1987	5.96	
Andrei Tiwontschik	Germany	1996		595
Maxim Tarasov	Russia	1997	5.95	
Jean Galfioine	France	1994		594

Source: The Top Ten of Everything 2000

For each of the questions below, record the measurement in both meters and centimeters.

2. What is the maximum pole vault height? _____ m _____ cm

3. What is the minimum pole vault height? _____ m _____ cm

4. What is the range of this data set? _____ m _____ cm

5. What is the mode of this data set? _____ m _____ cm

Challenge

6. What is the median of this data set? _____ m _____ cm

© 2002 Everyday Learning Corporation

Use with Lesson 4.7.

A cm/mm Ruler

Decimals and Metric Units

Symbols for Metric Units of Length	
meter	m
decimeter	dm
centimeter	cm
millimeter	mm

1 decimeter

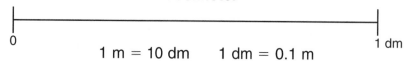

0   1 dm

1 m = 10 dm   1 dm = 0.1 m

10 centimeters

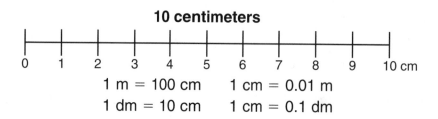

0   1   2   3   4   5   6   7   8   9   10 cm

1 m = 100 cm   1 cm = 0.01 m

1 dm = 10 cm   1 cm = 0.1 dm

100 millimeters

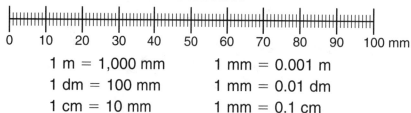

0   10   20   30   40   50   60   70   80   90   100 mm

1 m = 1,000 mm   1 mm = 0.001 m

1 dm = 100 mm   1 mm = 0.01 dm

1 cm = 10 mm   1 mm = 0.1 cm

Use your tape measure to help you
fill in the answers below.

Challenge

1. **a.** 5 cm = _____ mm   **b.** 4.2 cm = _____ mm   **c.** 0.8 cm = _____ mm

2. **a.** 30 mm = _____ cm   **b.** 64 mm = _____ cm   **c.** 5 mm = _____ cm

3. **a.** 3 m = _____ cm   **b.** 2.6 m = _____ cm   **c.** 0.43 m = _____ cm

4. **a.** 500 cm = _____ m   **b.** 780 cm = _____ m   **c.** 65 cm = _____ m

5. **a.** 4 m = _____ mm   **b.** 6.1 m = _____ mm   **c.** 0.750 m = _____ mm

6. Draw a line segment 12.5 centimeters long. Use a sharp pencil to get the
greatest accuracy.

Place-Value Number Lines

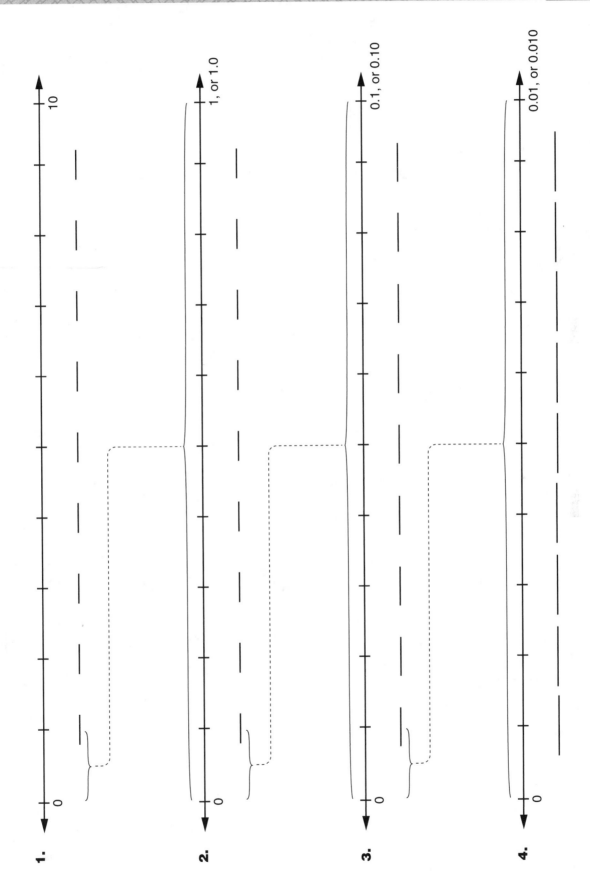

1.   10   0

2.   1, or 1.0   0

3.   0.1, or 0.10   0

4.   0.01, or 0.010   0

Place-Value Chart

1,000s	100s	10s	1s	.					
Thousands	Hundreds	Tens	Ones						

Use with Lesson 4.10.

Place-Value Flip Book

1. Cut each page along the dashed lines. – – – – – –

   Do NOT cut any of the solid lines!

2. Assemble with the pages in order.

3. Staple the assembled book. (Ask your teacher to help if you need it.)

4. Cut along the vertical dashed lines to
   separate the digits on each page.

Name _____   page 1

| | | | | |

page 2

0 0. 0 0 0

page 3

1 1. 1 1 1

Place-Value Flip Book (cont.)

page 4

2 2. 2 2 2

page 5

3 3. 3 3 3

page 6

4 4. 4 4 4

Use with Lesson 4.10.

Place-Value Flip Book (cont.)

page 7

| 5 | 5. | 5 | 5 | 5 |

page 8

| 6 | 6. | 6 | 6 | 6 |

page 9

| 7 | 7. | 7 | 7 | 7 |

Use with Lesson 4.10.

Place-Value Flip Book (cont.)

page 10

| 8 | 8. | 8 | 8 | 8 |

page 11

| 9 | 9. | 9 | 9 | 9 |

page 12

| Tens | Ones | Tenths | Hundredths | Thousandths |

Use with Lesson 4.10.

Beat the Calculator Gameboard

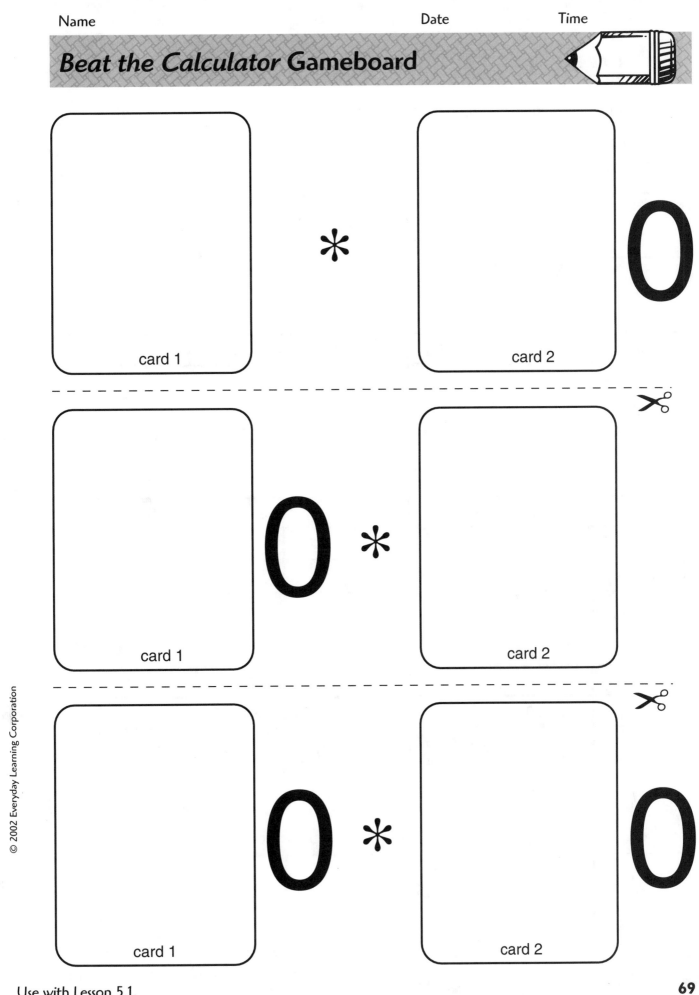

card 1   *   card 2   O

card 1   O   *   card 2

card 1   O   *   card 2   O

Multiplication and Division Fact Extensions

Solve the multiplication/division puzzles. Fill in the blank boxes.

Examples

*,/	300	2,000
2	600	4,000
3	900	6,000

*,/	80	50
4	320	200
8	640	400

1.

*,/	70	400
8		
9		

2.

*,/	5	7
8,000		
600		

3.

*,/	9	4
50		
7,000		

4.

*,/		600
7	3,500	
		2,400

5.

*,/		80
30	2,700	
		56,000

6.

*,/	4,000	
	36,000	
20		10,000

Make up and solve some puzzles of your own.

7.

*,/		

8.

*,/		

Use with Lesson 5.1.

Weights of Dogs

St. Bernard
140–200 pounds

Mastiff
150–160 pounds

Labrador retriever
55–75 pounds

Standard poodle
45–70 pounds

Siberian husky
35–60 pounds

Coonhound
50–60 pounds

Bearded collie
50–60 pounds

Rat terrier
12–35 pounds

Beagle
20–25 pounds

Basenji
22–24 pounds

Lhasa apso
13–15 pounds

Maltese
4–6 pounds

Multiplication Wrestling Worksheet

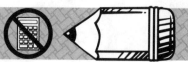

Round 1   Cards: _____   _____   _____   _____

Numbers formed: _____ * _____

Teams: (_____ + _____) * (_____ + _____)

Products: _____ * _____ = _____

_____ * _____ = _____

_____ * _____ = _____

_____ * _____ = _____

Total (add 4 products):   _____

Round 2   Cards: _____   _____   _____   _____

Numbers formed: _____ * _____

Teams: (_____ + _____) * (_____ + _____)

Products: _____ * _____ = _____

_____ * _____ = _____

_____ * _____ = _____

_____ * _____ = _____

Total (add 4 products):   _____

Round 3   Cards: _____   _____   _____   _____

Numbers formed: _____ * _____

Teams: (_____ + _____) * (_____ + _____)

Products: _____ * _____ = _____

_____ * _____ = _____

_____ * _____ = _____

_____ * _____ = _____

Total (add 4 products):   _____

Use with Lesson 5.2.

Adding Multidigit Numbers

1. 300
  + 80

2. 400
  + 260

3. 1,200
  + 400

4. 250
  + 75

5. 380
  + 940

6. 4,700
  + 900

7. 2,000
    400
  + 32

8. 4,000
    830
    500
  + 67

9. 6,400
    560
    320
  + 58

Extended Multiplication Facts

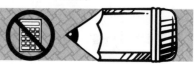

1. 6 * 7 = _____

6 * 70 = _____

60 * 7 = _____

60 * 70 = _____

600 * 7 = _____

60 * 700 = _____

2. 9 * 3 = _____

9 * 30 = _____

90 * 3 = _____

90 * 30 = _____

900 * 3 = _____

90 * 300 = _____

3. 4 * 8 = _____

4 * 80 = _____

40 * 8 = _____

40 * 80 = _____

400 * 8 = _____

40 * 800 = _____

4. 5 * _____ = 15

30 * _____ = 150

30 * _____ = 1,500

_____ * 50 = 150

_____ * 500 = 1,500

30 * _____ = 15,000

5. _____ * 9 = 54

_____ * 90 = 540

_____ * 90 = 5,400

60 * _____ = 540

6 * _____ = 5,400

6 * _____ = 54,000

6. 8 * _____ = 40

8 * _____ = 4,000

80 * _____ = 4,000

_____ * 50 = 400

_____ * 5 = 400

_____ * 500 = 400,000

Use with Lesson 5.2.

Number Puzzle

Cut out the number tiles at the bottom of the page. Use nine of the tiles to fill in the nine missing digits. One tile will be left over. Record your answers in the boxes.

9 ☐ − ☐ 5 = 1 1

3 ☐ 7 − ☐ 9 = ☐ 1 8

9 6 ☐ + 5 ☐ 5 = 1, 4 7 9

1 ☐ 6 + 9 3 = 1 9 ☐

Which digit was not used? _____

0	1	2	3	4	5	6	7	8	9

A Traveling Salesperson Problem

An Unsolved Problem in Mathematics and Computer Science

A salesperson plans to visit several cities. To save time and money, the trip should be as short as possible. If the salesperson is going to only a few cities, it would be easy to figure out the shortest possible route. But what if the trip includes 10 cities? There would be 3,628,800 possible routes!

Computers are often used to solve mathematical problems. A computer could be used to examine all the possible routes between 10 cities. However, if the salesperson needs to visit 100 cities, there is no computer that has enough power or memory to examine all the possible routes. Computer scientists are still trying to find ways to solve this problem without having to do an impossible number of calculations.

Try to think like a computer. Pick four cities on the map on journal page 119. Find the shortest route that would take you from one city to each of the other three. Remember, computers do not try out every route to find the shortest one. Computer scientists design programs that tell computers to estimate some routes and ignore any that do not make sense.

Cities to be visited:

_____   _____

_____   _____

Describe the shortest route between the four cities in the space below.

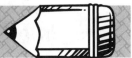

What Do Americans Eat?

Answer the following questions:

1. How many glasses of fruit juice did you drink in the last 7 days?   _____

2. How many hot dogs did you eat in the last 7 days?   _____

3. How many hamburgers did you eat in the last 7 days?   _____

Answer the following questions:

1. How many glasses of fruit juice did you drink in the last 7 days?   _____

2. How many hot dogs did you eat in the last 7 days?   _____

3. How many hamburgers did you eat in the last 7 days?   _____

Answer the following questions:

1. How many glasses of fruit juice did you drink in the last 7 days?   _____

2. How many hot dogs did you eat in the last 7 days?   _____

3. How many hamburgers did you eat in the last 7 days?   _____

Answer the following questions:

1. How many glasses of fruit juice did you drink in the last 7 days?   _____

2. How many hot dogs did you eat in the last 7 days?   _____

3. How many hamburgers did you eat in the last 7 days?   _____

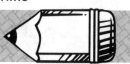

Rounding Practice

For Problems 1–3, write the lower number, the higher number, and the halfway number below each number line. Then write the answer to complete the sentence.

1. Round 3,546 to the nearest hundred.

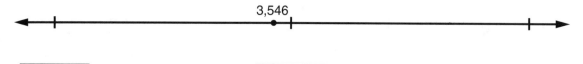

3,546 rounded to the nearest hundred is _____ .

2. Round 3,546 to the nearest ten.

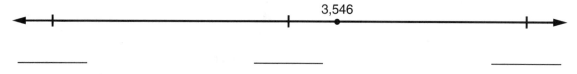

3,546 rounded to the nearest ten is _____ .

3. Round 3,546 to the nearest thousand.

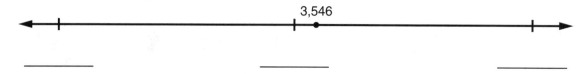

3,546 rounded to the nearest thousand is _____ .

4. Round 75,218 to the nearest thousand. _____

5. Round 58,083 to the nearest hundred. _____

6. Round 92,054 to the nearest hundred. _____

7. Round 888 to the nearest ten. _____

8. Round 99,621 to the nearest thousand. _____

9. Round 468,621 to the nearest thousand. _____

Use with Lesson 5.4.

Computational Estimation

1. Which of the following is closest to the product of 98 and 32?	30	300	3,000	30,000
2. Which of the following is closest to the sum of 591, 1,534, and 792?	1,800	2,300	2,800	3,100
3. Which of the following is closest to the difference between 714 and 382?	100	200	300	400

Solve the problems and show your work.

4. Carolyn has $5.00. She wants to buy the following for lunch: a hamburger for $1.95, french fries for 89 cents, and a fruit drink for $1.25. Does she have enough money?

_____

5. A school raised $423 at its bake sale. The money will be divided among 5 grade levels at the school. Will each grade level get more or less than $75?

_____

6. The average eye blinks once every 5 seconds. Is that more or less than one hundred-thousand times a day?

_____

Computation Grids

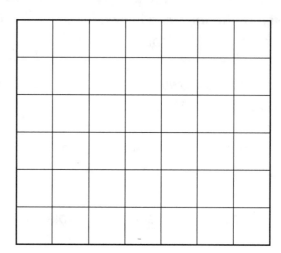

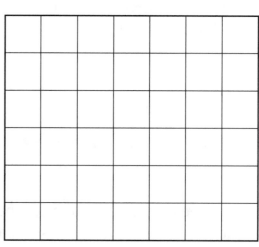

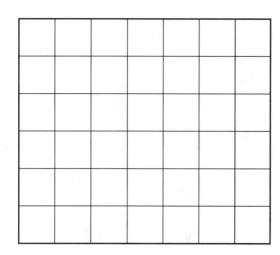

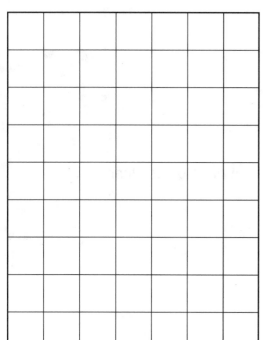

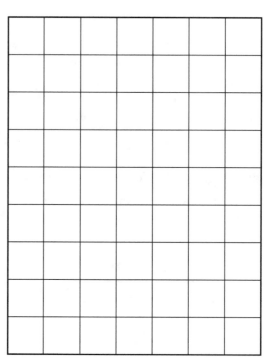

Use with Lesson 5.5.

Array Grid

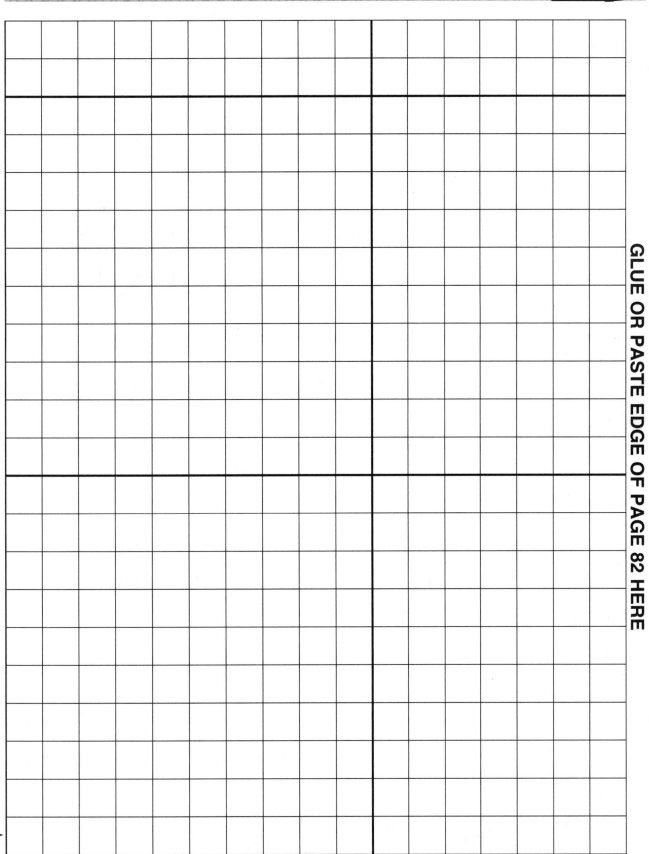

GLUE OR PASTE EDGE OF PAGE 82 HERE

© 2002 Everyday Learning Corporation

→ **Start here.**

Array Grid (cont.)

Use with Lesson 5.5.

Multiplication of Whole Numbers

1. A case of soda pop holds 24 cans. Thirty-three cases were purchased for the Hoffman School field day. How many cans of soda were purchased?

_____ cans

3. Complete the "What's My Rule?" table.

Rule
out = in * 7

in	out
8	
	420
	6,300
13	

2. Multiply.

a. 45 * 89 = _____

b. 314 * 23 = _____

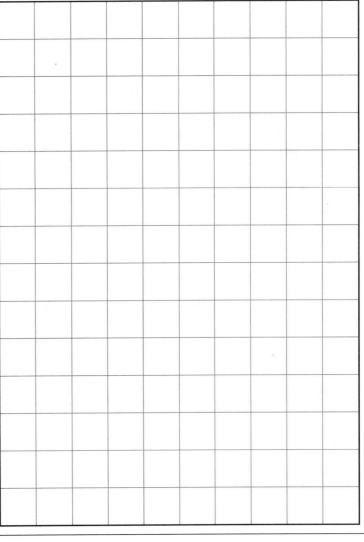

4. Write and solve a multiplication number story using the numbers 73 and 68.

_____

_____

_____

_____

Answer: _____
(unit)

A Multiplication Wrestling Competition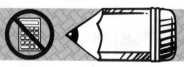

1. Twelve players entered a *Multiplication Wrestling* competition. The numbers they chose are shown in the following table. The score of each player is the product of the two numbers. For example, Aidan's score is 741, because 13 * 57 = 741. Which of the 12 players do you think has the highest score? _____

Group A	Group B	Group C
Aidan: 13 * 57	Indira: 15 * 73	Miguel: 17 * 35
Colette: 13 * 75	Jelani: 15 * 37	Rex: 17 * 53
Emily: 31 * 75	Kuniko: 51 * 37	Sarah: 71 * 53
Gunnar: 31 * 57	Liza: 51 * 73	Tanisha: 71 * 35

Check your guess with the following procedure. *Don't do any arithmetic for Steps 2 and 3.*

2. In each pair below, cross out the player with the lower score. Find that player's name in the table above and cross it out as well.

Aidan; Colette	Indira; Jelani	Miguel; Rex
Emily; Gunnar	Kuniko; Liza	Sarah; Tanisha

3. Two players are left in Group A. Cross out the one with the lower score.

Two players are left in Group B. Cross out the one with the lower score.

Two players are left in Group C. Cross out the one with the lower score.

Which 3 players are still left?

_____

4. Of the 3 players who are left, which player has the lowest score? _____
Cross out that player's name.

5. There are 2 players left. What are their scores? _____

_____

6. Who won the competition? _____

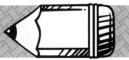

Computation Grids for Lattice Multiplication

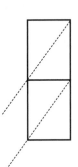 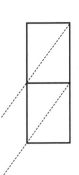 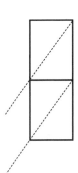

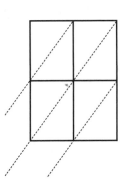 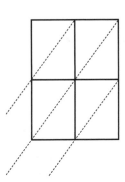 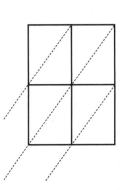

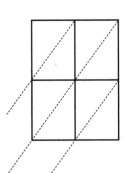 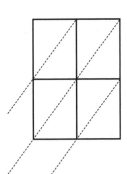 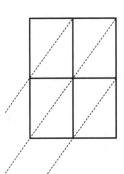

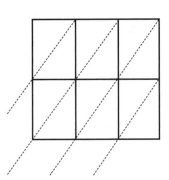 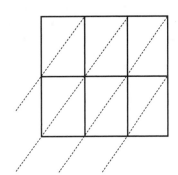 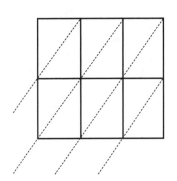

Use with Lesson 5.7.

A 50 by 40 Array

Use with Lesson 5.8.

Name _____ Date _____ Time _____

A Roomful of Dots

Suppose you filled your classroom from floor to ceiling with dot paper
(2,000 dots per sheet).

1. About how many dots do you think there would be on all the paper needed
to fill your classroom? Make a check mark next to your guess.

_____ less than a million

_____ between a million and half a billion

_____ between half a billion and a billion

_____ more than a billion

2. One ream of paper weighs about 5 pounds. About how many pounds would the
paper needed to fill your classroom weigh? Make a check mark next to your guess.

_____ less than 100,000 pounds

_____ between 100,000 pounds and 500,000 pounds

_____ between 500,000 pounds and a million pounds

_____ more than a million pounds

3. Work with your group to make more accurate estimates of the number of dots
and the weight of the dot paper needed to fill your classroom. Explain what you did.

My group's estimates:

Number of dots: _____   Weight of paper: _____

_____

_____

_____

_____

_____

_____

_____

_____

Representing Population Counts

Dot Paper Information

Each sheet of paper has 2,000 dots on it.
1 ream has 500 sheets.
1 carton contains 10 reams.

Pretend that each dot on a sheet of paper stands for 1 person.

1. How many people are represented by 1 ream of dot paper? _____

2. How many people are represented by 1 full carton of paper? _____

3. In the table below, round each population to the nearest million. Then write the number of full cartons and extra reams of dot paper needed to represent each country.

Country	Population	Round to Nearest Million	Number of Full Cartons	Number of Extra Reams
France	58,978,000			
Greece	10,707,000			
Hungary	10,186,000			
Iceland	273,000			
Italy	56,735,000			
Netherlands	15,808,000			
Norway	4,439,000			
Poland	38,609,000			
Spain	39,168,000			
United Kingdom	59,113,000			

4. The population of Poland is about 10 times the population of which country in the table?

_____

5. True or false? The population of Italy is about $\frac{1}{5}$ the *total population* of all the other countries in the table. Explain your answer.

_____

_____

Use with Lesson 5.10.

Computation-Tile Problems

Cut out the 20 computation tiles at the bottom of the page. Use them to help you solve the problems.

1. Use five odd-number tiles to make the largest possible sum.

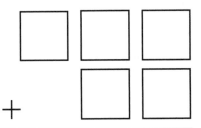

2. Use five even-number tiles (that include 0) to make the smallest possible sum. Do not use 0 as the first digit.

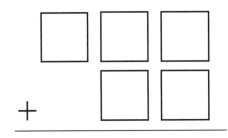

3. Use five odd-numbered tiles to make the smallest possible difference.

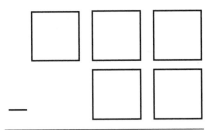

4. Use five even-numbered tiles (that include 0) to make the largest possible difference. Do not use 0 as the first digit.

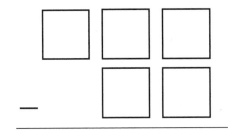

5. Use each of the tiles 0 through 9 once to find the missing digits in these number sentences.

a. $7\ \boxed{} - \boxed{}\ 3 = 36$

b. $9\ \boxed{}\ 2 - \boxed{}\ 56 = 82\ \boxed{}$

c. $7\ \boxed{}\ 4 + \boxed{}\ 15 = 1{,}289$

d. $1\ \boxed{}\ 4 + 8\ \boxed{} = \boxed{}\ 14$

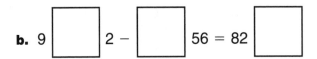

0	1	2	3	4	5	6	7	8	9
0	1	2	3	4	5	6	7	8	9

Use with Lesson 5.12.

Name Date Time

My Multiplication Strategy

1. Solve the problem below. Show your work.

2. Tell how you solved this problem.

Use with Lesson 5.12.

Estimation Problems

Here is some information you will need to answer Problems 1–3:

- You can cover a sheet of paper with about 6 one-dollar bills.

- There are 500 sheets in 1 ream of paper.

- There are 10 reams in 1 carton of paper.

- One ream of paper weighs about 5 pounds.

- Your suitcase holds about as many bills as a carton of paper.

1. Imagine if you had 1 million dollars in $1 bills. Could that money fit into your suitcase? Explain your answer.

   Ask: About how many $1 bills would fit in the suitcase?

   _____

   _____

   _____

   _____

   _____

   _____

2. What if the money in $100 bills? Would the money fit in the suitcase? Explain your answer.

   _____

   _____

   _____

   _____

   _____

   _____

Estimation Problems (cont.)

3. Do you think you would be able to carry 1 million dollars in $100 bills? Explain your answer.

Ask: About how many pounds would the money weigh?

_____

_____

_____

_____

_____

4. Imagine you found 10 suitcases of money and you wanted to count it in the shortest amount of time. If you were given the choice of counting the money in either 1 million minutes or 1 thousand weeks, which would you choose? Why?

_____

_____

_____

_____

_____

_____

Use with Lesson 5.12.

Equal Groups

1 [   ] = _____   10 [s] = _____   1 [   ] = _____   10 [s] = _____

2 [s] = _____   20 [s] = _____   2 [s] = _____   20 [s] = _____

3 [s] = _____   30 [s] = _____   3 [s] = _____   30 [s] = _____

4 [s] = _____   40 [s] = _____   4 [s] = _____   40 [s] = _____

5 [s] = _____   50 [s] = _____   5 [s] = _____   50 [s] = _____

---

1 [   ] = _____   10 [s] = _____   1 [   ] = _____   10 [s] = _____

2 [s] = _____   20 [s] = _____   2 [s] = _____   20 [s] = _____

3 [s] = _____   30 [s] = _____   3 [s] = _____   30 [s] = _____

4 [s] = _____   40 [s] = _____   4 [s] = _____   40 [s] = _____

5 [s] = _____   50 [s] = _____   5 [s] = _____   50 [s] = _____

---

1 [   ] = _____   10 [s] = _____   1 [   ] = _____   10 [s] = _____

2 [s] = _____   20 [s] = _____   2 [s] = _____   20 [s] = _____

3 [s] = _____   30 [s] = _____   3 [s] = _____   30 [s] = _____

4 [s] = _____   40 [s] = _____   4 [s] = _____   40 [s] = _____

5 [s] = _____   50 [s] = _____   5 [s] = _____   50 [s] = _____

---

1 [   ] = _____   10 [s] = _____   1 [   ] = _____   10 [s] = _____

2 [s] = _____   20 [s] = _____   2 [s] = _____   20 [s] = _____

3 [s] = _____   30 [s] = _____   3 [s] = _____   30 [s] = _____

4 [s] = _____   40 [s] = _____   4 [s] = _____   40 [s] = _____

5 [s] = _____   50 [s] = _____   5 [s] = _____   50 [s] = _____

Easy Multiples

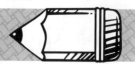

200 * _____ = _____

100 * _____ = _____

50 * _____ = _____

20 * _____ = _____

10 * _____ = _____

5 * _____ = _____

1 * _____ = _____

200 * _____ = _____

100 * _____ = _____

50 * _____ = _____

20 * _____ = _____

10 * _____ = _____

5 * _____ = _____

1 * _____ = _____

200 * _____ = _____

100 * _____ = _____

50 * _____ = _____

20 * _____ = _____

10 * _____ = _____

5 * _____ = _____

1 * _____ = _____

200 * _____ = _____

100 * _____ = _____

50 * _____ = _____

20 * _____ = _____

10 * _____ = _____

5 * _____ = _____

1 * _____ = _____

Writing Multiplication and Division Stories

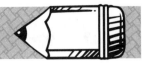

Work with a partner or in a small group.

Each of you makes up a multiplication or division number story. Use large numbers or very small numbers—numbers you would want to calculate with a calculator rather than with paper and pencil. Be sure your problem makes sense.

Then trade and solve each other's problems.

Problem: _____

_____

_____

_____

Solution: _____

_____

_____

- -

Name _____ Date _____ Time _____

Writing Multiplication and Division Stories

Work with a partner or in a small group.

Each of you makes up a multiplication or division number story. Use large numbers or very small numbers—numbers you would want to calculate with a calculator rather than with paper and pencil. Be sure your problem makes sense.

Then trade and solve each other's problems.

Problem: _____

_____

_____

_____

Solution: _____

_____

Grid Search Grids

Use Grids 1 and 2 to play a game.

My Pieces
(Grid 1)

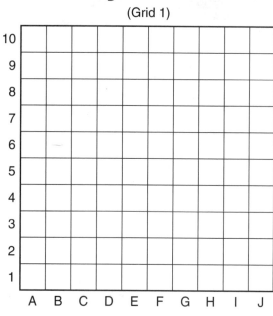

Opponent's Pieces
(Grid 2)

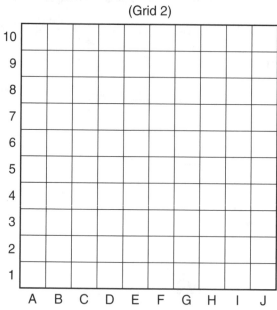

Use Grids 1 and 2 below to play another game.

My Pieces
(Grid 1)

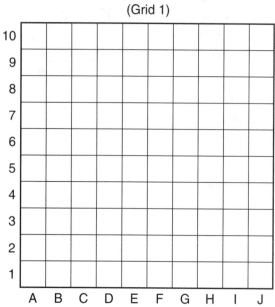

Opponent's Pieces
(Grid 2)

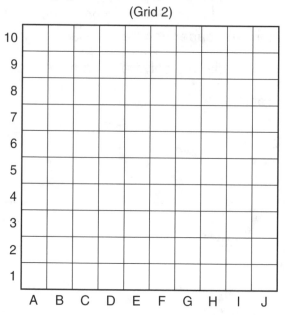

Use with Lesson 6.5.

Flying to Europe

The table below shows the time it takes to fly between five capitals in Europe.
Use this information to answer the questions below.

Travel Times

	Berlin	Lisbon	London	Paris	Warsaw
Berlin	———	4 hr 10 min	1 hr 45 min	1 hr 30 min	1 hr
Lisbon	4 hr 10 min	———	2 hr 35 min	2 hr 25 min	4 hr 55 min
London	1 hr 45 min	2 hr 35 min	———	50 min	2 hr 20 min
Paris	1 hr 30 min	2 hr 25 min	50 min	———	2 hr 30 min
Warsaw	1 hr	4 hr 55 min	2 hr 20 min	2 hr 30 min	———

1. You have just arrived in Lisbon. You decide to visit 3 historic Summer
   Olympic sites: Paris, site of the 1924 Olympics; Berlin, site of the 1936
   Olympics; and London, site of the 1948 Olympics. First, you fly from Lisbon
   to Paris; then from Paris to Berlin; and last, from Berlin to London. What is
   the total amount of time you were in the air?

   _____ hr _____ min

2. From London, you decide to visit Warsaw. How much longer is your flight
   from London to Warsaw than was your flight from Berlin to London?

   _____ hr _____ min

3. It's time to fly back to the United States. You have to get back to Paris to
   catch your flight home. If you leave Warsaw Friday afternoon at 2:15 P.M.,
   at what time will you arrive in Paris?

   _____ (A.M. or P.M.?)

4. Your flight was delayed leaving Warsaw. You didn't arrive in Paris until 10:15 P.M.
   At what time did you actually leave Warsaw?

   _____ (A.M. or P.M.?)

360° Angle Measurer

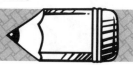

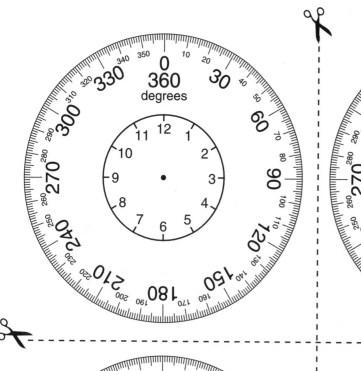

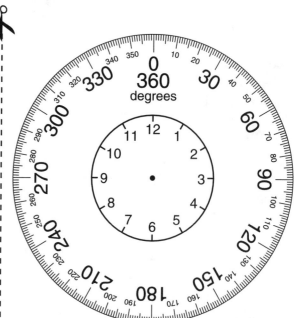

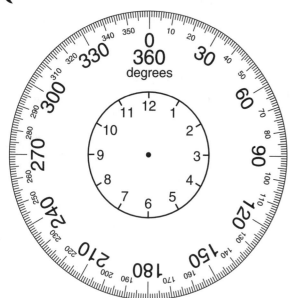

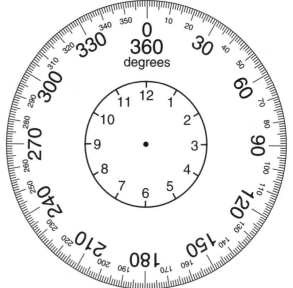

Use with Lesson 6.7.

Latitude and Longitude

Use the world map and globe in your classroom to answer the questions below.

1. Find the latitude and longitude of each of these locations.

Geographical Reference Numbers

Location	Latitude	Longitude
your hometown or city	_____ °_____	_____ °_____
Cairo, Egypt	_____ °_____	_____ °_____
Sydney, Australia	_____ °_____	_____ °_____

2. What is located at the following latitudes and longitudes?

56°N, 38°E _____   42°N, 88°W _____

1°S, 33°E _____   33°S, 71°W _____

3. The **Torrid Zone** is that part of Earth where the sun can be seen straight overhead. The equator is in the middle of the Torrid Zone. The boundaries of the Torrid Zone are called the **Tropic of Cancer** and the **Tropic of Capricorn.** Find the Tropic of Cancer and the Tropic of Capricorn on the map or globe. Describe their locations.

_____

_____

_____

_____

_____

4. Pretend you are flying from the North Pole to the South Pole along the 30° West longitude semicircle. Over which land areas does your flight take you?

_____

_____

Use with Lesson 6.10.

My Division Strategy

1. Solve the problem below. Show your work.

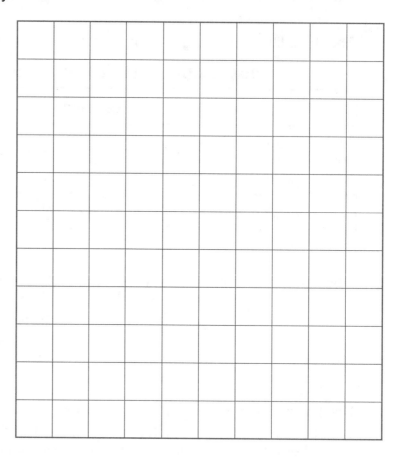

2. Tell how you solved this problem.

_____

_____

_____

_____

_____

_____

_____

_____

_____

_____

Measuring Angles

Three students measured the angle below.

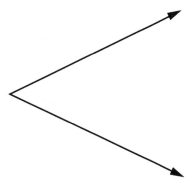

- Tonya used her half-circle protractor. She said the angle measures about 50°.

- Alexi used his half-circle protractor. He said the angle measures about 130°.

- José used his full-circle protractor. He said the angle measures about 310°.

Use both your half-circle protractor and your full-circle protractor to measure the angle.

Do you agree with Tonya, Alexi, or José? _____

Why? _____

_____

_____

_____

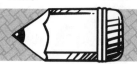

Constructing an Equilateral Triangle

An **equilateral triangle** is a triangle in which all 3 sides are the same length. Here is one way to construct an equilateral triangle using a compass and straightedge.

Step 1: Draw line segment *AB*.

Step 2: Place the anchor of the compass on point *A* and the pencil on point *B*. Without changing the compass opening, make a mark above the line segment.

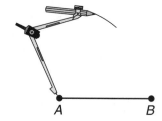

Step 3: Place the anchor on point *B*. Keeping the same compass opening, make a second mark that crosses the first mark. Label the point where the two marks meet *C*.

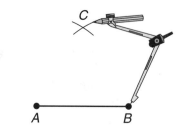

Step 4: Connect point *C* with points *A* and *B*.

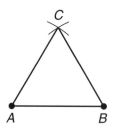

Use your compass and straightedge to construct a very large equilateral triangle on a separate sheet of paper. Cut out your triangle. Divide it into 6 equal parts. Color $\frac{1}{6}$ of it. Tape or paste your triangle on the back of this sheet.

Hint: One way to divide the triangle into 6 equal parts is to put two vertices (corners) together and fold the triangle in half. Then unfold it. Repeat this, using two other vertices. Repeat a third time, using two other vertices.

Collections

There are many words in the English language that name collections of things. For example, we speak of a **pack** of wolves, a **set** of math problems, and a **string** of pearls.

1. Here is a list of special "collection" words. Use them to fill in the blanks in the descriptions below. Look up any words you don't know in a dictionary.

"Collection" words:

brood	crew	flight	litter	school	team
bunch	fleet	flock	pride	swarm	troop

Collections of things:

A <u> litter </u> of kittens

A _____ of hens

A _____ of scouts

A _____ of bees

A _____ of workers

A _____ of oxen

A _____ of sheep

A _____ of fish

A _____ of stairs

A _____ of lions

A _____ of ships

A _____ of grapes

2. What might go with these collection words?

A band of <u> musicians </u>   A couple of _____

A pod of _____   A gaggle of _____

A herd of _____   A carton of _____

Polygons

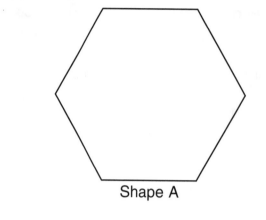

Shape A

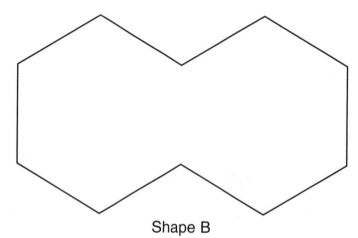

Shape B

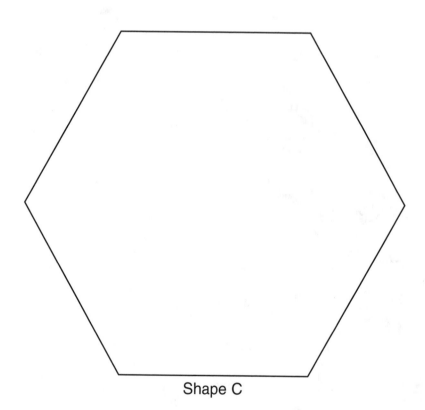

Shape C

Use with Lesson 7.3.

Tangram Puzzle

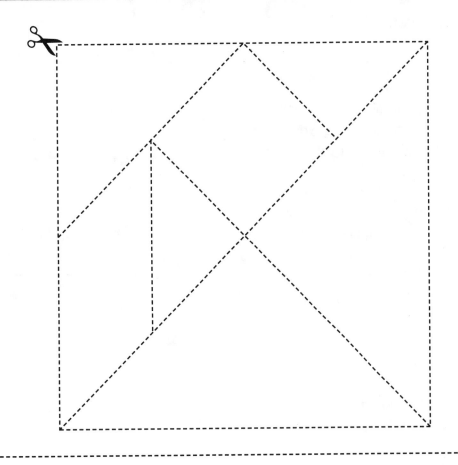

Use with Lesson 7.3.

Line Segments

1. Draw a line segment $4\frac{1}{2}$ inches long.

2. If you made this line segment $\frac{1}{4}$ inch
   longer **at each end,** how long would the
   new segment be? Use your ruler to figure this out.   _____ inches

3. If you removed $\frac{1}{4}$ inch from one end
   of the original line segment, how long
   would the new segment be?   _____ inches

4. Draw a line segment $2\frac{1}{8}$ inches long.

5. How much would you need to add to the
   segment to make it 3 inches long?   _____ inch

6. How much would you need to add to the
   segment to make it $2\frac{1}{2}$ inches long?   _____ inch

7. Which is longer—the first line segment you drew in Problem 1 or a line segment
   $4\frac{3}{8}$ inches long? _____

   It is longer by how much? _____ inch

8. Which is longer—the line segment you drew in Problem 4 or a line segment
   $2\frac{3}{16}$ inches long? _____

   It is longer by how much? _____ inch

Use with Lesson 7.4.

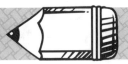

Clock Face

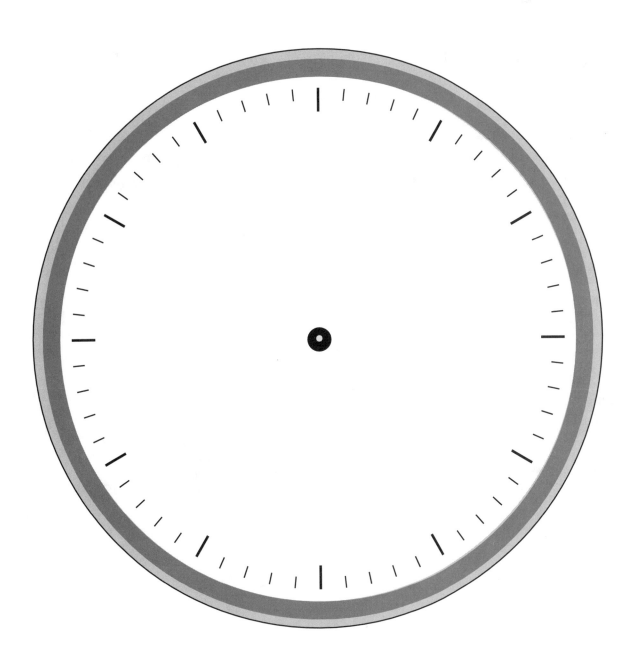

Use with Lesson 7.5.   **107**

More Clock Fractions

Write the fraction represented on each clock face.

1.

2.

3.

_____ _____ _____

Shade each clock face to show the fraction. Start shading at the line segment.

4.

$\dfrac{1}{20}$

5.

$\dfrac{1}{30}$

6.

$\dfrac{1}{60}$

Use the clock faces, if you wish, to help you solve these problems.

7.

$\dfrac{7}{15} + \dfrac{3}{10} =$ _____

8.

$\dfrac{19}{20} + \dfrac{1}{60} =$ _____

9.

$\dfrac{20}{30} - \dfrac{2}{5} =$ _____

10.

$\dfrac{35}{60} - \dfrac{1}{10} =$ _____

Use with Lesson 7.5.

Base-10 Grids

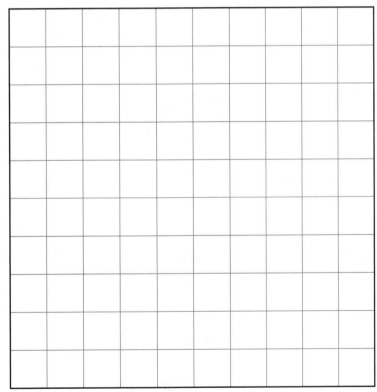

Use with Lesson 7.8.

Base-10 Block Designs

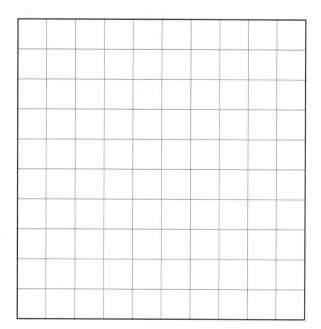

Decimal: _____

Fraction: _____

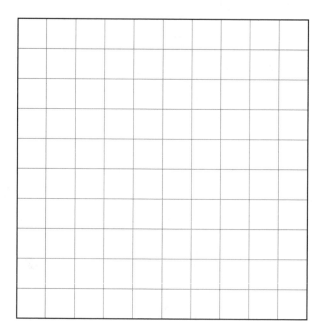

Decimal: _____

Fraction: _____

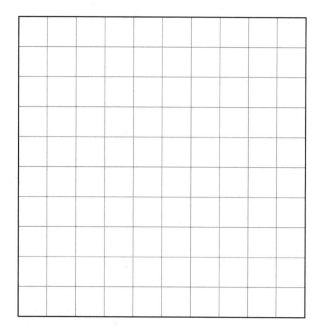

Decimal: _____

Fraction: _____

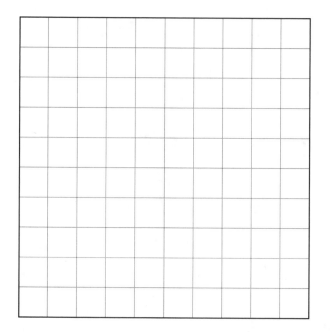

Decimal: _____

Fraction: _____

Use with Lesson 7.8.

Spinner Experiments

1. Use a paper clip and pencil to make a spinner.

   a. Spin the paper clip 4 times. Record the number of times it lands on the shaded part and on the white part.

shaded	white

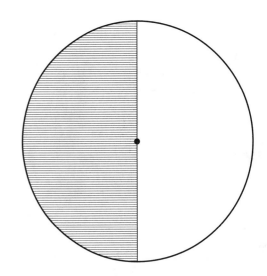

   b. Record the number of times the paper clip lands on the shaded part and on the white part **for the whole class.**

shaded	white

2. Make another spinner. Color the circle blue and red so that the paper clip is **twice as likely** to land on blue as on red.

   a. Spin the paper clip 4 times. Record the number of times it lands on blue and on red.

blue	red

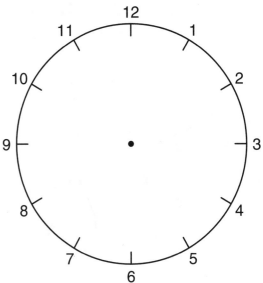

   b. Record the number of times the paper clip lands on blue and on red **for the whole class.**

blue	red

   c. What would you expect after spinning the paper clip 300 times?

blue	red

A Cube-Drop Experiment

How to Color the Grid

Color	Number of Squares
yellow	1
red	4
green	10
blue	35
white	50
Total	**100**

Color the squares in the grid above.

The table at the right shows the number of squares you should end up with for each color.

Use with Lesson 7.12.

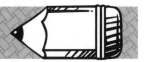

Results for 50 Cube Drops

Results for 50 Cube Drops	
Color	Number of Drops
yellow	
red	
green	
blue	
white	
Total	50

Results for 50 Cube Drops	
Color	Number of Drops
yellow	
red	
green	
blue	
white	
Total	50

Results for 50 Cube Drops	
Color	Number of Drops
yellow	
red	
green	
blue	
white	
Total	50

Results for 50 Cube Drops	
Color	Number of Drops
yellow	
red	
green	
blue	
white	
Total	50

Results for 50 Cube Drops	
Color	Number of Drops
yellow	
red	
green	
blue	
white	
Total	50

Results for 50 Cube Drops	
Color	Number of Drops
yellow	
red	
green	
blue	
white	
Total	50

Use with Lesson 7.12.

Class Results for 1,000 Cube Drops

Color	S1	S2	S3	S4	S5	S6	S7	S8	S9	S10	S11	S12	S13	S14	S15	S16	S17	S18	S19	S20	Number of drops	Percent
yellow																						
red																						
green																						
blue																						
white																						
Total	50	50	50	50	50	50	50	50	50	50	50	50	50	50	50	50	50	50	50	50	1,000	100%

Students

Use with Lesson 7.12.

My Fraction Addition Strategy

1. Solve the problem below. Show your work.

2. Tell how you solved this problem.

_____

_____

_____

_____

_____

_____

My Fraction Subtraction Strategy

1. Solve the problem below. Show your work.

2. Tell how you solved this problem.

_____

_____

_____

_____

_____

_____

Name   Date   Time

Geoboard Perimeters

On a geoboard, make rectangles or squares with the
perimeters given below. Record the lengths of a longer side
and shorter side of each shape.

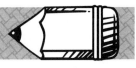

1
unit

1
unit

Perimeter (units)	Longer side (units)	Shorter side (units)
12		
12		
12		
14		
14		
14		
16		
16		
16		
16		

Use with Lesson 8.1.   **117**

© 2002 Everyday Learning Corporation

Name   Date   Time

Geoboard Perimeters

On a geoboard, make rectangles or squares with the
perimeters given below. Record the lengths of a longer side
and shorter side of each shape.

1
unit

1
unit

Perimeter (units)	Longer side (units)	Shorter side (units)
12		
12		
12		
14		
14		
14		
16		
16		
16		
16		

© 2002 Everyday Learning Corporation

Grid Paper ($\frac{1}{4}$ in.)

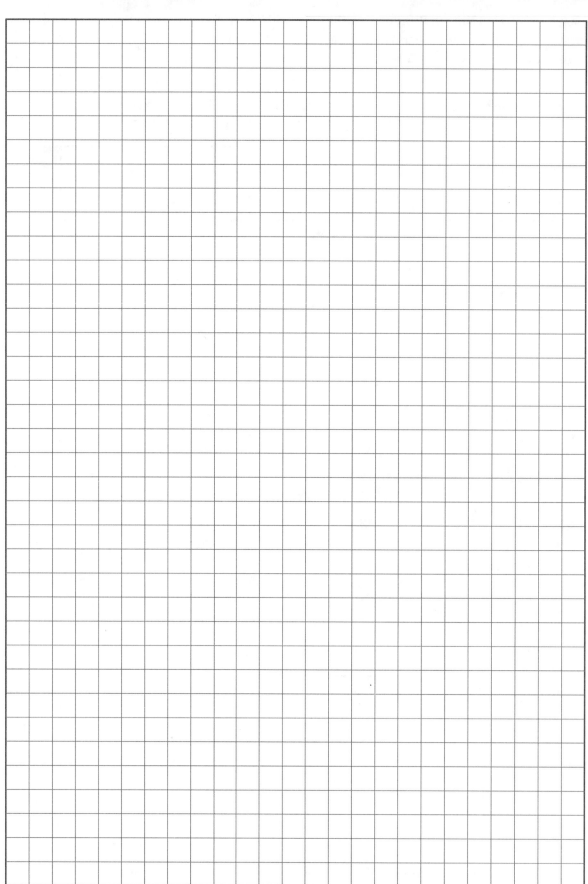

Use with Lesson 8.2.

My Bedroom Floor Plan

Make a scale drawing of your bedroom floor. Round your measurements to the nearest $\frac{1}{4}$ foot (3 inches).

Scale: $\frac{1}{2}$ inch represents 1 foot.

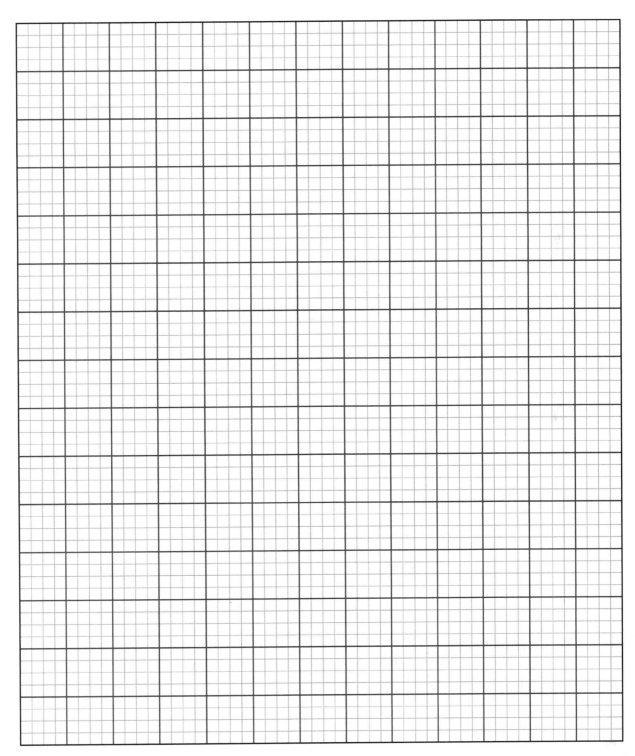

My Bedroom Floor Plan (cont.)

Make a scale drawing of each piece of furniture in your bedroom. Round your measurements to the nearest $\frac{1}{4}$ foot (3 inches). Cut out the scale drawings and tape them in place onto your scale drawing of your bedroom floor.

Scale: $\frac{1}{2}$ inch represents 1 foot.

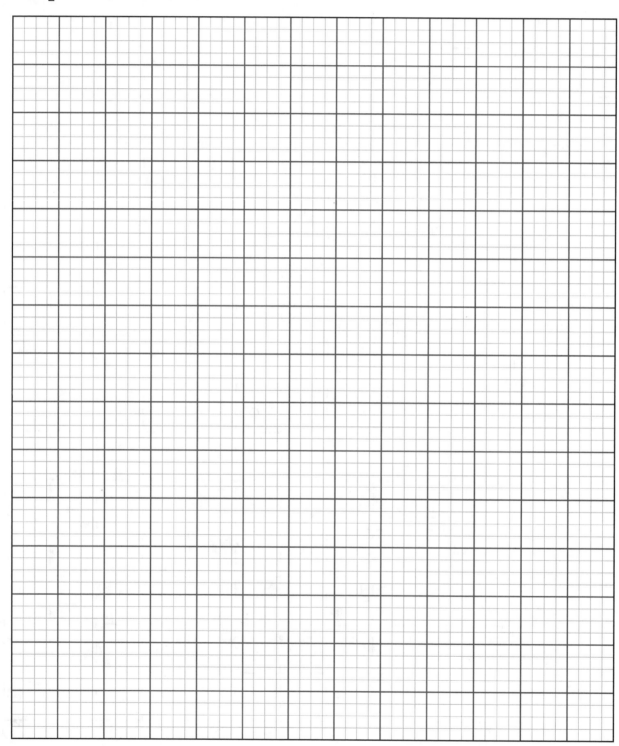

Use with Lesson 8.2.

Grid Paper (1 in.)

Use with Lesson 8.4.

Areas of Parallelograms

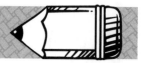

Cut out Parallelogram A. (Use the second Parallelogram A if you make a mistake.) Cut it into 2 pieces so that it can be made into a rectangle. Tape the rectangle onto page 250 in your journal.

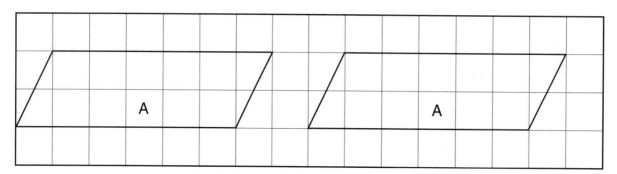

Do the same with Parallelograms B, C, and D.

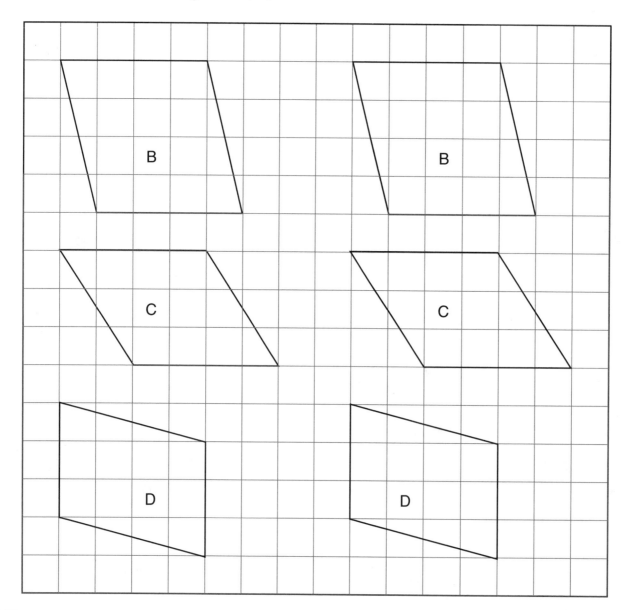

© 2002 Everyday Learning Corporation

         Use with Lesson 8.6.

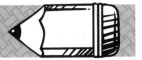

Areas of Triangles

Cut out Triangles A and B. Tape them together at the shaded corners to form a parallelogram. Tape the parallelogram in the space next to Triangle A on page 254 in your journal.

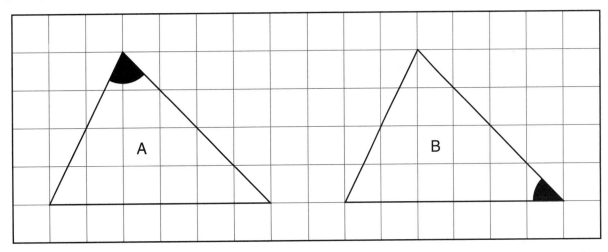

Do the same with the other 3 pairs of triangles.

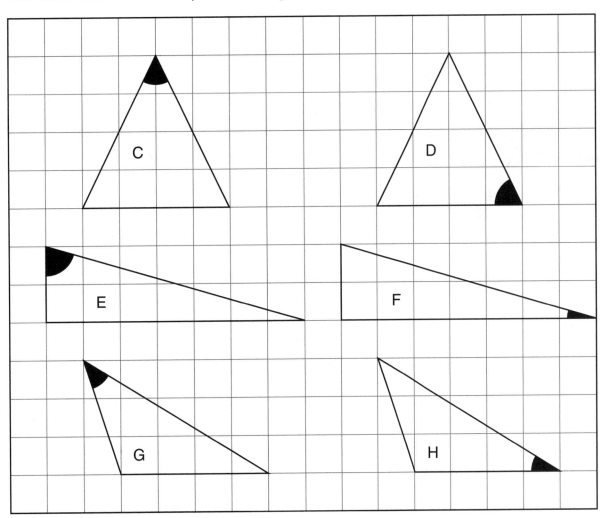

Use with Lesson 8.7.

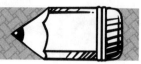

Comparing Areas

1. Cut out the hexagon below. Then cut out the large equilateral triangle. You should end up with one large triangle and three smaller triangles.

2. Use the large triangle and the three smaller triangles to form a rhombus.

   a. Is the area of the rhombus the same as the area of the hexagon you started with? _____

   b. Is it possible for two different shapes to have the same area? _____

3. Put the pieces back together to form a hexagon with an equilateral triangle inside.

   How can you show that the area of the hexagon is twice the area of the large triangle?

   _____

   _____

   _____

- ✂

There are 4 triangles in the hexagon.

- The large triangle is called an **equilateral triangle.** All 3 sides are the same length.

- The smaller triangles are called **isosceles triangles.** Each of these triangles has 2 sides that are the same length.

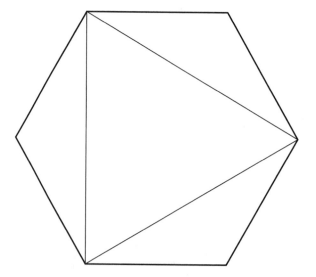

Mammal Species

One of the major achievements of science is a system for classifying plants and animals. It was developed by Carolus Linnaeus (luh • knee´ • us) over 200 years ago. It is still in use today. In this system, a group of animals that are similar in form and that reproduce together is called a *species.* (The plural of *species* is *species.*)

Linnaeus's Classification System

	Bear	**Rhinoceros**
Kingdom	Animalia	Animalia
Phylum	Chordata	Chordata
Class	Mammalia	Mammalia
Order	Carnivora	Perissodactyla
Family	Ursidae	Rhinocerotidae
Genus and Species	*Ursus arctos* (Brown bear), *Ursus americanus* (American black bear), *Ursus maritimus* (Polar bear), *Selenarctos thibetanus* (Asiatic black bear), *Melursus ursinus* (Sloth bear), *Tremarctos ornatus* (Spectacled bear), *Helarctos malayanus* (Sun bear)	*Rhinoceros unicornis* (Indian rhino), *Rhinoceros sondaicus* (Javan rhino), *Dicerorhinus sumatrensis* (Sumatran rhino), *Diceros bicornis* (Black rhino), *Ceratotherium simum* (White or Square-lipped rhino)

Scientists have identified over 4,000 species of mammals. According to this system, jackrabbits of the northern plains form one species. Snowshoe hares of the western mountains form another.

Species that share a number of features are grouped into *genera* (plural of *genus*), and genera are grouped into *families.* There are 44 different rabbit and hare species. Each species has some unique feature that makes it different from all other species in the rabbit and hare family.

Number of Species in the Family

Koala 1		Dolphin 32
Elephant 2		Deer 34
White whale 3		Rabbit & hare 44
Great ape 4		Kangaroo & wallaby 50
Rhinoceros 5		Opossum 75
Porpoise 6		Monkey 127
Bear 7		Shrew 246
Pig 9		Squirrel 267
Hedgehog & moonrat . . . 17		Bat 950
Armadillo 20		Mouse & rat 1,082

Source: Simon and Schuster's Guide to Mammals

Use with Lesson 8.8.

Area and Perimeter

1. Find the area of the polygon below *without* counting squares.
   Hint: Divide the polygon into figures for which you can calculate
   the areas: rectangles, parallelograms, and triangles. Use a formula
   to find the area of each of the figures.

   Total area of polygon = _____ cm²

2. Find the perimeter of the polygon. Use a centimeter ruler.

   Perimeter = _____ cm

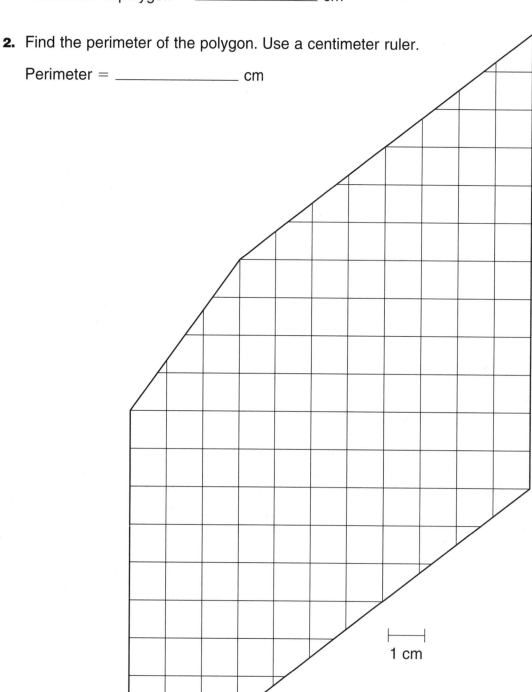

1 cm

Making Enlargements

Imagine that you used a copying machine to enlarge the original shapes below and on *Math Masters,* page 128 to twice their original size. Find the perimeter of each original shape and of its enlargement.

1 cm

1.   Original   Enlargement (double size)

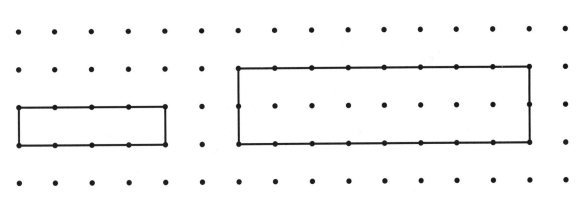

a. Perimeter = _____ cm   **b.** Perimeter = _____ cm

c. How many small rectangles can fit inside the large rectangle? _____ small rectangles

d. Draw the small rectangles inside the large rectangle.

2.   Original   Enlargement (double size)

a. Perimeter = _____ cm   **b.** Perimeter = _____ cm

c. Area = _____ cm²   **d.** Area = _____ cm²

Making Enlargements (cont.)

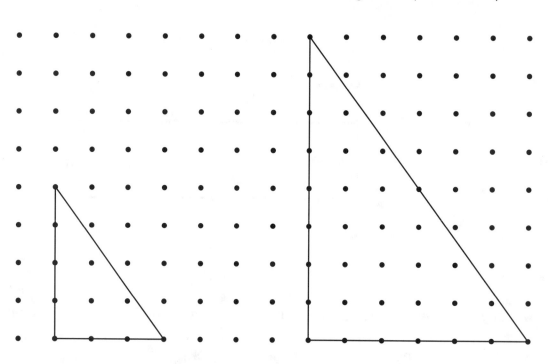

1 cm

3.   Original   Enlargement (double size)

Use a centimeter ruler to measure the longest side of each triangle.

a. Perimeter of original = _____ cm

b. Perimeter of enlargement = _____ cm

c. How many small triangles can fit
inside the large triangle?   _____ small triangles

d. Draw the small triangles inside the large triangle.

4. **a.** When you enlarge a shape to twice
its original size, how many times larger
is the perimeter of the larger shape?   _____ times larger

    b. How many times larger is its area?   _____ times larger

Use with Lesson 8.9.

Perimeter and Area

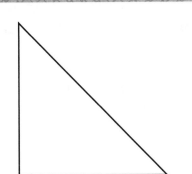 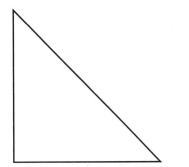 

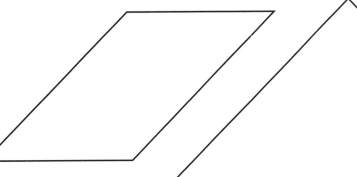

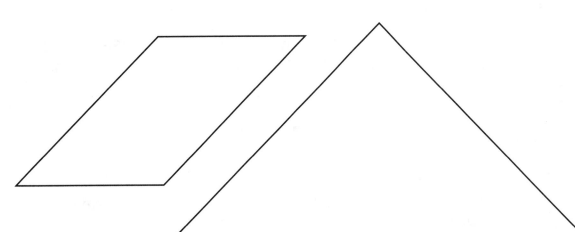

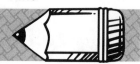

Perimeter and Area (cont.)

Cut out and use only the shapes in the *top half* of *Math Masters,* page 129 to complete Problems 1–5.

1. Make a square out of 4 of the shapes. Draw the square on the centimeter dot grid on *Math Masters,* page 131. Your picture should show how you put the square together.

2. Make a triangle out of 3 of the shapes. One of the shapes should be the shape you did *not* use to make the square in Problem 1. Draw the triangle on *Math Masters,* page 131.

3. Find the area of the following:

   a. the small triangle   _____ cm²

   b. the square   _____ cm²

   c. the parallelogram   _____ cm²

4. a. What is the perimeter of the large square you
      made in Problem 1?   _____ cm

   b. What is the area of that square?   _____ cm²

5. What is the area of the large triangle you
   made in Problem 2?   _____ cm²

Challenge

6. Cut out the 5 shapes in the bottom half of *Math Masters,* page 129 and add them to the other shapes. Use at least 6 pieces each to make the following shapes.

   a. a square   b. a rectangle

   c. a trapezoid   d. any shape you choose

Tape your favorite shape together and then tape it onto the back of this sheet. Next to the shape, write its perimeter and area.

Perimeter and Area (cont.)

1.

2.

Use with Lesson 8.9.

Many Names for Percents

100%

That's _____ out of every 100.　　Fraction name: $\dfrac{}{100}$　　Decimal name: _____

✂ -

100%

That's _____ out of every 100.　　Fraction name: $\dfrac{}{100}$　　Decimal name: _____

- -

100%

That's _____ out of every 100.　　Fraction name: $\dfrac{}{100}$　　Decimal name: _____

- -

100%

That's _____ out of every 100.　　Fraction name: $\dfrac{}{100}$　　Decimal name: _____

- -

100%

That's _____ out of every 100.　　Fraction name: $\dfrac{}{100}$　　Decimal name: _____

© 2002 Everyday Learning Corporation

Base-10 Block Designs

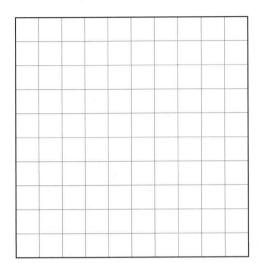

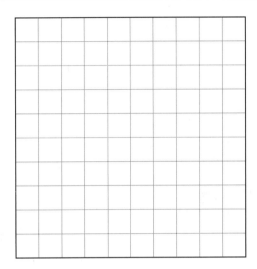

Fraction: ☐/100

Decimal: _____

Percent: _____%

Fraction: ☐/100

Decimal: _____

Percent: _____%

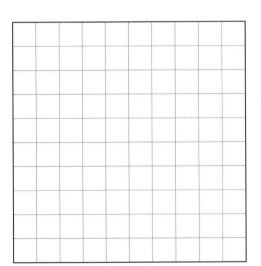

Fraction: ☐/100

Decimal: _____

Percent: _____%

Fraction: ☐/100

Decimal: _____

Percent: _____%

Use with Lesson 9.1.

Fractions, Decimals, and Percents

Fill in the missing numbers. If the grid is not shaded, then shade the grid.

100%
large square

1. Ways of showing _____ :

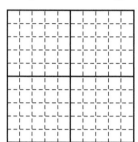

$\dfrac{\boxed{}}{4}$ is shaded. $\dfrac{\boxed{}}{100}$

0._____ _____%

2. Ways of showing _____ :

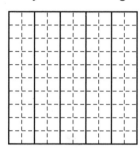

$\dfrac{\boxed{}}{5}$ is shaded. $\dfrac{\boxed{}}{100}$

0._____ _____%

3. Ways of showing _____ :

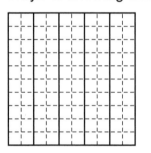

$\dfrac{\boxed{}}{5}$ is shaded. $\dfrac{\boxed{}}{100}$

0._____ _____%

4. Ways of showing _____ :

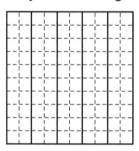

$\dfrac{\boxed{}}{5}$ is shaded. $\dfrac{\boxed{}}{100}$

0._____ _____%

5. Ways of showing _____ :

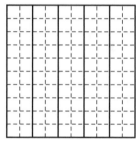

$\dfrac{\boxed{}}{5}$ is shaded. $\dfrac{\boxed{}}{100}$

0._____ _____%

6. Ways of showing _____ :

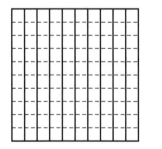

$\dfrac{\boxed{}}{10}$ is shaded. $\dfrac{\boxed{}}{100}$

0._____ _____%

7. Ways of showing _____ :

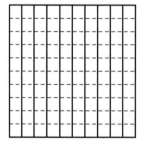

$\dfrac{\boxed{}}{10}$ is shaded. $\dfrac{\boxed{}}{100}$

0._____ _____%

8. Ways of showing _____ :

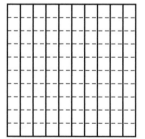

$\dfrac{\boxed{}}{10}$ is shaded. $\dfrac{\boxed{}}{100}$

0._____ _____%

Use with Lesson 9.2.

"Easy" Equivalents

$\frac{1}{2}$	0.50	50%	$\frac{1}{4}$	0.25	25%
$\frac{3}{4}$	0.75	75%	$\frac{1}{5}$	0.20	20%
$\frac{2}{5}$	0.40	40%	$\frac{3}{5}$	0.60	60%
$\frac{4}{5}$	0.80	80%	$\frac{1}{10}$	0.10	10%
$\frac{3}{10}$	0.30	30%	$\frac{7}{10}$	0.70	70%
$\frac{9}{10}$	0.90	90%	$\frac{2}{2}$	1	100%

Fraction, Decimal, Percent Equivalencies

1. Write 3 equivalent fractions for each of the following fractions.

a. $\frac{5}{6}$ _____

b. $\frac{15}{25}$ _____

c. $\frac{1}{10}$ _____

d. $\frac{18}{20}$ _____

2. Complete.

	Fraction	Decimal	Percent
a.	$\frac{9}{10}$	_____	_____
b.	_____	0.75	_____
c.	_____	_____	30%

3. Shade more than $\frac{2}{5}$, but less than $\frac{1}{2}$ of the square.

Write the value of the shaded part as a fraction, decimal, and percent.

Fraction: _____

Decimal: _____

Percent: _____

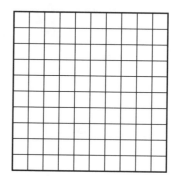

4. Name a percent value

a. greater than $\frac{1}{5}$ and less than $\frac{1}{2}$.

_____

b. less than $\frac{8}{10}$ and greater than $\frac{3}{4}$.

_____

5. Insert >, <, or = to make each number sentence true.

a. $\frac{1}{2}$ _____ 55%

b. 0.63 _____ $\frac{4}{5}$

c. $\frac{5}{6}$ _____ $\frac{9}{10}$

d. 27% _____ $\frac{3}{12}$

e. 80% _____ 0.92

Use with Lesson 9.3.

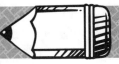

Fraction, Decimal, Percent Equivalencies (cont.)

1. Write 5 names for $\frac{9}{12}$.

_____

_____

_____

_____

_____

2. Insert $<$, $>$, or $=$ to make each number sentence true.

   a. 0.45 _____ 27%

   b. $\frac{5}{6}$ _____ 0.90

   c. 25% _____ $\frac{5}{20}$

   d. 0.82 _____ 32%

   e. $\frac{5}{4}$ _____ 1.00

3. Write an equivalent fraction, decimal, or percent.

	Fraction	Decimal	Percent
a.	_____	1.00	_____
b.	_____	_____	29%
c.	$\frac{2}{5}$	_____	_____
d.	$\frac{96}{120}$	_____	_____

4. Write four numbers between 1.65 and 1.75.

_____

_____

_____

_____

5. Shade more than $\frac{34}{100}$ of the square and less than $\frac{42}{100}$.

Write a decimal and a percent for the shaded part.

Decimal: _____

Percent: _____

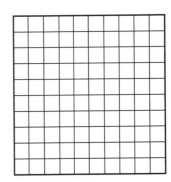

Discount Number Stories

1. A store is having a sale on gym shoes.

- The regular price of the High Flyers is $50. Now they are on sale for $38.

- The Zingers are $15 off the regular price. When not on sale, the Zingers cost $75 a pair.

Which pair has the greater percent of discount? Explain your answer.

_____

_____

_____

_____

_____

2. The same store is also having a sale on tennis rackets.

- The regular price of the Smasher is $54.00. It is on sale for 25% off the regular price.

- The regular price of the Fast Flight is $75.00. It is on sale for 20% off the regular price.

For which tennis racket are you getting more money taken off the regular price? Explain your answer.

_____

_____

_____

_____

Deforestation

Deforestation, the clearing of forest land, is taking place in many parts of the world. Each circle below represents all the forest land that was left in that country in 1990. The shaded part shows the percent of forest land that was cleared between 1990 and the year 2000.

Brazil   Costa Rica   Ghana   Honduras   Indonesia

Malaysia   Mexico   Nicaragua   Philippines   Thailand

Which countries lost

1. 50% of their forests? _____

2. 25% of their forests? _____

3. less than 25% of their forests? _____

4. more than 25% but less than 50% of their forests? _____

5. more than 50% but less than 75% of their forests? _____

6. more than 75% but less than 100% of their forests? _____

Use with Lesson 9.4.

Renaming Fractions as Percents

According to the Cat Fancier's Association, 65,183 cats were registered in the United States in 1997. Of the 36 breeds registered, the table below shows the top ten.

1. Use a calculator to find what percent of 65,183 registered cats belongs to each breed. Round the percents to the nearest whole percent.

Breed	Number of Cats Registered	Percent of Total Number of Cats Registered
Persian	39,119	
Maine coon	4,819	
Siamese	2,657	
Abyssinian	2,308	
Exotic	2,037	
Oriental	1,337	
Scottish fold	1,202	
American shorthair	1,072	
Birman	1,007	
Burmese	939	

Source: The Top 10 of Everything 1999

2. Describe the procedure that you used to round the percents to the nearest whole percent.

_____

_____

_____

3. Explain why the percents do not add up to 100%.

_____

_____

_____

Trivia Survey Data Chart

Class Results for the Trivia Survey

Question	Yes	No	Total	$\frac{Yes}{Total}$	% Yes
1. Monday					
2. movies					
3. breakfast					
4. map					
5. fast food					
6. read					
7. meter					
8. liver					

Use with Lesson 9.6.

Map of Region 4

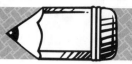

Title: _____

Russia

Turkey

Iran

China

Japan

India

Bangladesh

Vietnam

Thailand

Australia

Color-Coded Map for Percent of Literacy

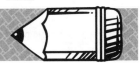

List the countries in Region 4 from *largest* to *smallest* according to the **percent of the population that is literate.** On *Math Masters,* page 142, write a title for the map. Then color these countries using the color code shown below.

Rank	Country	Percent of Literacy	Color Code
1	*Australia*	*100%*	blue
2	*Japan*	*100%*	blue
3			blue
4			green
5			green
6			green
7			green
8			red
9			red
10			red

Multiplying Whole Numbers

Multiply. Use your favorite method.

1. 7 * 68 = _____

2. 534 * 6 = _____

3. _____ = 58 * 67

4. _____ = 75 * 86

5. 33 * 275 = _____

6. 74 * 322 = _____

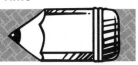

Dividing Whole Numbers

Solve each division problem. Write the answer as a mixed number by writing the remainder as a fraction.

1. 79 / 6 = _____

2. 92 / 3 = _____

3. _____ = 573 / 4

4. _____ = 896 / 6

5. 739 / 22 = _____

6. 945 / 18 = _____

Name   Date   Time

Grid Paper (2 cm)

Use with Lesson 9.10.

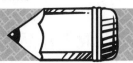

My Decimal Division Strategy

1. Solve the problem below. Show your work.

2. Tell how you solved this problem.

_____

_____

_____

_____

_____

_____

_____

_____

_____

_____

_____

_____

My Decimal Multiplication Strategy

1. Solve the problem below. Show your work.

2. Tell how you solved this problem.

_____

_____

_____

_____

_____

_____

_____

_____

_____

_____

Bzzzzz ...

Beetrice, the bee, wants to gather pollen from each flower and then return to her hive. Use your transparent mirror to help Beetrice fly around.

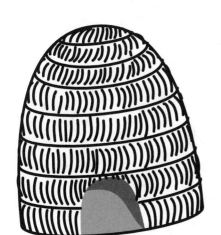

Build a Clown

Use a transparent mirror to put a hat on the clown's head. When the hat is where you want it, draw the hat. Do the same thing with the other missing parts to complete the clown picture. Then color the picture and cut it out.

Polygon Review

1. Match each polygon below with its name. Place the correct letter on the line next to the polygon.

Three of the polygons have more than one name. The square, for example, is also a parallelogram. For these three polygons, write the letters for all the names they can have.

_____    **a.** kite

_____ 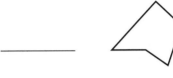   **b.** hexagon

_____   **c.** equilateral triangle

_____    **d.** rectangle

_____   **e.** rhombus

_____ 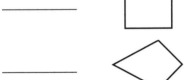   **f.** pentagon

_____    **g.** right triangle

_____    **h.** octagon

_____   **i.** parallelogram

_____   **j.** square

_____ 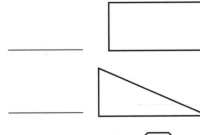   **k.** trapezoid

2. Which of the polygons above are regular polygons?

Finding Lines of Reflection

Dart Game

Practice before you play the game on *Math Masters,* page 153. One partner chooses Dart A and the other partner Dart B. Try to hit the target with your own dart, using the transparent mirror. **Do not practice with your partner's dart.**

Now play the game with your partner.

Directions Take turns. When it is your turn, use the other dart — the one you did not use for practice. Try to hit the target by placing the transparent mirror on the page, but **do not look through the mirror.** Then both you and your partner look through the mirror to see where the dart hit the target. Keep score.

Pocket-Billiards Game

Practice before you play the game on *Math Masters,* page 154. Choose a ball (1, 2, 3, or 4) and a pocket (A, B, C, D, E, or F). Try to get the ball into the pocket, using the transparent mirror.

Now play the game with a partner.

Directions Take turns. When it is your turn, say which ball and which pocket you have picked: for example, "Ball 2 to go into Pocket D." Try to get the ball into the pocket by placing the transparent mirror on the billiard table, **but do not look through the mirror.** Then both you and your partner look through the mirror to check whether the ball has gone into the pocket.

Dart Game

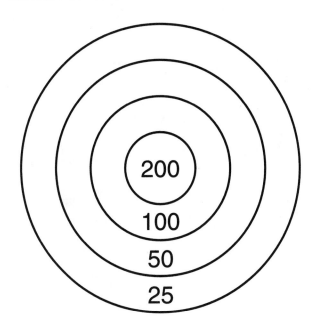

200

100

50

25

Scoreboard 1

Player 1	Player 2

Scoreboard 2

Player 1	Player 2

Scoreboard 3

Player 1	Player 2

Pocket–Billiards Game

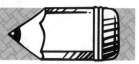

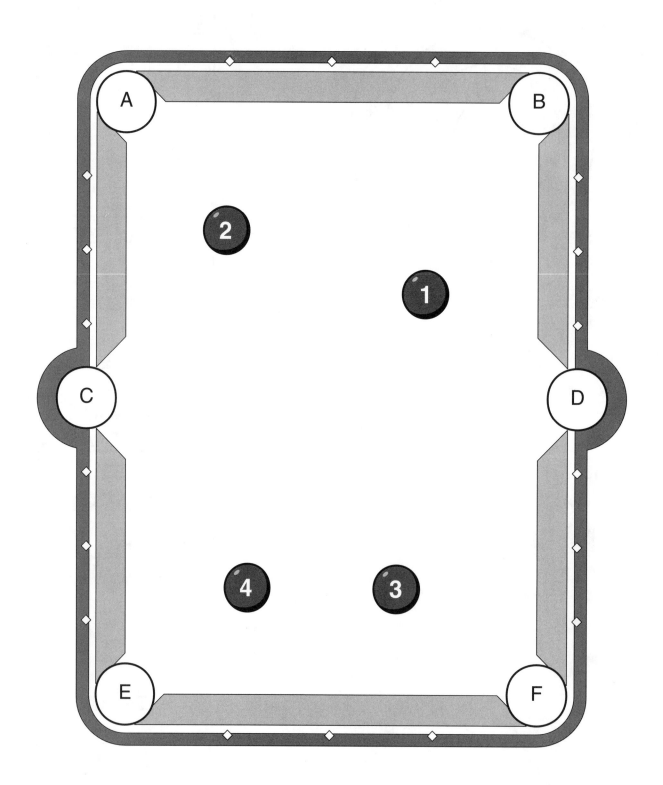

Use with Lesson 10.2.

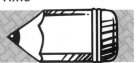

Reflections

1. Use a transparent mirror to draw the reflected image of the head of the dog.

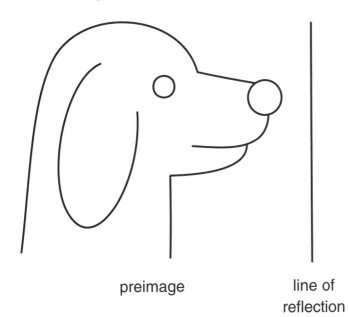

preimage   line of   image
                    reflection

2. Draw a picture on the left of the line. Ask your partner to use a transparent mirror to draw the reflected image of your picture.

preimage   line of   image
                    reflection

Use with Lesson 10.3.   **155**

Half-Pictures

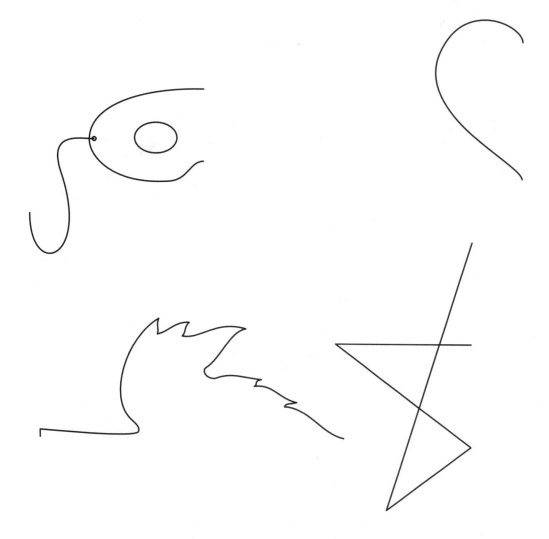

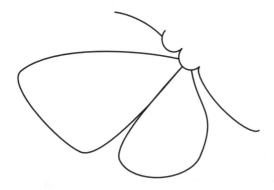

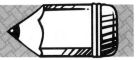

Symmetric Pictures

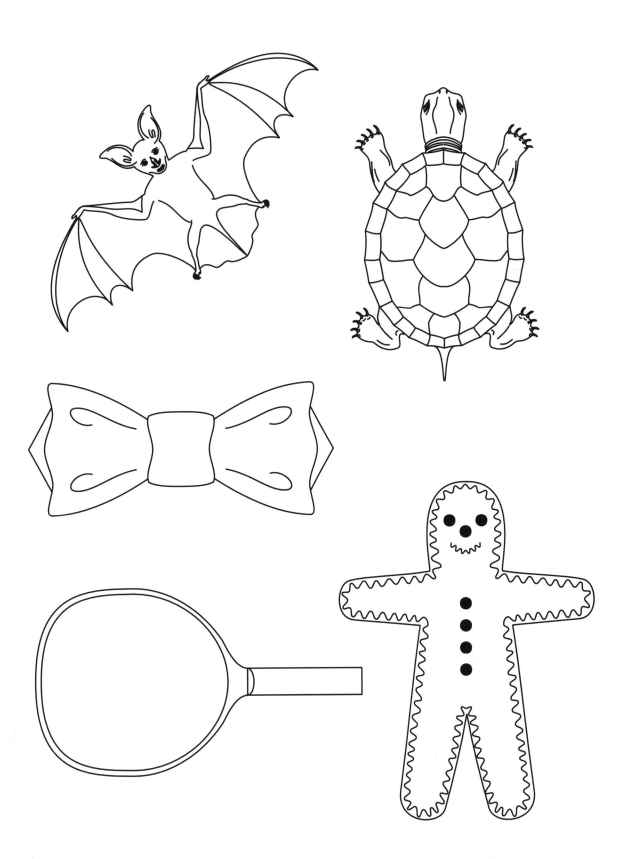

Polygons A–E

E

C

B

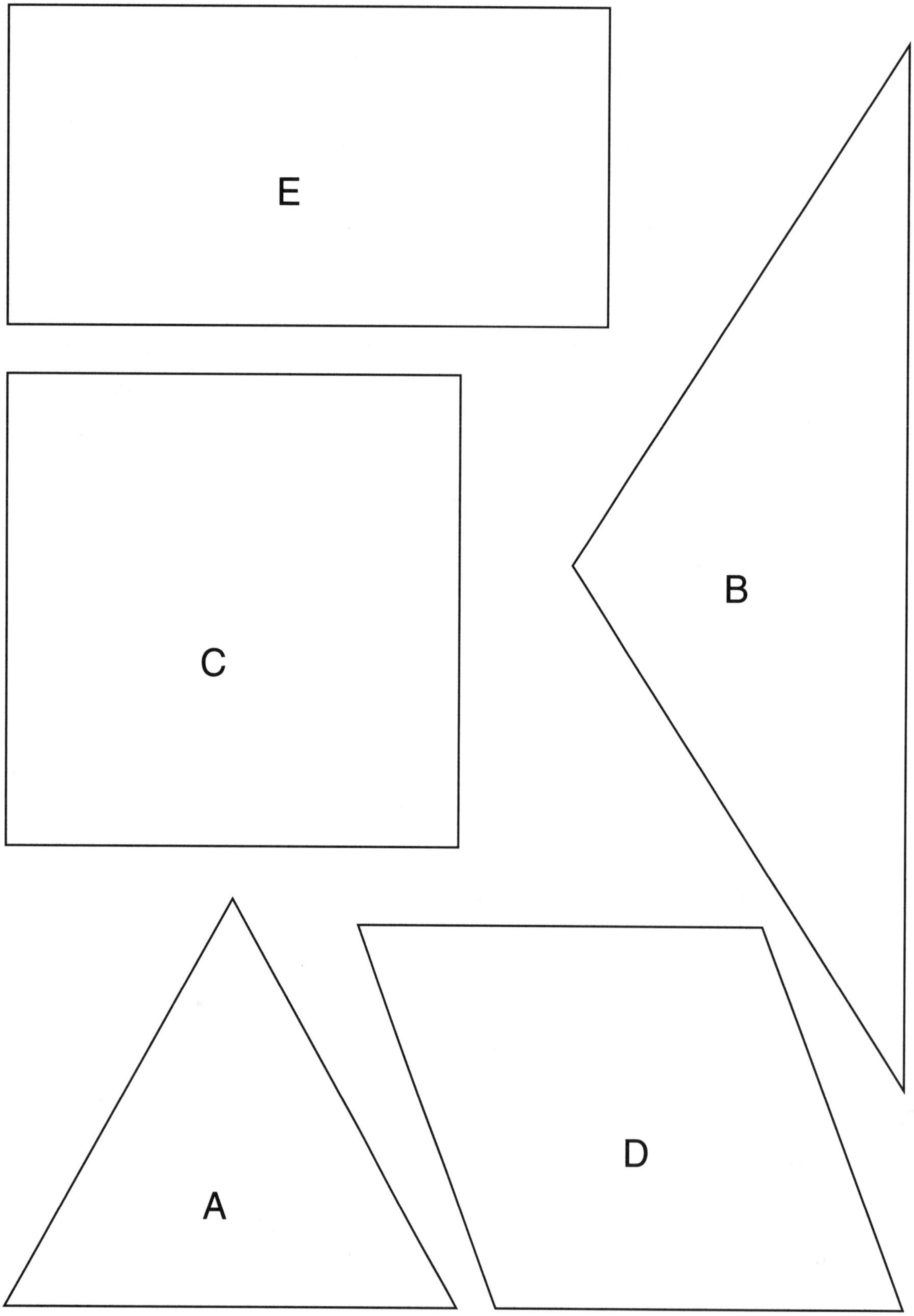

A

D

Use with Lesson 10.4.

Polygons F–J

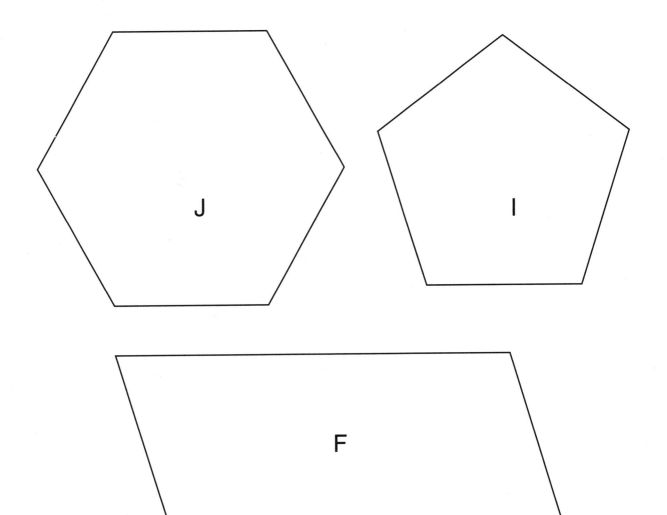

J

I

F

G

H

Use with Lesson 10.4.

Turn Symmetry

A shape that looks the same after it has been turned by less than a full turn has **turn symmetry.**

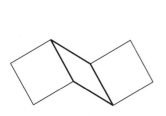
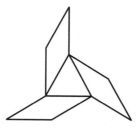
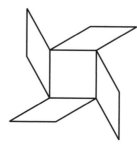

$\frac{1}{2}$-turn symmetry $\frac{1}{3}$-turn symmetry $\frac{1}{4}$-turn symmetry

1. Use tape and pattern blocks to make shapes that have turn symmetry. Use your Geometry Template to draw your shapes below. Underneath each shape, write the smallest turn that leaves the shape looking the same.

2. A corporate logo is a symbol that stands for a company. Look through magazines and newspapers for corporate logos that have turn symmetry. Copy them or cut them out and tape them onto the back of this page. Underneath each logo, write the smallest turn that leaves the logo looking the same.

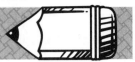

Frieze Patterns

A frieze pattern is a design made of shapes that are lined up. Frieze patterns are often found on the walls of buildings, on the borders of rugs and tiled floors, and on clothing.

In many frieze patterns, the same design is reflected over and over. For example, the following frieze pattern was used to decorate a sash worn by a Mazahua woman from San Felipe Santiago in the state of New Mexico. The strange-looking beasts in the frieze are probably meant to be horses.

Some frieze patterns are made by repeating (translating) the same design instead of reflecting it. These patterns look as if they were made by sliding the design along the strip. An example of such a frieze pattern is the elephant and horse design below that was found on a woman's sarong from Sumba, Indonesia. All the elephants and horses are facing in the same direction.

The following frieze pattern is similar to one painted on the front page of a Koran in Egypt about 600 years ago. (The Koran is the sacred book of Islam.) The pattern is more complicated than the two above. It was created with a combination of reflections, rotations, and translations.

Use with Lesson 10.5.

Patterns in My World

Patterns are all around you. Tiles on a floor or wall often form a pattern. Here are some tile patterns you might find:

   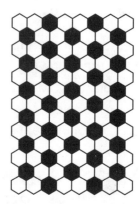

Look around your home. Can you find some tile patterns? If you can, copy them. If there are no tile patterns, look for other patterns on heating grates, furniture, wallpaper, and so on. If you can't find patterns, make up your own.

1. A pattern:

Where I found it: _____

2. A pattern:

Where I found it: _____

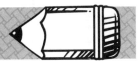

Making Frieze Patterns

1. Use an index card as a template for making frieze patterns.

   a. Trim your index card to make a 3-inch by 3-inch square.

   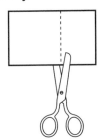

   b. Draw a simple design in the middle of the square.

   c. Cut out your design. If you need to cut through the edge of the index card, then use tape to repair the cut.

2. Make a frieze pattern with your template.

   a. Draw a long line on a large sheet of paper.

   b. Put your template at the left end of the line.

   c. Trace the shape of the design you cut out. Make a mark on the line at the right edge of the template.

   d. Move your template to the right along the line. Line up the left side of the template with the mark you made on the line.

   e. Repeat Steps c and d. To make more complicated patterns, give your template a turn or a flip every time you move it.

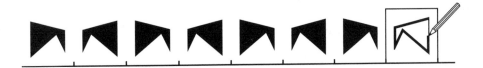

Positive and Negative Numbers

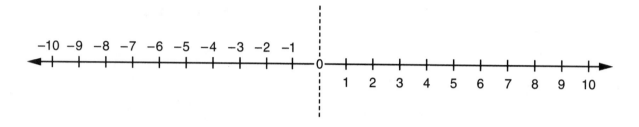

Place your transparent mirror on the dashed line that passes through 0 on the number line above. Look through the mirror. What do you see?

What negative number image do you see

above 1? _____   above 2? _____   above 8? _____

Use with Lesson 10.6.

--- ✂

Positive and Negative Numbers

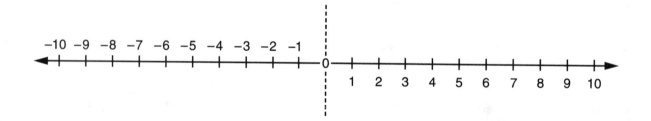

Place your transparent mirror on the dashed line that passes through 0 on the number line above. Look through the mirror. What do you see?

What negative number image do you see

above 1? _____   above 2? _____   above 8? _____

Use with Lesson 10.6.

Ledger

Transaction	Start	Change	End/Start of Next Transaction

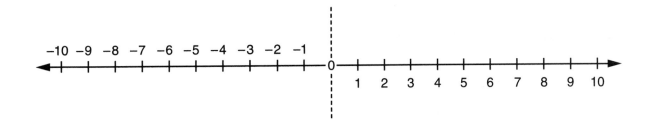

Credits/Debits Game Recording Sheets

Game 1

Recording Sheet

	Start	Change	End/Next Start
1	+ $10		
2			
3			
4			
5			
6			
7			
8			
9			
10			

Game 2

Recording Sheet

	Start	Change	End/Next Start
1	+ $10		
2			
3			
4			
5			
6			
7			
8			
9			
10			

-22 -21 -20 -19 -18 -17 -16 -15 -14 -13 -12 -11 -10 -9 -8 -7 -6 -5 -4 -3 -2 -1 0 1 2 3 4 5 6 7 8 9 10 11 12 13 14 15 16 17 18 19 20 21 22

Use with Lesson 10.6.

Interpreting a Cartoon

Ruthie's brother doesn't think she understands "fraction-of" problems. He knows that half of eight is four. However, Ruthie does know quite a bit about line symmetry. Can you explain her answers? You may want to draw a picture.

_____

_____

_____

_____

Use with Lesson 10.7.

Ounces and Grams

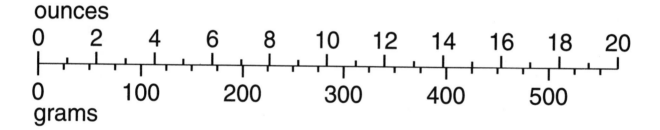

Use with Lesson 11.1.

Name _____ Date _____ Time _____

Mammal Weights

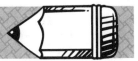

The table below shows typical weights, in pounds and kilograms, of different mammals. The weight of a typical fourth grader is also included.

Mammal	Pounds	Kilograms	Mammal	Pounds	Kilograms
Blue whale	300,000	140,000	Human adult	150	70
African elephant	12,000	5,400	**Fourth grader**	**65**	**30**
Giraffe	2,400	1,100	Raccoon	25	10
Bison	1,800	810	House cat	10	5
Arabian camel	1,200	540	Domestic rabbit	3	1.5
Zebra	650	290	Squirrel	1	0.5
Tiger	500	230	Mouse	0.25	0.1
Mountain gorilla	450	200	Pygmy shrew	0.01	0.005
White-tailed deer	400	180			

Source (for nonhumans): Simon and Schuster's Guide to Mammals

1. For each of the following mammals, tell about how many fourth graders it would take to equal the weight of each mammal.

Mammal	Typical Weight (in kilograms)	Approximate Number of Fourth Graders
Zebra		About _____
Mountain gorilla		About _____
Tiger		About _____
Human adult		About _____
Bison		About _____
Blue whale		About _____

2. On the back of this page, write additional mammal comparisons. For example, about how many pygmy shrews would it take to equal the weight of a typical fourth grader?

Use with Lesson 11.1.

Square Pyramid Template

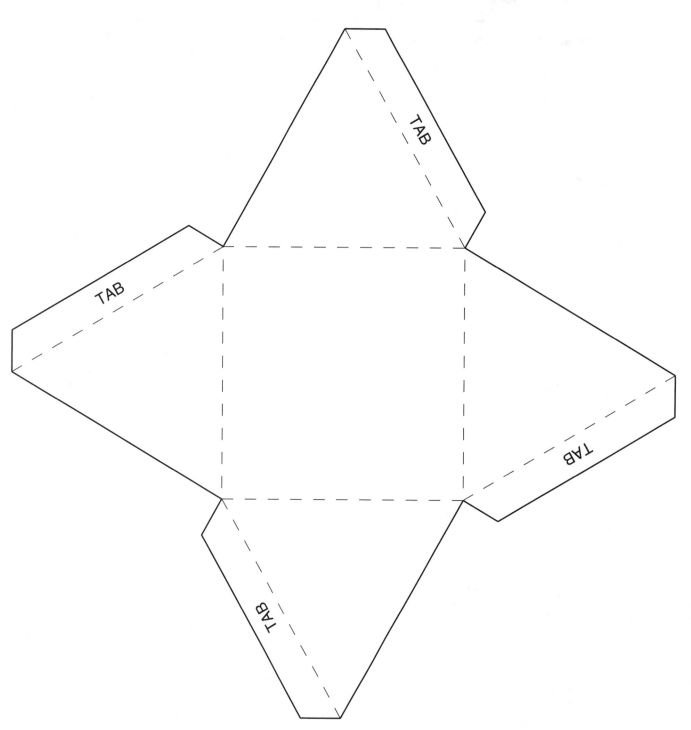

Use with Lesson 11.2.

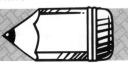

Triangular Prism Template

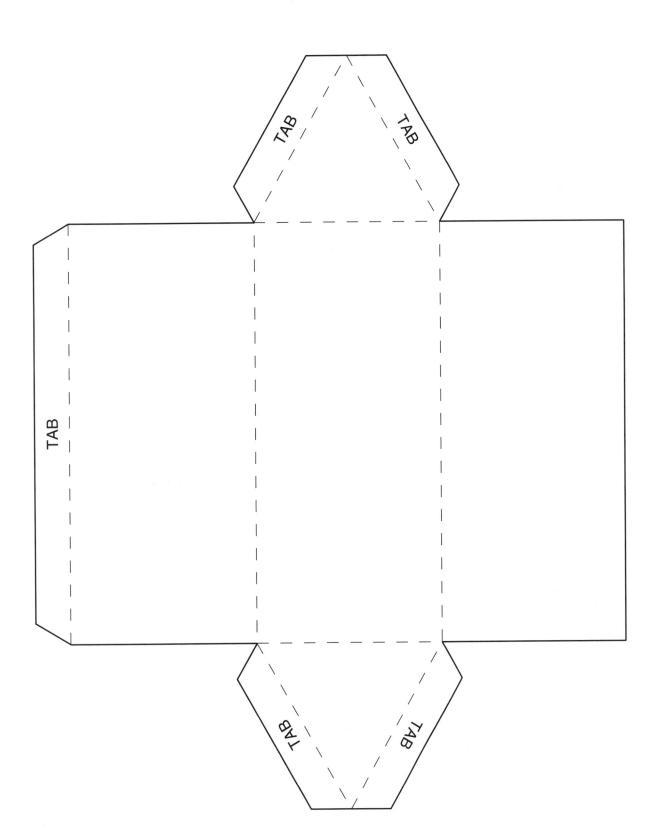

Use with Lesson 11.2.

Cone Template

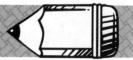

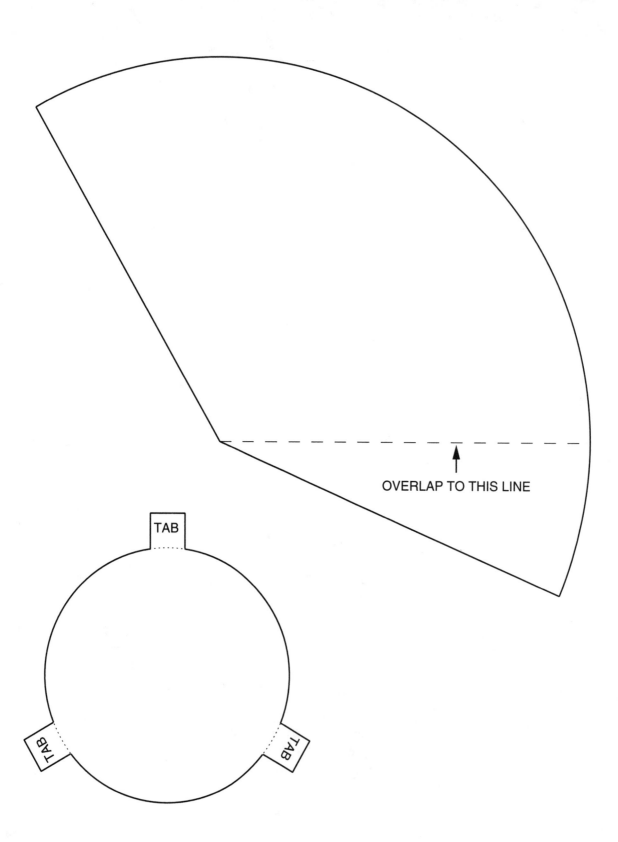

↑ OVERLAP TO THIS LINE

TAB

TAB

TAB

Use with Lesson 11.2.

Geometry Review

Match each description of a geometric figure in Column I with its name in Column II.
Some of the items in Column II do not have a match.

I

II

a. a polygon with 4 right angles
and 4 sides of the same length

_____ octagon

_____ rhombus

b. any polygon that has 4 sides

_____ right angle

c. a quadrilateral with exactly one pair
of opposite sides that are parallel

_____ acute angle

d. lines that never intersect

_____ trapezoid

e. a parallelogram with all sides
the same length and that is not
a rectangle

_____ hexagon

_____ square

f. a polygon with 8 sides

_____ equilateral triangle

g. two lines that are at right angles
to each other

_____ perpendicular lines

h. a polygon with 5 sides

_____ parallel lines

_____ pentagon

i. an angle that measures 90°

_____ isosceles triangle

j. a triangle with all sides
the same length

_____ quadrangle (or quadrilateral)

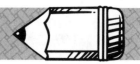

Comparing Geometric Solids

In each of the following lists, tell how the underlined geometric solid is different from the other two solids. Try to give more than one difference.

1. <u>rectangular prism</u>, cone, cylinder

    a. _____

    b. _____

2. <u>cylinder</u>, square pyramid, cone

    a. _____

    b. _____

3. <u>square pyramid</u>, cylinder, cone

    a. _____

    b. _____

4. <u>sphere</u>, cone, cylinder

    a. _____

    b. _____

174   Use with Lesson 11.2.

Name   Date   Time

Comparing Geometric Solids

In each of the following lists, tell how the underlined geometric solid is different from the other two solids. Try to give more than one difference.

1. <u>rectangular prism</u>, cone, cylinder

    a. _____

    b. _____

2. <u>cylinder</u>, square pyramid, cone

    a. _____

    b. _____

3. <u>square pyramid</u>, cylinder, cone

    a. _____

    b. _____

4. <u>sphere</u>, cone, cylinder

    a. _____

    b. _____

174   Use with Lesson 11.2.

Triangular Pyramid Template

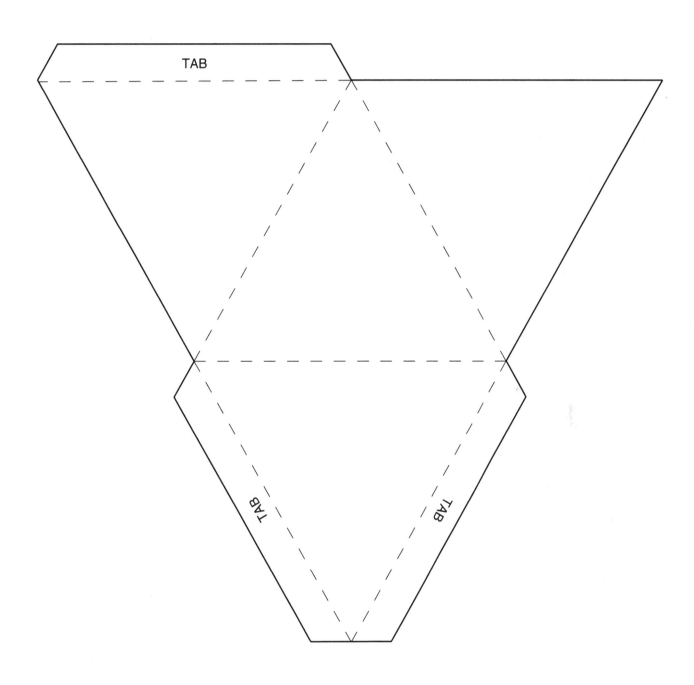

TAB

TAB

TAB

Cube Template

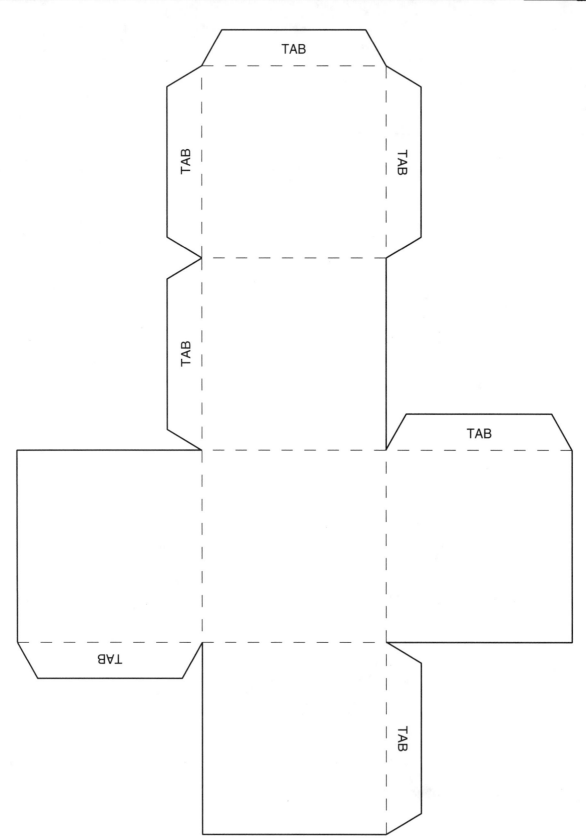

© 2002 Everyday Learning Corporation

Use with Lesson 11.3.

Geometry Riddles

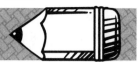

Riddle 1

I am a geometric solid.

I have six faces.

All of my faces are squares.

What am I? _____

Riddle 2

I am a geometric solid.

I have 2 surfaces.

My base is formed by a circle.

I come to a point at the top.

What am I? _____

Riddle 3

I am a polyhedron.

I have the fewest number of faces
of all the polyhedrons.

All of my faces are triangular.

I come to a point at the top.

What am I? _____

Geometry Riddles (cont.)

Riddle 4

I am a polyhedron.

My faces are pentagons.

I am useful for calendars.

My picture is on page 89 of the *Student Reference Book*.

What am I? _____

Riddle 5

I am a polyhedron.

I have two triangular bases.

My other faces are rectangles.

Sometimes I am used for keeping doors open.

What am I? _____

Riddle 6

I am a geometric solid.

I have only one surface.

My one surface is curved.

I have no base.

What am I? _____

© 2002 Everyday Learning Corporation

Drawing a Cube

Knowing how to draw is a useful skill in mathematics. There are several ways to draw a cube. Here are a few ways. Try them and experiment on your own.

A Basic Cube

Draw a square.

Draw another square that overlaps your first square. The second square should be the same size as the first.

Connect the corners of your two squares as shown. This picture doesn't look much like a real cube. One problem is that the picture shows all 12 edges, even though not all the edges of a real cube can be seen at one time. Another problem is that it's hard to tell which face of the cube is in front.

A Better Cube

Begin with a square.

Next, draw 3 parallel line segments going right and up from three corners of your square. The segments should all be the same length.

Finally, connect the ends of the 3 line segments.

This cube is better than before, but it shows only the edges and corners, not the faces. If you want, try shading your cube to make it look more realistic.

Drawing a Cube (cont.)

A Cube with Hidden Edges

Sometimes people draw cubes and other shapes with dashed line segments.
The dashed line segments show edges that are hidden. Here is one way to draw
a cube with hidden edges. Use a pencil.

Draw a square.

Draw a faint square that overlaps your first square.
The second square should be the same size as the first.

Connect the corners of your 2 squares with faint line
segments.

Trace over 5 of your faint line segments with solid lines
and 3 with dashed lines. The dashed line segments show
the 3 edges that are hidden.

Making a Model of a Tetrahedron

In a **regular geometric solid,** the faces are all copies of one regular polygon that have the same size. The following directions tell how to make a model of a regular triangular pyramid, or regular tetrahedron. Each face is formed by an equilateral triangle.

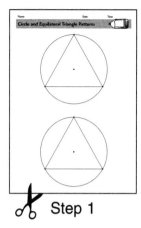

Step 1

Cut out 4 circles with equilateral triangles from two copies of *Math Masters,* page 182, "Circle and Equilateral Triangle Patterns."

Step 1

Step 2

Fold each circle along all three sides of the triangle.

Step 2

Step 3

Lay down one of your paper circles and unfold it so that the three curved flaps stick up. It will be the base.

Steps 3 and 4

Step 4

Take another paper circle. Match one side of its triangle with a side of the triangle on the base. Use staples, tape, or glue to fasten the two curved flaps together.

Step 5

In the same way, attach the other two paper circles to other sides of the base.

Step 5

Step 6

Fold up the three paper circles that you attached to the base. The triangles come together to form the tetrahedron. Either push all the flaps inside and tape the edges together, or leave two or three flaps outside and tape or glue them to the tetrahedron.

Step 6

Finished

Use with Lesson 11.3.   **181**

Circle and Equilateral Triangle Patterns

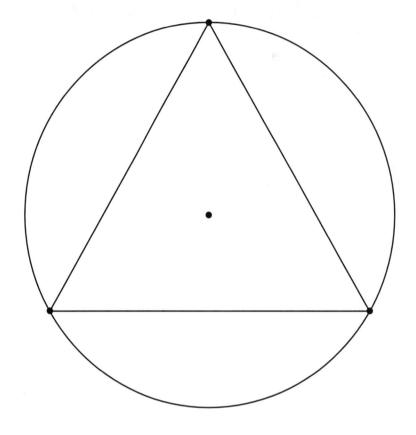

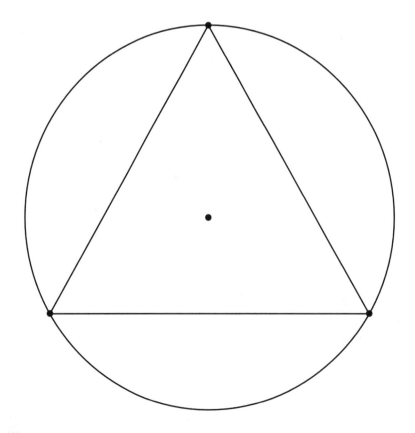

Use with Lesson 11.3.

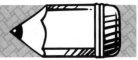

What Is Volume?

Use your dictionary to find as many different meanings of the word *volume* as you can.

Write each definition below. For each definition, write a sentence containing the word *volume*.

Meaning of *volume*	**Sentence that uses the word *volume***
1. _____	_____
_____	_____
_____	_____
	_____
2. _____	_____
_____	_____
_____	_____
	_____
3. _____	_____
_____	_____
_____	_____
	_____
4. _____	_____
_____	_____
_____	_____

Area of a Rectangle

1. Write a **formula** for the area of a rectangle. In your formula, use *A* for area. Use *l* and *w* for length and width, or *b* and *h* for base and height.

_____

2. Draw a rectangle with sides 3 centimeters and 9 centimeters.

3. Use the formula to find the area of the rectangle you drew.

Area = _____ square centimeters

Area of a Rectangle

1. Write a **formula** for the area of a rectangle. In your formula, use *A* for area. Use *l* and *w* for length and width, or *b* and *h* for base and height.

_____

2. Draw a rectangle with sides 3 centimeters and 9 centimeters.

3. Use the formula to find the area of the rectangle you drew.

Area = _____ square centimeters

Building Prisms

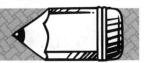

1. Use centimeter cubes to build the shaded prism shown on the 3-dimensional grid below.

Volume = _____ cm³

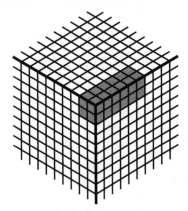

2. Build a different prism that has the same volume as the prism in Problem 1. Shade the grid to show the prism. Record the results in the table on *Math Masters*, page 186.

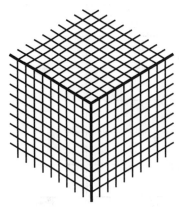

Use centimeter cubes to build the following rectangular prisms. Then shade the grids to show the prisms you built. Record the results in the table on *Math Masters*, page 186.

3. Build a prism that has a volume of 36 cm³ with a height of 3 cm.

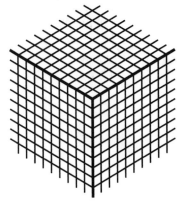

4. Build a prism that has a volume of 36 cm³ with a height of 6 cm.

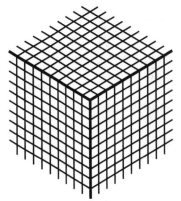

5. Build a prism that has a volume of 36 cm³ with a 2 cm square base.

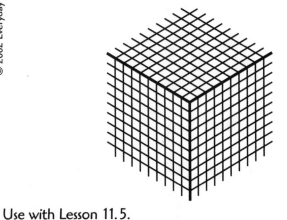

6. Build a prism that has a volume of 27 cm³.

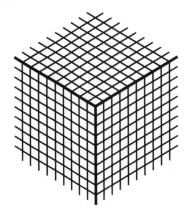

Use with Lesson 11.5.

Building Prisms (cont.)

Record the results from *Math Masters*, page 185 in the table below.

Prism	length of Base	width of Base	height of Prism	Volume
1	6 cm	2 cm	2 cm	24 cm^3
2				
3				
4				
5				
6				

Formula for the volume of a rectangular prism:

_____

l is the length of the base.

w is the width of the base.

h is the height of the prism.

Volume units are cubic units.

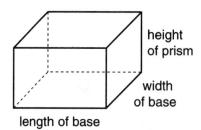

height of prism

width of base

length of base

Use with Lesson 11.5.

Credits/Debits Game (Advanced Version) Recording Sheets

Game 1

	Start	Change		End, and next start
		Addition or Subtraction	**Credit or Debit**	
1	+ $10			
2				
3				
4				
5				
6				
7				
8				
9				
10				

Game 2

	Start	Change		End, and next start
		Addition or Subtraction	**Credit or Debit**	
1	+ $10			
2				
3				
4				
5				
6				
7				
8				
9				
10				

Use with Lesson 11.6.

Positive and Negative Numbers

One way to add and subtract positive and negative numbers is to imagine you are walking on a number line.

- The first number tells you where to start.
- The operation sign (+ or −) tells you which way to face:
  + means face toward the positive end of the number line.
  − means face toward the negative end of the number line.
- If the second number is negative (has a − sign), then you walk backward. Otherwise, you walk forward.
- The second number tells you how many steps to walk.
- The number where you stop is the answer.

Example −4 + 3

- Start at −4.
- Face toward the positive end of the number line.
- Walk forward 3 steps.
- You are now at −1. So −4 + 3 = −1.

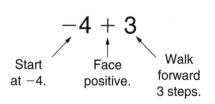

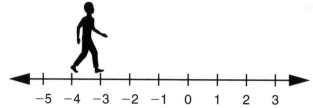

Example 5 − (−2)

- Start at 5.
- Face toward the negative end of the number line.
- Walk backward 2 steps.
- You are now at 7. So 5 − (−2) = 7.

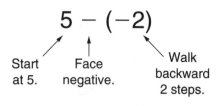

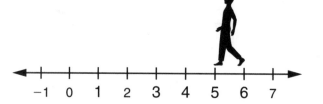

Solve.

1. −4 + (−3) = _____   **2.** 6 − 9 = _____   **3.** −4 − (−6) = _____

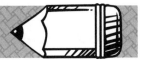

A Record Rainfall

According to the National Weather Service, the most rain that fell in the United States in a 24-hour period was 42 inches. This happened in Alvin, Texas, on July 25 and 26, 1979.

Imagine that it rained 42 inches in your classroom. About how many pounds would the water weigh?

Work with your group to solve the problem.

> *Hints:* 1 cubic foot of water weighs about 62.5 pounds.
> 1 ton equals 2,000 pounds.

1. About how many pounds would 42 inches of rainwater in your classroom weigh?

About _____ pounds

2. About how many tons is that?

About _____ tons

3. What information did you use to solve the problem? How did you find this information?

_____

_____

_____

_____

_____

4. Explain what you did to solve the problem.

_____

_____

_____

_____

_____

Use with Lesson 11.8.

Rate Tables

For each problem, fill in the rate table. Then answer the question below the table.

1. _____

_____
_____ ? _____ _____
(unit)

2. _____

_____
_____ ? _____ _____
(unit)

3. _____

_____
_____ ? _____ _____
(unit)

4. _____

_____
_____ ? _____ _____
(unit)

Use with Lesson 12.2.

Mammal Speeds

Introduction

The speed at which mammals walk or run is important for many of them. It helps them avoid or run from danger. Speed also helps a predator when it hunts other animals for food. Speed is useful when mammals search for food, water, or shelter.

The speed of mammals varies widely. The fastest mammals, including some antelopes and gazelles, can run two to three times as fast as the fastest human. On the other hand, some mammals move very slowly. Can you think of any? (Remember that a turtle is not a mammal.) A three-toed sloth might take 43 minutes to travel the length of a football field.

Some mammals can maintain fast speeds for long distances. Antelopes, zebras, and horses, as well as dolphins and whales, can travel for hours at average speeds of 20 miles per hour or more. Most mammals, however, are not marathon runners. They sprint, or move quickly, over short distances.

How does your speed compare to the speed of other mammals?

It couldn't happen, of course, but suppose that you, an elephant, and a cheetah were to race a distance of 100 yards, or 300 feet. Which of you would win? Which would come in second? Third?

My Prediction: First _____ Second _____ Third _____

On the line below, show the winner crossing the finish line. (Use "C" for the cheetah, "E" for the elephant, and "Me" for yourself.) Show where you think the second-place and third-place mammals will be when the fastest mammal crosses the finish line.

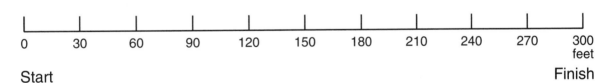

| | | | | | | | | | | |
0   30   60   90   120   150   180   210   240   270   300
feet

Start   Finish

What information would help you predict the winner?

_____

_____

_____

Mammal Speeds (cont.)

Check whether your prediction is correct.

The table below will help you figure out who would win the race and by how much.

Top Sprint Speeds (approximate) in Feet per Second	
Fourth grader . . . 20 ft/sec	Polar bear . . . . . . 58 ft/sec
Squirrel . . . . 18 ft/sec	Elephant . . . . 36 ft/sec
House cat. . . . . . 45 ft/sec	Quarter horse . . . 70 ft/sec
Cheetah . . . . . . 102 ft/sec	Fast human . . . . 30 ft/sec

Source (for nonhumans): International Wildlife

Rewrite the data above in the Mammal Speeds Table below.
Put the fastest mammal first, the second-fastest second, and so on.

Mammal Speeds Table	
Mammal	**Top Sprint Speed** (approximate)
1.	ft/sec
2.	ft/sec
3.	ft/sec
4.	ft/sec
5.	ft/sec
6.	ft/sec
7.	ft/sec
8.	ft/sec

Mammal Speeds (cont.)

According to the figures in the Mammal Speeds Table, how would the 300-foot race among an elephant, a cheetah, and a fourth grader turn out?

First _____ Second _____ Third _____

About how long does the winner of the race take to run 300 feet?

About _____ seconds

About how far do the second-place and third-place mammals run in the time it takes the winner to run 300 feet?

Second-place mammal   About _____ feet

Third-place mammal   About _____ feet

Would it be a close race?   _____

Draw a diagram of your findings. On the line below, show which mammal will win the race and where the second-place and third-place mammals will be when the fastest mammal crosses the finish line.

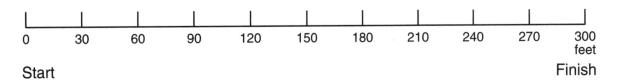

How good was your prediction? _____

Further Explorations

1. About how many times faster is the first-place mammal

   a. than the second-place mammal?   _____

   b. than the third-place mammal?   _____

2. According to the Mammal Speeds Table, a fourth grader can run faster than a squirrel. Does this mean that you could catch a squirrel by running after it? Why or why not?

   _____

   _____

   _____

Unit-Price Labels

Go to a grocery store or supermarket that displays the unit price of the items stocked on the shelves. Choose at least 6 items. For each item, record the following information in the table below:

Vita-C Orange Juice 12 oz	Price-Rite Supermarket
4673 KEHE / 12	$1.49
‖ ▌‖‖▌ ‖‖ ‖ ▌‖‖▌‖ ‖ ▌‖ ‖▌ ‖‖ ▌‖‖	
0 74401 11241	12.4¢ per oz

- the name of the item

- the amount (for example, 1 pound, 1 box of 8 items, 12 fluid ounces)

- the total price of the item

- the unit price (for example, 12.4¢/oz)

Item	Amount	Total Price	Unit Price
Vita-C Orange Juice	12 oz	$1.49	12.4¢/oz

Use with Lesson 12.3.

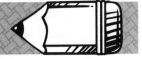

Mammal Heart Rates

Your heart pumps blood throughout your body. The blood carries heat, nutrients, and oxygen. It also takes away waste.

The rate at which a mammal's heart pumps is determined by the size and efficiency of the heart, as well as by the mammal's need for heat, nutrients, and oxygen. These needs are affected by the mammal's size and amount of activity. A mammal's heart rate can tell you about the mammal's size and the kind of life it leads.

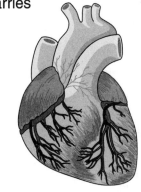

How fast does your heart beat?

1. If you know how, find your own heart rate; otherwise, use an estimated rate of 80 or 90 beats per minute. Record the rate below.

My heart beats about _____ times per minute.

Do you think mammals smaller than you have a slower or faster heart rate? _____

Examine the chart to find out.

Mammal Heart-Rate Data		
Mammal	**Heartbeats per Minute**	**Weight in Pounds**
Pygmy shrew	1,200	0.01
Mouse	650	0.25
Guinea pig	280	0.75
House cat	110	10
Human		
Newborn	110–160	7
7-year-old	90	50
Adult	60–80	160
Senior citizen	50–65	140
Tiger	40	500
African elephant	25	12,000
Gray whale	8	60,000

Source: Sportworks

Use with Lesson 12.3.

Mammal Heart Rates (cont.)

2. Do heart rate and weight seem to be related? If so, how?

_____

_____

3. Compare your heart rate to the rates of smaller mammals.

    a. A mouse's heart beats about   _____ times as fast as mine.

    b. A guinea pig's heart beats about   _____ times as fast as mine.

    c. A house cat's heart beats about   _____ times as fast as mine.

    d. It seems as though smaller mammals have _____ (faster or slower) heart rates than I have.

4. Compare your heart rate to the rates of larger mammals.

    a. A tiger's heart rate is about   _____ (what fraction?) of mine.

    b. An African elephant's heart rate is about   _____ (what fraction?) of mine.

    c. A gray whale's heart rate is about   _____ (what fraction?) of mine.

    d. It seems as though larger mammals have _____ (faster or slower) heart rates than I have.

One reason smaller mammals have faster heart rates is that they lose body heat more quickly than larger mammals. Their hearts have to pump quickly to keep a supply of warm blood constantly circulating throughout their bodies.

In order to create this heat, smaller mammals must eat a lot. They tend to be more active than larger mammals, because they are always searching for food. This makes their hearts work even harder. One result of a quicker heart rate is that smaller mammals tend to live shorter lives. The constant activity wears them out.

Use with Lesson 12.3.

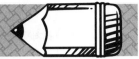

Mammal Heart Rates (cont.)

Challenge

5. Could you use what you have learned to estimate a squirrel's heart rate and a bison's heart rate? Write down your ideas and discuss them with your classmates. What other information might be helpful?

_____

_____

_____

_____

_____

_____

_____

My Estimates

6. a. I estimate that a squirrel's heart might beat about _____ times in a minute.

  b. I think this because _____

_____

_____

7. a. I estimate that a bison's heart might beat about _____ times in a minute.

  b. I think this because _____

_____

_____

See if you can find data to check your predictions.

Supermarket Sleuths

1. The Price-Rite Supermarket usually sells a
16-ounce box of rice for $0.85 and a 32-ounce
box for $1.37. One week, the store put the 16-ounce
box on sale for $0.72. Which is the better buy, the
16-ounce box at the sale price or the 32-ounce
box at the regular price? Explain your answer.

_____

_____

_____

_____

When two different sizes of the same item are sold at the regular price, the larger size
is usually the better buy. Supermarkets often put the smaller size of some items on
sale. However, the item on sale is not always the better buy.

2. Go to a supermarket and choose 5 items that are *on sale*. In the table below,
record the information both for the item *on sale* and for another size of the
same item sold at the *regular price*. Decide which is the better buy and write
your choice in the last column.

Item	Size on Sale	Size at Regular Price	Better Buy
rice	72¢ for 16 oz	$1.37 for 32 oz	32-oz size

Use with Lesson 12.5.

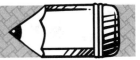

Cookie Problems

You may use a calculator to solve the problems.

Part A: Cynthia and Fred volunteered to buy cookies for the class party. They needed to buy enough cookies for 26 students and 1 teacher. They found a 1-pound see-through package of butter cookies and counted the cookies in the package—there were 3 rows with 15 cookies per row. They thought that they should buy enough so that each person could have 5 cookies.

1. How many packages of butter cookies would they need to buy?

_____

Explain how you found your answer.

_____

_____

_____

_____

Part B: After thinking it over, Cynthia and Fred decided that they did not want to buy butter cookies. Instead, they would buy 4 different kinds of cookies and would try to spend as little money as possible. They wanted to buy a total of 3 pounds of cookies. They walked down the cookie aisle and copied the price and weight on the package of each different kind of cookie on the shelves. Here are their data:

mint creams . . . . $2.79/lb   chocolate chip . . . . $2.39/12 oz

fudge marshmallow . . . . . $1.69/12 oz   oatmeal . . . . $2.03/17 oz

sugar wafers . . . . $2.99/8 oz   windmill $2.59/lb

vanilla wafers . . . . $1.39/11 oz   ginger snaps . . . . 60¢/8 oz

toffee bars . . . . $1.79/9 oz   vanilla cream . . . . $3.19/20 oz

Cookie Problems (cont.)

2. Study the data Cynthia and Fred collected. Which 4 kinds of cookies should they buy? Remember that the cookies should weigh about 3 pounds in all and that they should cost as little as possible.

Kind of Cookie	Number of Packages	Cost of Packages	Number of Ounces

Explain how you figured out the answer.

_____

_____

_____

_____

_____

_____

_____

3. What is the total weight of the cookies you selected? _____ oz

4. What is their total cost? $_____

5. What is the cost per ounce of all the cookies you selected? _____ ¢ per oz

                                                     Use with Lesson 12.7.

Globe Pattern

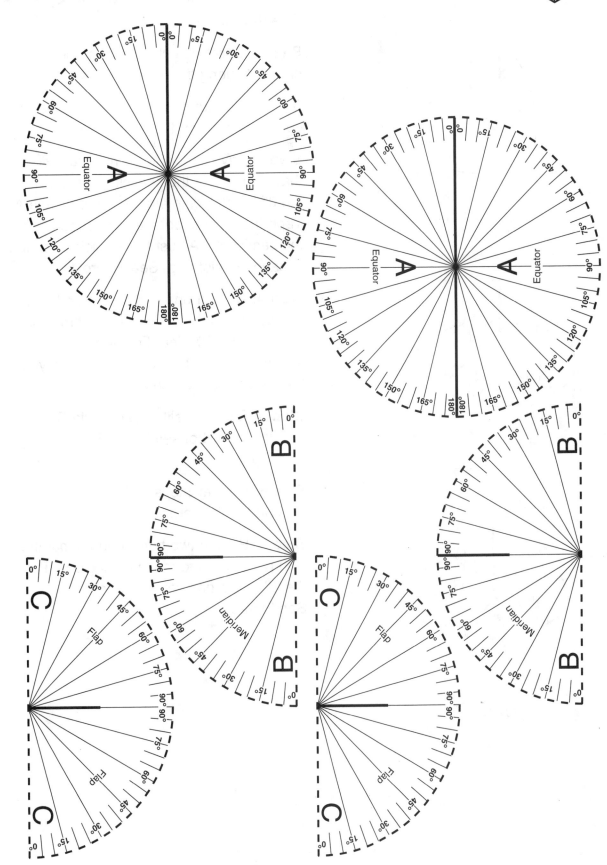

Use with Project 1.

How to Make a Cutaway Globe

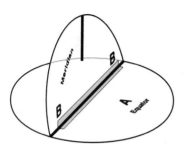

Figure 1

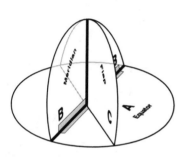

Figure 2

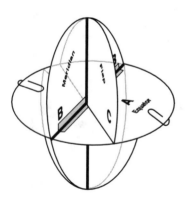

Figure 3

Directions:

Step 1: Carefully cut out one of the circles A along the dashed lines.

Step 2: Cut out one of the semicircles B; cut the thin slit on the semicircle.

Step 3: Lay semicircle B on circle A so that the base of the semicircle aligns with the 0° to 180° diameter shown on circle A. Tape the pieces together on both sides of the semicircle. Adjust the semicircle so that it stands straight up. See Figure 1.

Step 4: Cut out one of the semicircles C and cut along the slit. Fold the semicircle in half at the 90° line. Fold it back and forth several times at the same place until you have made a good crease.

Step 5: Slide the slit of semicircle C through the slit of semicircle B. See Figure 2.

Step 6: Repeat Steps 1–5 to make a second hemisphere.

Step 7: Put the two hemispheres together with paper clips to make a full globe. Put the 0° labels on circles A together. See Figure 3.

Use with Project 1.

A Paper Compass

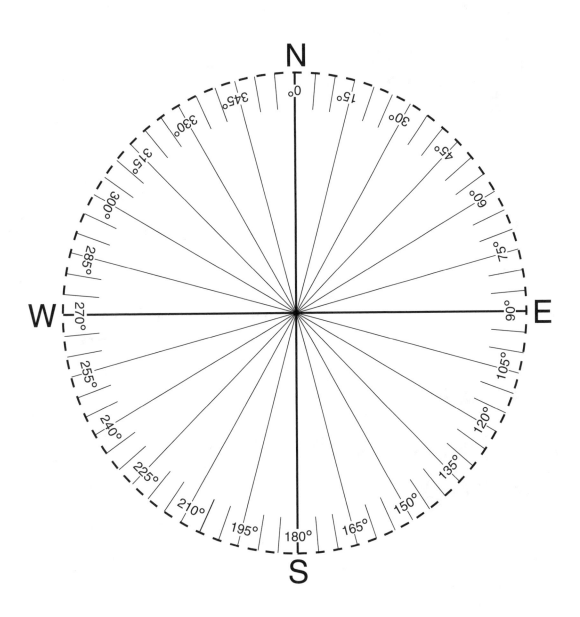

Making a Compass

In ancient times, sailors had only the sun, moon, and stars to aid them in navigation. The most important navigational instrument was the **compass.** The compass was invented more than 1,000 years ago. The first compass was a small bar of magnetized iron that floated on a reed in a bowl of water. The magnet in the iron would make the reed point to the magnetically charged North Pole. Using a compass, sailors could tell in which direction they were traveling.

You, too, can make a floating compass.

First, magnetize a steel sewing needle by stroking it with one pole of a strong bar magnet. Slowly stroke the needle from end to end **in one direction only.** Be sure to lift your hand up in the air before coming down for another stroke.

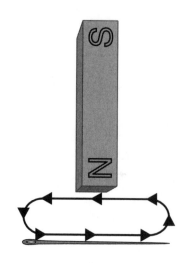

Slice a round ($\frac{1}{2}$-inch-thick) piece from a cork stopper. Cut a groove across the center of the top of the cork. Put the needle in the groove. Place the cork into a glass, china, or aluminum dish filled with water. Add a teaspoon of detergent to the water. The detergent will lower the surface tension of the water and prevent the cork from moving to one side of the dish and staying there.

The needle will behave like a compass needle. It will assume a North-South position because of Earth's magnetic field.

Source: Science for the Elementary School. New York: Macmillan, 1993.

Use with Project 2.

A Carnival Game

1. The class "quilt" of colored grids is placed on the floor and used as a target mat. The player stands about five feet from the mat and tosses a centimeter cube onto the mat. If the cube does not land on the mat, the player gets another turn. If the cube lands on more than one color, the color that is covered by most of the cube is used. The player may win a money prize, depending upon the color on which the cube lands. For each play, the player must buy a ticket for 10 cents.

Suppose that you bought 50 tickets.

a. How much would you pay for 50 tickets? _____

Suppose that your 50 tosses landed on the colors you recorded in the table at the bottom of page 225 of *Math Journal 2.*

b. How much prize money would you have won? _____

c. Would you have won or lost money on the game? _____

How much? _____

2. Suppose that the class decided to use the game to raise money to buy computer software. Pretend that students sold 1,000 tickets and that the cubes landed on the colors as shown on the board or on *Math Masters,* page 114.

a. How much would the class collect on the sale of tickets? _____

b. How much prize money would the class have to pay? _____

c. How much money would the class have raised? _____

A Carnival Game (cont.)

3. Work with your group to make up your own version of the Carnival Game.

   a. Record how much you would charge for a ticket and what the prizes would be for each color.

<table>
<tr><td>

Ticket Price

_____ per toss

</td><td>**Prizes**

yellow _____

red _____

green _____

blue _____

white _____</td></tr>
</table>

   b. Use the results for 1,000 cube drops shown on the board or on *Math Masters,* page 114 to answer the following questions:

      Would the class have won or lost money?   _____

      How much?   _____

4. Suppose that the class ran your game on Parents' Night.

   a. How many tickets do you estimate the class would sell?   _____

   b. How much money would the class get from ticket sales?   _____

   c. About how much money should you expect to pay in prizes?   _____

   d. About how much money should the class expect to earn?   _____

Patchwork Quilts

Throughout American history, women have worked together to make **patchwork quilts.** Because cloth was expensive and scarce, quilts were often made out of pieces of worn-out clothing or leftovers from another project. The quilters began by sewing together pieces of different colors, shapes, and textures to create a square pattern. Then they made more "patchwork" squares with the same pattern. When they had enough squares, they sewed them together to form the top of the quilt. Next they added a layer of wool fleece or cotton, called *batting,* and a cloth backing. They made a "sandwich" of the three layers—the backing on the bottom, the batting in the middle, and the patchwork on the top. They stretched the "sandwich" on a wooden frame and sewed the three layers together with tiny stitches.

The quilt was put together at a party, called a **quilting bee.** While cutting and sewing, the women would tell stories and share what went on in their lives. When the quilt was finished, the men joined the women for supper and dancing.

Many patchwork patterns have become traditions. Their names and designs have come from the everyday lives of the people who created them. For example, the "Buggy Wheel" pattern was probably inspired by a trip in a buggy. Along with walking and riding horses, buggies were a popular form of transportation in early America.

Buggy Wheel

Although early quilters may not have studied geometry in school, we can see geometry in many of their designs. Patchwork quilting involves the cutting of fabric into various geometric shapes and sewing them together into patterns. The pattern may be repeated over and over to form a quilt, or it may be rotated or reflected as the patches are assembled. Many patchwork patterns, such as the "Buggy Wheel" and "Does and Darts" patterns, are symmetric. Others, such as the "Crazy Quilt," seem to have been created at random.

Does and Darts

The beauty of a quilt lies in its uniqueness. No two patches need ever be the same because there are many possible arrangements of fabrics and colors.

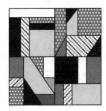
Crazy Quilt

Symmetric Patterns

Each pattern to the right of the "Pinwheel" pattern below has been colored in a different way. Notice how each color arrangement changes the number of lines of symmetry.

Pinwheel Pattern

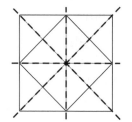 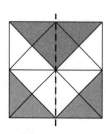 

lines of
symmetry: ___4___   ___2___   ___1___   ___0___

For each pattern below, draw all the lines of symmetry and record the number of lines of symmetry.

1. Bow-Tie Pattern

 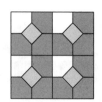 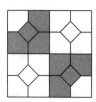

lines of
symmetry: _____   _____   _____   _____

2. Ohio Star Pattern

  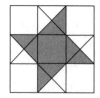

lines of
symmetry: _____   _____   _____   _____

3. Pineapple Log Cabin Pattern

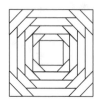 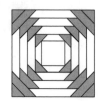 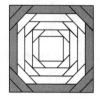 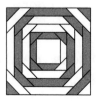

lines of
symmetry: _____   _____   _____   _____

Use with Project 4.

Traditional 9-Patch Patterns

Some patterns, called **9-Patch Patterns,** look like they are made up of 9 squares. You can make your own 9-Patch Pattern on a 3 by 3 grid.

Take out *Math Masters,* pages 210 and 211. Color 6 squares on *Math Masters,* page 210 in one color and the other 6 in a different color. Cut out the 12 squares. Then make triangles by cutting 6 of the squares in half along a diagonal. Make rectangles by cutting the other 6 squares in half along a line through the middle.

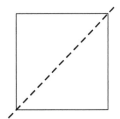 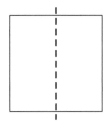

Now arrange some of the pieces on the grid on *Math Masters,* page 211 to make a pattern. Follow the directions below. When you have completed a pattern, draw and color it on one of the 3 by 3 grids below.

1. Make 1 or 2 patterns having 4 lines of symmetry.

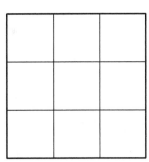 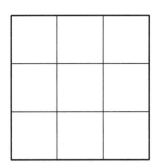

2. Make 1 or 2 patterns having 2 lines of symmetry.

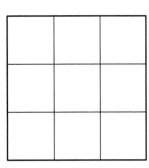 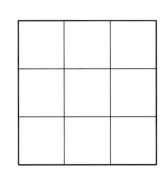

3. Make 1 or 2 patterns having no lines of symmetry.

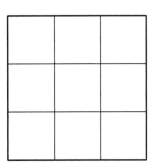

9-Patch Pattern Pieces

✂

Use with Project 4.

9-Patch Grid

Name   Date   Time

Rotating Patterns

Many traditional American quilts are made by rotating the square patterns as they are assembled into a quilt.

The first patchwork pattern below is a variation of the traditional "Grandmother's Fan" pattern. The patterns to the right of it show the pattern after it has been rotated clockwise a $\frac{1}{4}$, $\frac{1}{2}$, and $\frac{3}{4}$ turn.

starting position $\frac{1}{4}$ turn $\frac{1}{2}$ turn $\frac{3}{4}$ turn

This is what part of the quilt might look like if some of the patterns are rotated:

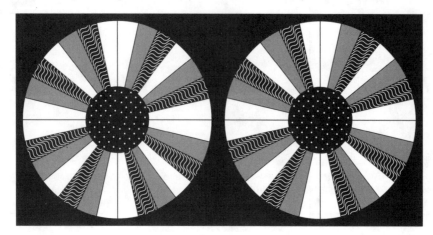

The "Wrench" pattern at the right, also known as the "Monkey Wrench," is a classic pattern that can be found in Amish and Mennonite quilts. Describe what it would look like if it were rotated a $\frac{1}{4}$, $\frac{1}{2}$, and $\frac{3}{4}$ turn.

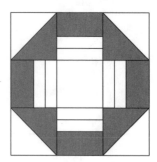

_____

_____

How many lines of symmetry does it have? _____

Use with Project 4.

Making a Quilt

As you study the traditional 9-Patch Patterns on this page, think about the following questions:

- Do you see where some of the patterns might have gotten their names?

- What are some similarities and differences among the patterns?

- How many lines of symmetry does each pattern have?

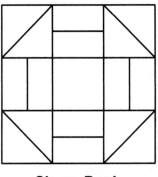

Churn Dash

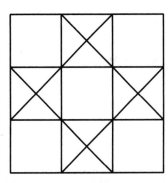

Ohio Star

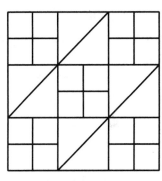

Jacob's Ladder

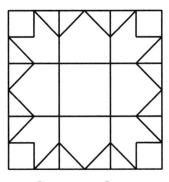

Storm at Sea

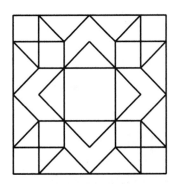

Weather Vane

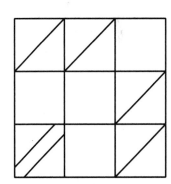

Maple Leaf

Making a Quilt (cont.)

Work with two partners to make a quilt.

1. Each of you needs three copies of *Math Masters,* page 216. Cut out the 3 by 3 grid on each sheet. **Make sure you include the border with the dots!**

2. Cut out the quilting pattern shapes on *Math Masters,* page 215.

3. With your partners, choose one of the patterns on *Math Masters,* page 213. Decide on a way to color it. The colored pattern your group chooses **should not have more than two lines of symmetry.** Each group member should then copy this design onto three 3 by 3 grids. Use the pieces you cut out of *Math Masters,* page 215 to trace the pattern onto the 3 by 3 grids. Then color the pattern. Or you can trace the pieces onto colored paper, cut out the tracings, and paste them onto the 3 by 3 grids. Your group should end up with nine square "patches" that **look exactly alike.**

4. Punch holes through the dots along the border of the patches.

5. Lay all nine square patches on the floor and arrange them so that some of the square patterns are rotated. When your group has agreed on an arrangement, line up the holes on the edges of the squares. Then fasten the pieces together by weaving yarn in and out of the holes. If you wish, make a ruffle for your quilt out of a strip of crepe paper. Pleat and glue the ruffle around the outer edges of the quilt.

Here is an example of a quilt with the "Maple Leaf" pattern:

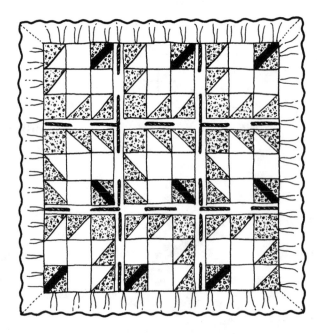

Quilting Pattern Shapes

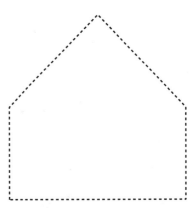

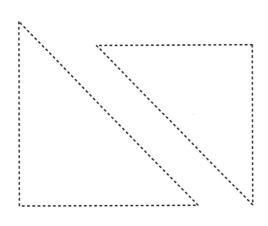

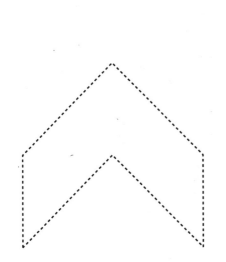
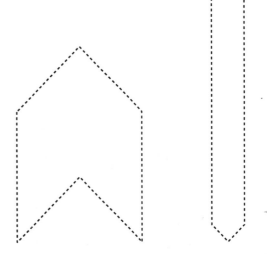

Use with Project 4.

9-Patch Grid with Border

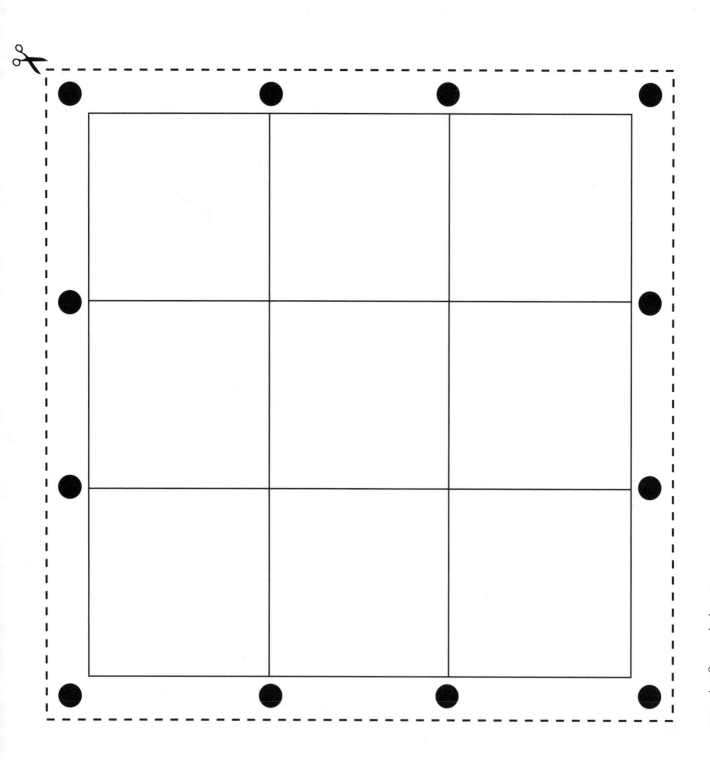

Use with Project 4.

Which Soft Drink Would You Buy?

For each set of soft-drink cups, record the following information:

- The name of the place from which the cups come

- The size of the cup (small, medium, or large)

- The price

- The capacity in fluid ounces

Then calculate each unit price in cents per fluid ounce, rounded to the nearest tenth of a cent.

Soft-Drink Cups from

Size	Price	Capacity (fl oz)	Unit Price (¢/fl oz)

Soft-Drink Cups from

Size	Price	Capacity (fl oz)	Unit Price (¢/fl oz)

Soft-Drink Cups from

Size	Price	Capacity (fl oz)	Unit Price (¢/fl oz)

Consumer Report: Best Soft-Drink Prices

Imagine that you have been assigned by *Kids' Consumer Reports* to investigate and report on the prices of soft drinks. Use the information your group recorded on *Math Masters,* page 217 to prepare a group report for the magazine. Your report might contain graphs, tables, and pictures. Try to answer some of the following questions in your report:

- Do small (or medium or large) cups at different places contain the same amount?

- Are prices similar for similar sizes? (For example, are the small-size drinks about the same price at different places?)

- Which places have the least expensive soft drinks? The most expensive soft drinks?

- Is the largest size always the best value?

- Which types of businesses offer better values? (For example, do restaurants generally offer better values than movie theaters?)

- What would you recommend to consumers? Do some places offer free refills? If so, how would this affect your recommendation?

_____

_____

_____

_____

_____

_____

_____

_____

_____

_____

_____

(Continue on the back.)

Blueprints

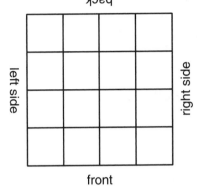

Sample Blueprint

back

1	2	2	2
0	0	0	1
0	1	1	1
0	2	2	1

left side   right side

front

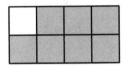

front view

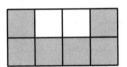

left-side view

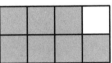

back view

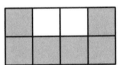

right-side view

Blueprint Mat

back

left side   right side

front

✂ --

Group _____

Cut the sheet apart along the dashed line. Build your own structure on the Blueprint Mat (upper right). Then record the front view and the left-side view in the grid squares below. Leave your structure so that other students can find it, using these views.

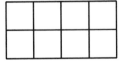

front view

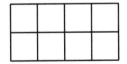

left-side view

If you make a mistake, use the grids below to draw the corrected views.

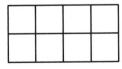

front view

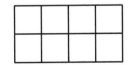

left-side view

Use with Project 6.

Building Structures

1. Use the blueprint at the right to build a structure on the Blueprint Mat (*Math Masters,* page 219). Use centimeter cubes.

back

2	1	1	0
0	0	0	0
1	2	0	1
0	1	1	0

left side   right side

front

  a. Compare your structure to the structure built by your partner. They *should* look the same.

  b. Draw all four views of your structure by shading squares.

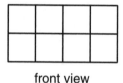

front view   left-side view   back view   right-side view

  c. Compare your views to those drawn by your partner. They *should* be the same.

2. Build any structure you wish on your Blueprint Mat. *Reminder:* Use no more than two centimeter cubes on a square.

back

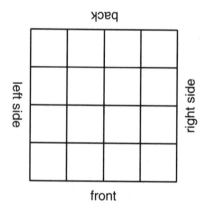

left side   right side

front

  a. Record your structure on the blueprint at the right.

  b. Draw all four views of your structure by shading the squares below. Ask your partner to check your work.

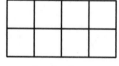 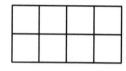 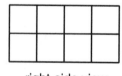 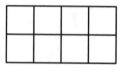

front view   left-side view   back view   right-side view

  c. Compare the views of opposite sides of your structure.

3. Here is the front view of a structure. Draw its back view.

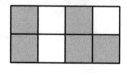 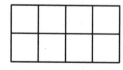

front view   back view

Use with Project 6.

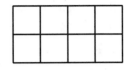

More Structures

1. Here are two views of a structure. Draw its other two views.

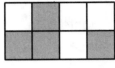
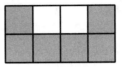
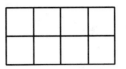
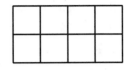

front view   left-side view   back view   right-side view

2. Here is the front view, as well as the left-side view, of a structure.

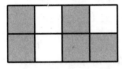
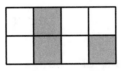

front view   left-side view

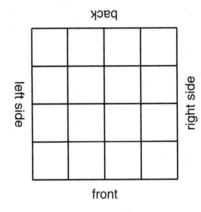

a. Build a structure that has these views. Record it on the blueprint at the right.

b. Compare your structure and blueprint to your partner's. Are they the same?

3. Work with your partner. Use the following front view and left-side view to build three different structures. Record each structure on one of the blueprints.

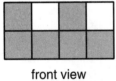

front view

left-side view

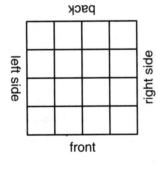
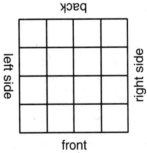
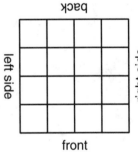

4. a. Is it possible to build two different structures from the same front and left-side views? _____

   b. Is it possible to build two different structures from the same front, left-side, back, and right-side views? _____

The ancient Maya used a writing system made of pictures. The Maya had words and numerals for numbers, just as we do. Below are the Maya picture words and numerals for 0–10, and the pronunciation of those words.

Maya picture words	Maya numerals/ pronunciation	
	0 mi	zero
	1 hun	one
	2 ca	two
	3 ox	three
	4 can	four
	5 ho	five
	6 uac	six
	7 uuc	seven
	8 uaxac	eight
	9 bolon	nine
	10 lahun	ten

Numbers, Maya Style

The Maya are the native people who have lived for thousands of years in a 120,000-square-mile area of Central America stretching from the Valley of Mexico through Guatemala. Today there are about 6 million Maya in Central America.

The ancient Maya civilization reached its height in A.D. 250 and flourished for more than 600 years. The Maya people built large cities and tall limestone pyramids where they performed religious ceremonies. They traded cloth, cacao beans for making chocolate, and other items throughout Central America. Children, parents, grandparents, and even great-grandparents all lived together, and everyone helped with the housework and farming. The ancient Maya had no schools. Children learned everything by watching and helping adults.

The ancient Maya invented a number system using place value with dots and dashes to represent numbers, and a special symbol for zero. Their numbers read from top to bottom.

In our place-value system, we group numbers by tens and powers of ten. When we write a number like 2,457, we really mean $(2 * 1,000) + (4 * 100) + (5 * 10) + (7 * 1)$. The Maya place-value system works similarly with 20s and powers of 20. But while we use 10 different symbols to write all of our numbers (the digits 0–9), the ancient Maya used only three symbols.

Maya Number Symbols

(symbol)	0
•	1
—	5

Our Place-Value System	Maya Place-Value System
10,000s (10 * 10 * 10 * 10)	160,000s (20 * 20 * 20 * 20)
1000s (10 * 10 * 10)	8000s (20 * 20 * 20)
100s (10 * 10)	400s (20 * 20)
10s	20s
1s	1s

To write the number 837 using the Maya system, put a 2 in the 400s place, a 1 in the 20s place, and 17 in the 1s place:

$$2 * 400 = 800$$
$$1 * 20 = 20$$
$$17 * 1 = + 17$$
$$837$$

Use with Project 7.

Family Letter

Introduction to Fourth Grade Everyday Mathematics®

Welcome to *Fourth Grade Everyday Mathematics.* It is part of an elementary school mathematics curriculum developed by the University of Chicago School Mathematics Project (UCSMP).

Everyday Mathematics offers students a broad background in mathematics. Some approaches in this program may differ from those you used as a student. However, the approaches the authors use are based on research results, field-test experiences, and the mathematics that students will need in the twenty-first century. Following are some program highlights:

▷ A problem-solving approach that uses mathematics in everyday situations

▷ A balance of independent activities that develop confidence and self-reliance, and partner and small-group activities that promote cooperative learning

▷ Concepts and skills introduced and reviewed throughout the school year, promoting retention through a variety of exposures

▷ Concepts and skills developed through hands-on activities

▷ Opportunities to discuss and communicate mathematically

▷ Frequent practice using games as an alternative to tedious drills

▷ Opportunities for home and school communication

Fourth Grade Everyday Mathematics emphasizes the following content:

Algebra and Uses of Variables Reading, writing, and solving number sentences

Algorithms and Procedures Exploring addition, subtraction, multiplication, and division methods; inventing individual procedures and algorithms; and experimenting with calculator procedures

Coordinate Systems and Other Reference Frames Using numbers in reference frames: number lines, coordinates, times, dates, latitude and longitude, and elevation above and below sea level

Exploring Data Collecting, organizing, displaying, and interpreting numerical data

Functions, Patterns, and Sequences Designing, exploring, and using geometric and number patterns

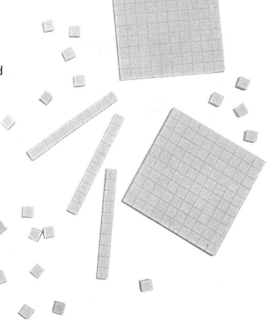

Geometry and Spatial Sense Developing an intuitive sense about 2- and 3-dimensional objects, their properties, uses, and relationships

Measures and Measurement Exploring and using metric and U.S. customary measures: linear, area, volume, weight; and exploring geographical measures

Numbers, Numeration, and Order Relations Reading, writing, and using whole numbers, fractions, decimals, percents, and negative numbers; and exploring scientific notation

Operations, Number Facts, and Number Systems Practicing addition and subtraction to proficiency; and developing multiplication and division skills

Problem Solving and Mathematical Modeling Investigating methods for solving problems using mathematics in everyday situations, such as travel, shopping, health, and sports

Math Experiences Your Child Will Have This Year

The mathematics program we are using this year—*Everyday Mathematics*—will help your child appreciate how mathematics affects our daily lives and will prepare your child for making sound decisions in areas that involve mathematics. Experiences your child will have include the following:

▷ Collecting, displaying, and interpreting numerical information—for example, about the climate in the United States and other parts of the world; about the way people in other countries live; about mammals; and about the students in the class themselves

▷ Exploring the role of mathematics in geography—for example, using latitude and longitude to locate places in the world; using a map scale to find distances; and using a time-zone map to compare the time of day in various locations

▷ Developing methods for estimating the lengths, heights, and weights of objects; and practicing making accurate measurements

▷ Examining several methods for adding, subtracting, multiplying, and dividing numbers; and becoming proficient at using one of these methods for each operation

▷ Beginning the study of algebra and continuing the study of geometry

▷ Predicting the outcomes of events that occur by chance and checking the predictions by performing experiments

Throughout the year, you will receive Family Letters informing you of the mathematical content to be studied in each unit. Letters may include definitions of new terms as well as suggestions for at-home activities designed to reinforce skills. We are looking forward to an exciting year filled with discovery. You will enjoy seeing your child's mathematical understanding grow.

Use with Lesson 1.1.

Unit 1: Naming and Constructing Geometric Figures

During the next two to three weeks, the class will study the geometry of 2-dimensional shapes. Students will examine definitions and properties of various shapes and the relationships between and among these shapes. Students will use compasses to construct shapes and to create their own geometric designs. In the process, they will develop an appreciation for geometric patterns and their many uses.

Please keep this Family Letter for reference as your child works through Unit 1.

Vocabulary

Important terms in Unit 1:

concave (nonconvex) polygon A polygon in which at least one vertex is "pushed in."

concave polygon

convex polygon A polygon in which all vertices are "pushed outward."

convex polygon

endpoint A point at the end of a line segment or a ray. A line segment is normally named using the letter labels of its end points.

line segment A straight path joining two points. The two points are called the endpoints of the segment.

parallelogram A quadrilateral that has two pairs of parallel sides. Opposite sides of a parallelogram are congruent.

polygon A closed, 2-dimensional figure that is made up of line segments joined end to end. The line segments of a polygon may not cross.

quadrangle or quadrilateral A polygon that has four sides and four angles.

ray A straight path that extends infinitely from a point called its endpoint.

rhombus A quadrilateral whose sides are all the same length.

trapezoid A quadrilateral that has exactly one pair of parallel sides.

vertex The point where the rays of an angle, the sides of a polygon, or the edges of a polyhedron meet.

Do-Anytime Activities

1 Help your child discover everyday uses of geometry as found in art, architecture, jewelry, toys, and so on.

2 See how many words your child can think of that have Greek/Latin prefixes such as *tri-, quad-, penta-, hexa-, octa-,* and so on.

3 Help your child think of different ways to draw or make figures without the use of a compass, protractor, or straightedge. For example, you can trace the bottom of a can to make a circle, bend a straw to form a triangle, or make different shapes with toothpicks.

4 Challenge your child to draw or build something, such as a toothpick bridge, using triangle and square shapes. Or show pictures of bridges and point out the triangle shapes used in bridges to provide support.

Use with Lesson 1.1.

As You Help Your Child with Homework

As your child brings assignments home, you may want to go over the instructions together, clarifying them as necessary. The answers listed below will guide you through this unit's Study Links.

Study Link 1.2

1. Answers vary.

2. Answers vary.

Study Link 1.3

1. **a.** 12 **b.** 8

2. **a.** 6 **b.** 12 **c.** 4

Study Link 1.4

1. Sample answer:

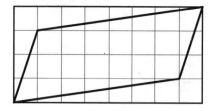

2. **a.** yes **b.** yes **c.** yes **d.** no

3. Sample answer:

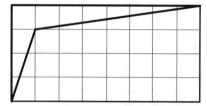

4. Sample answer:

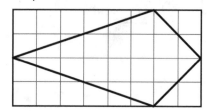

Study Link 1.5

a. D and O

b. All capital letters except D and O

c. Answers vary.

d. Answers vary.

Study Link 1.6

_f_ octagon

_e_ rhombus

_h_ right angle

_c_ trapezoid

_a_ square

_i_ equilateral triangle

_d_ parallel lines

_g_ pentagon

_b_ quadrangle

Study Link 1.7

1. Answers vary.

2. Answers vary.

Study Link 1.8

1. rhombus

2. rectangle

3. equilateral triangle

4. Answers vary.

Use with Lesson 1.1.

Name Date Time

Geometry in Your Home

Study Link 1.2

SRB 76 94

1. List at least 5 things in your home that remind you of line segments.

____

____

____

____

____

2. Look for geometric patterns in your home. Sketch at least two of the patterns that you find. Write a description of the pattern for each of your drawings.

Shape Search

1. Study the figure at the right.

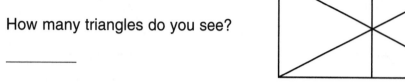

   a. How many triangles do you see?

   _____

   b. How many triangles have
      a right angle?

   _____

2. Study the figure at the right.

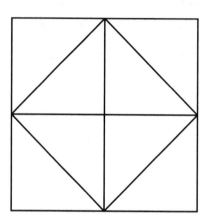

   a. How many squares do you see?

   _____

   b. How many triangles?

   _____

   c. How many rectangles
      that are not squares?

   _____

3. Make a 4 by 4 array of dots on the back of this page, like this but bigger:

      • • • •

      • • • •

      • • • •

      • • • •

Make up a geometry puzzle like the one in Problem 2. Draw line segments
to connect some of the dots in your array. Then ask someone to count the
number of triangles in your puzzle.

Classifying Quadrangles

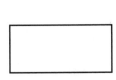
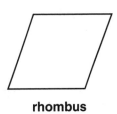
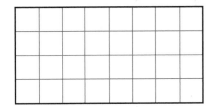

square   **rectangle**   **rhombus**   **trapezoid**

1. A parallelogram is a quadrangle that has 2 pairs of parallel sides. Draw a parallelogram at the right.

2. Answer *yes* or *no.* Then explain your answers to a friend or someone at home.

    a. Is a rectangle a parallelogram? _____

    b. Is a square a parallelogram? _____

    c. Is a square a rhombus? _____

    d. Is a trapezoid a parallelogram? _____

3. Draw a quadrangle that has at least 1 right angle.

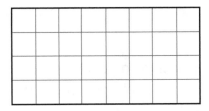

4. Draw a quadrangle that has 2 pairs of equal sides but is NOT a parallelogram.

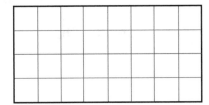

A Polygon Alphabet

Can you design an alphabet using only polygons? Try reading this message:

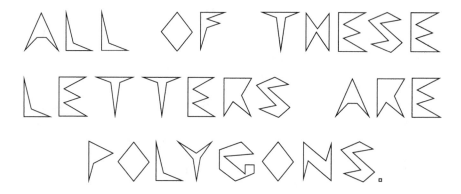

Now try designing your own alphabet. You can start with the samples above and finish the alphabet, or design your own versions of all 26 letters. Start with all capital letters. You'll have to simplify, because a polygon can't have any curves, and it can't have any "holes."

For example, if you look at the letter "P" in the sample above, you see that there is no opening in the upper part. Making it look like this, Ᵽ, would make it easier to read, but it wouldn't be a polygon!

Write the alphabet you designed on the back of this paper. When your alphabet is finished, look at all of the letters and ask yourself the following questions:

a. Which letters are convex polygons?

b. Which letters are nonconvex (concave) polygons?

c. Do any of your letters have special names as polygons?

d. Which letters were most difficult to design? Why?

Use your alphabet to write a message to someone who is not in your class. Was that person able to read it? Report back to the class.

If you enjoyed this activity, you can continue by designing the 26 lowercase (small) letters and the 10 digits, as well.

Definition Match

Match each description of a geometric figure in Column I with its name in Column II. Some of the items in Column II don't have a match.

I   **II**

a. a polygon with 4 right angles and 4 sides of the same length

_____ octagon

_____ rhombus

b. a polygon with 4 sides, none of which are the same size

_____ right angle

c. a quadrilateral with exactly one pair of opposite sides that are parallel

_____ trapezoid

_____ hexagon

d. lines that never intersect

_____ square

e. a parallelogram with all sides the same length, but not a rectangle

_____ equilateral triangle

_____ perpendicular lines

f. a polygon with 8 sides

_____ parallel lines

g. a polygon with 5 sides

_____ pentagon

h. an angle that measures 90°

_____ isosceles triangle

i. a triangle with all sides the same length

_____ quadrangle

Use with Lesson 1.6.

The Radius of a Circle

1. Find a circular object. Trace it in the space below.

   a. Draw a point to mark the approximate center of the circle.
   Then draw a point on the circle.

   b. Use a straightedge to draw the **radius** that connects these points.

   c. Measure the radius to the nearest $\frac{1}{4}$ inch.

   The radius of the circle is _____ inches.

2. Find another circular object. Trace it in the space below.

   a. Draw a point to mark the approximate center of the circle.
   Then draw a point on the circle.

   b. Use a straightedge to draw the **radius** that connects these points.

   c. Measure the radius to the nearest millimeter.

   The radius of the circle is _____ millimeters.

Use with Lesson 1.7.

Polygon Riddles

Answer each riddle. Then draw a picture of the shape in the space to the right.

1. I am a polygon.

I am a quadrangle.

All of my sides are the same length.

None of my angles are right angles.

What am I? _____

2. I am a quadrangle.

I have two pairs of parallel sides.

All of my angles are right angles.

I am not a square.

What am I? _____

3. I am a polygon.

All of my sides have the same measure.

All of my angles have the same measure.

I have three sides.

What am I? _____

4. Make up your own polygon riddle using 4 clues. Make two of the clues hard and two of the clues easy. Ask a friend or someone at home to solve your polygon riddle.

_____

_____

_____

_____

Family Letter

Unit 2: Using Numbers and Organizing Data

Your child is about to begin this year's work with numbers. Throughout the school year, the class will examine what numbers mean and how they are used in everyday life to convey information and solve problems.

In today's world, numbers are all around us—in newspapers and magazines and on TV. We use them

- to count things (*How many people are in the room?*)

- to measure things (*How tall are you?*)

- to create codes (*What is your Social Security number?*)

- to locate things in reference frames (*What time is it?*)

- to express rates, scales, and percents (*How many miles per gallon does your car get? What percent voted for Jamie?*)

The class will experience many different situations in which numbers are used. Your child will collect examples of numbers throughout the year and record the most interesting ones in a journal.

While we often deal with numbers one at a time, there are times when we need to interpret a whole collection of numbers. The class will learn to organize such collections of numbers in tables and graphs and to draw conclusions about them.

Computation is an important part of problem solving. Fortunately, we are no longer restricted to paper-and-pencil methods of computation: We can use calculators to solve lengthy problems or computer programs to solve very complex ones. Your child will have many opportunities for practicing mental and paper-and-pencil methods of computation, for using a calculator, and for deciding which is most appropriate for solving a particular problem.

Many of us were taught that there is just one way to do computations. For example, we may have learned to subtract by "borrowing." We may not have realized that there are other ways of subtracting numbers. While students will not be expected to learn more than one method, they will examine several different methods and realize that there are often several ways to arrive at the same result. They will have the option of learning a method they find most comfortable, or even inventing one of their own.

Mathematics games will be used throughout the school year to practice various arithmetic skills. Through games, practice becomes a thinking activity to be enjoyed. The games your child will play in this unit will provide practice with renaming numbers, with addition, and with subtraction. They require very little in the way of materials, so you may play them at home as well.

Please keep this Family Letter for reference as your child works through Unit 2.

Use with Lesson 1.9.

Vocabulary

Important terms in Unit 2:

algorithm A set of step-by-step instructions for doing something, such as carrying out a computation or solving a problem.

base ten The property of our number system that results in each place having a value of 10 times the place to its right.

column-addition method A method for adding numbers in which the addends' digits are first added in each place-value column separately and then 10-for-1 trades are made until each column has only one digit. Lines are drawn to separate the place-value columns.

	100s	10s	1s
	2	4	8
+	1	8	7
Add the columns:	3	12	15
Adjust the 1s and 10s:	3	13	5
Adjust the 10s and 100s:	4	3	5

equivalent names Different names for the same number. For example, 2 + 6, 4 + 4, 12 − 4, 18 − 10, 100 − 92, 5 + 1 + 2, eight, VIII, and ⫽⫽⫽ ⫽⫽⫽ are *equivalent names* for 8.

line plot A sketch of data in which check marks, Xs, or other marks above a number line show the frequency of each value.

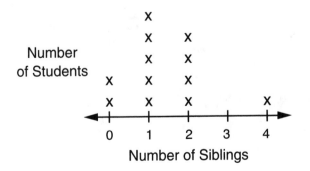

mean The sum of a set of numbers divided by the number of numbers in the set. The mean is often referred to simply as the *average*.

median The middle value in a set of data when the data are listed in order from least to greatest. If there is an even number of data points, the median is the *mean* of the two middle values.

mode The value or values that occur most often in a set of data.

name-collection box A diagram that is used for writing equivalent names for a number.

8
2 + 6
4 + 4
VIII
eight

partial-sums method A way to add in which sums are computed for each place (ones, tens, hundreds, and so on) separately, and are then added to give the final answer.
Example: 496 + 229 + 347 = ?

```
                                      496
                                      229
                                    + 347
Add the hundreds: 400 + 200 + 300 →   900
     Add the tens:   90 + 20 + 40 →   150
     Add the ones:     6 + 9 + 7  →    22
    Find the total:  900 + 150 + 22 → 1,072
```

range The difference between the maximum and the minimum in a set of data.

whole numbers The numbers 0, 1, 2, 3, 4, and so on.

Use with Lesson 1.9.

Do-Anytime Activities

To work with your child on the concepts taught in this unit, try these interesting and rewarding activities:

1 Have your child see how many numbers he or she can identify in newspapers, magazines, advertisements, or news broadcasts.

2 Have your child collect and compare the measurements (height and weight) or accomplishments of favorite professional athletes.

3 Look up the different time zones of the United States and the world, quizzing your child on what time it would be at that moment at a particular location.

4 Have your child look for different representations of the same number. For example, he or she may see the same money amounts expressed in different ways, such as 50¢, $0.50, or 50 cents.

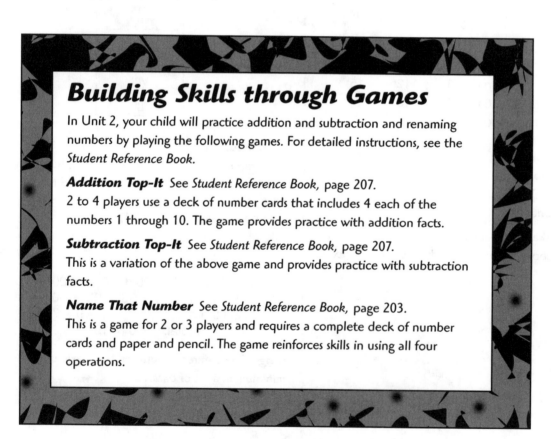

Building Skills through Games

In Unit 2, your child will practice addition and subtraction and renaming numbers by playing the following games. For detailed instructions, see the *Student Reference Book.*

Addition Top-It See *Student Reference Book*, page 207.
2 to 4 players use a deck of number cards that includes 4 each of the numbers 1 through 10. The game provides practice with addition facts.

Subtraction Top-It See *Student Reference Book*, page 207.
This is a variation of the above game and provides practice with subtraction facts.

Name That Number See *Student Reference Book*, page 203.
This is a game for 2 or 3 players and requires a complete deck of number cards and paper and pencil. The game reinforces skills in using all four operations.

Use with Lesson 1.9.

As You Help Your Child with Homework

As your child brings assignments home, you may want to go over the instructions together, clarifying them as necessary. The answers listed below will guide you through some of the Study Links in this unit.

Study Link 2.2

4. Sample answers:
10 + 10 + 10 + 10
100 − 60

5. Sample answers:
18 × 2
40 − 4

Study Link 2.3

1. 876,504,000

5. a. 4,499,702   **c.** 30,457,300

6. a. 496,708   **c.** 19,410,366

Study Link 2.4

2. 581,970,000   **3.** 97,654,320

6. 97,308,080

Study Link 2.5

2. 27   **3.** 8   **4.** 2   **5.** 6   **6.** 5

Study Link 2.6

1.

Class Data on Computer Time

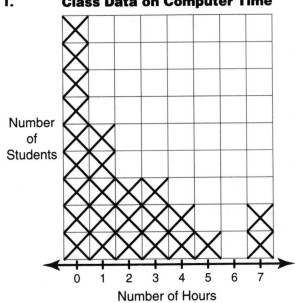

Number of Students

Number of Hours
Spent on the Computer Each Week

2. a. 7   **b.** 0   **c.** 7   **d.** 0   **e.** 1

3. Answers vary.

Study Link 2.7

Sample problem using the partial-sums method:

1. 152   **2.** 510

3. 613   **4.** 1,432

	4	9	3
+	9	3	9
1	3	0	0
	1	2	0
+		1	2
1	4	3	2

Sample problem using the column-addition method:

7. 136   **8.** 720

9. 225   **10.** 720

	8	9
+	4	7
12	16
13	6
1	3	6

Study Link 2.8

1. a. 645   **b.** 19   **c.** 626   **d.** 151

2. giraffe, Asian elephant, and rhinoceros

3. 90   **4.** dog   **5.** mouse

Study Link 2.9

Sample problem using the trade-first subtraction method:

1. 68   **2.** 382   **3.** 367

	8	16
	9	6
−	2	8
	6	8

Sample problem using the partial-differences subtraction method:

1. 29   **2.** 57   **3.** 406

	8	4
−	5	5
+	3	0
−		1
	2	9

Numbers Everywhere

Read pages 2 and 3 in your *Student Reference Book*.

Find examples of numbers—all kinds of numbers. Look in newspapers and magazines. Look in books. Look on food packages. Ask people in your family for examples.

Write your numbers below. If an adult says you may, cut out the numbers and tape them onto the back of this page.

Be sure you write what the numbers mean.

Example Mount Everest is 29,028 feet high. It is the world's tallest mountain.

_____

_____

_____

_____

_____

_____

_____

_____

_____

_____

_____

_____

_____

_____

_____

_____

_____

Name   Date   Time

Many Names for Numbers

1. Cross out the names that do not belong in the name-collection box below.

2. Write the name for this name-collection box.

3. Write five names for 64.

28
67 − 39
4 × 7
2 × 8
$\frac{56}{2}$
100 ÷ 4

413 − 281
50 + 40 + 42
150 − 18
66 × 2
133 − 1

64

4. Pretend that the 4-key is broken on your calculator. Write six ways to display the number 40 on the calculator without using the 4-key. Try to use different numbers and operations.

Example 2 × 2 × 10

_____   _____   _____

_____   _____   _____

5. Now pretend that the 3-key and the 6-key are broken. Write six ways to display the number 36 without using these keys.

_____   _____   _____

_____   _____   _____

Place Value in Whole Numbers

1. Write the number that has

   6 in the millions place,
   4 in the thousands place,
   7 in the ten-millions place,
   5 in the hundred-thousands place,
   8 in the hundred-millions place, and
   0 in the remaining places.

   ___ ___ ___, ___ ___ ___, ___ ___ ___

2. Write the number that has

   7 in the ten-thousands place,
   3 in the millions place,
   1 in the hundred-thousands place,
   8 in the tens place,
   2 in the ten-millions place, and
   0 in the remaining places.

   ___ ___, ___ ___ ___, ___ ___ ___

3. Compare the two numbers you wrote in Problems 1 and 2.

   Which is greater? _____

4. The 6 in 46,711,304 stands for 6 __*million*__, or __6,000,000__.

   a. The 4 in 508,433,529 stands for 400 _____, or _____.

   b. The 8 in 182,945,777 stands for 80 _____, or _____.

   c. The 5 in 509,822,119 stands for 500 _____, or _____.

   d. The 3 in 450,037,111 stands for 30 _____, or _____.

5. Write the number that is 1 million more.

   a. 3,499,702 _____

   b. 12,877,000 _____

   c. 29,457,300 _____

   d. 149,691,688 _____

6. Write the number that is 1 million less.

   a. 1,496,708 _____

   b. 5,321,589 _____

   c. 20,410,366 _____

   d. 450,620,500 _____

More Place Value in Whole Numbers

1. Write the numbers in order from smallest to largest.

15,964   1,509,460   150,094,400
1,400,960   15,094,600

_____

_____

_____

_____

_____

2. Write the number that has

5 in the hundred-millions place,
7 in the ten-thousands place,
1 in the millions place,
9 in the hundred-thousands place,
8 in the ten-millions place, and
0 in all other places.

___ ___ ___ , ___ ___ ___ , ___ ___ ___

3. Write the largest number you can. Use each digit just once.

3 5 0 7 9 2 6 4 _____

4. Write the value of the digit 8 in each numeral below.

a. 80,007,941 _____

b. 835,099,714 _____

c. 8,714,366 _____

d. 860,490 _____

5. Write each number using digits.

a. four hundred eighty-seven million, sixty-three _____

b. fifteen million, two hundred ninety-seven _____

6. Answer the following riddle:

I am an 8-digit number.

• The digit in the thousands place is the result of dividing 64 by 8.
• The digit in the millions place is the result of dividing 63 by 9.
• The digit in the ten-millions place is the result of dividing 54 by 6.
• The digit in the tens place is the result of dividing 40 by 5.
• The digit in the hundred-thousands place is the result of dividing 33 by 11.
• All the other digits are the result of subtracting any number from itself.

What number am I? ___ ___ , ___ ___ ___ , ___ ___ ___

Collecting Data

1. Make a list of all the people in your family. Include all the people living at home now. Also include any brothers or sisters that live somewhere else. The people who live at home do not have to be related to you. Don't forget to write your name in the list.

   You will need this information to learn about the sizes of families in your class.

   Names of people in my family:

   _____   _____   _____

   _____   _____   _____

   _____   _____   _____

   _____   _____   _____

   How many people are in your family? _____

The tally chart at the right shows the number of books that some fourth grade students read over the summer.

Use the information to answer the questions below.

2. How many students reported the

   number of books they read? _____

3. What is the **maximum** (the largest

   number of books reported)? _____

4. What is the **minimum** (the smallest

   number of books reported)? _____

5. What is the **range**? _____

6. What is the **mode** (the most frequent

   number of books reported)? _____

Number of Books Reported	Number of Students
2	///
3	////
4	
5	//// //
6	//// /
7	//
8	////

Line Plots

Mrs. Chen's students estimated the amount of time they spend on the computer each week. The tally chart below shows the data they collected.

Number of Hours on the Computer per Week	Number of Students
0	＃＃ ////
1	＃＃
2	///
3	///
4	//
5	/
6	
7	//

1. Construct a line plot for the data.

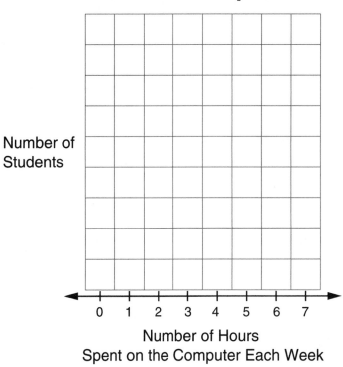

Class Data on Computer Time

Number of Students

0   1   2   3   4   5   6   7
Number of Hours
Spent on the Computer Each Week

2. Find the following landmarks for the data:

   a. What is the maximum number of hours spent on the computer

     each week? _____ hours

   b. What is the minimum number of hours spent on the computer

     each week? _____ hours

   c. What is the range? _____ hours

   d. What is the mode? _____ hours

   e. What is the median number of hours spent on the computer

     each week? _____ hours

3. Estimate the amount of time that you spend on the computer

   each week. _____ hours

Addition of Multidigit Numbers

Use the partial-sums addition method to solve Problems 1–6.

1. 67 + 85 = _____

2. _____ = 439 + 71

3. _____ = 227 + 386

4. _____ = 493 + 939

5. 732 + 1,788 = _____

6. 4,239 + 1,508 = _____

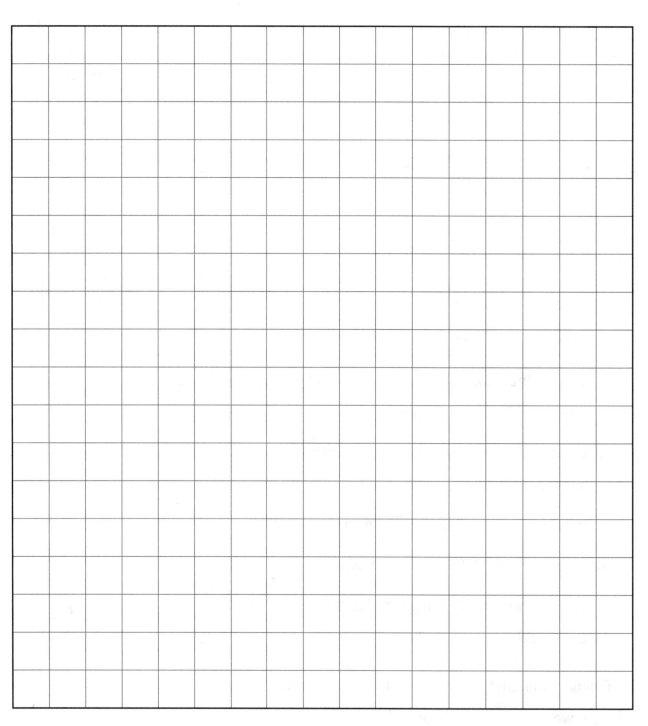

Use with Lesson 2.7.

Addition of Multidigit Numbers (cont.)

Use the column-addition method to solve Problems 7–12.

7. 89 + 47 = _____

8. _____ = 634 + 86

9. 148 + 77 = _____

10. _____ = 481 + 239

11. _____ = 746 + 827

12. 508 + 1,848 = _____

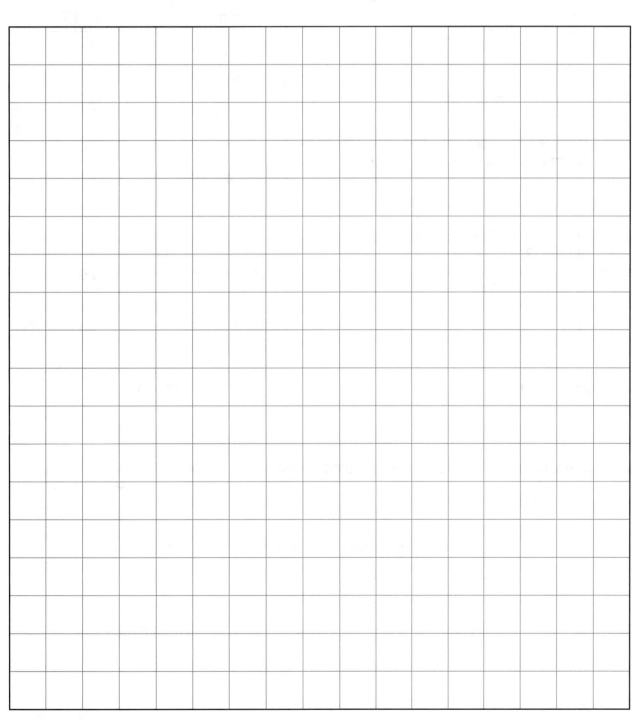

Gestation Period

The period between the time an animal becomes pregnant and the time its baby is born is called the **gestation period.** The table below shows the number of days in the average gestation period for some animals.

1. For the gestation periods listed in the table ...

   a. What is the maximum number of days?

   _____ days

   b. What is the minimum number of days?

   _____ days

   c. What is the range (the difference between the maximum and the minimum)?

   _____ days

   d. What is the median (middle number of days)?

   _____ days

Average Gestation Period (in days)	
Animal	**Number of Days**
dog	61
giraffe	457
goat	151
human	266
Asian elephant	645
mouse	19
squirrel	44
rhinoceros	480
rabbit	31

Source: World Almanac

2. Which animals have an average gestation period that is longer than 1 year?

   _____

3. How much longer is the average gestation period for a goat than for a dog?

   _____ days

4. Which animal has an average gestation period that is about twice as long as a rabbit's? _____

5. Which animal has an average gestation period that is about half as long as a squirrel's? _____

Name _____ Date _____ Time _____

Use the trade-first subtraction method to solve the problems.

1. 96 − 28 = _____

2. _____ = 469 − 87

3. _____ = 732 − 365

4. 4,321 − 75 = _____

5. 5,613 − 2,724 = _____

6. _____ = 600 − 438

Subtraction of Multidigit Numbers (cont.)

Use the partial-differences subtraction method to solve the problems.

1. _____ = 84 − 55   **2.** 136 − 79 = _____

3. _____ = 573 − 167   **4.** _____ = 506 − 282

5. _____ = 5,673 − 1,194   **6.** 3,601 − 1,063 = _____

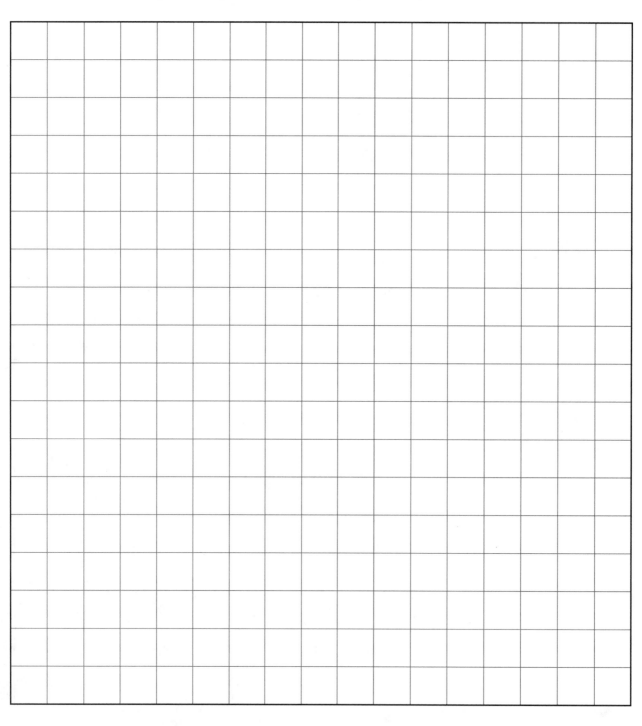

Use with Lesson 2.9.

Family Letter

Unit 3: Multiplication and Division; Number Sentences and Algebra

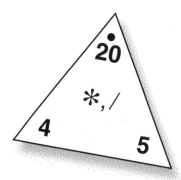

One of our goals in the coming weeks is to finish memorizing the multiplication facts for single-digit numbers. To help students master the facts, they will play several math games. Ask your child to teach you one of the games described in his or her *Student Reference Book,* and play a few rounds together. The class will also take a series of 50-facts tests. Because correct answers are counted only up to the first mistake (and not counted thereafter), your child may at first receive a low score. If this happens, don't be alarmed. Before long, scores will improve dramatically. Help your child set a realistic goal for the next test, and discuss what can be done to meet that goal.

Your child will use Multiplication/Division Fact Triangles to review the relationship between multiplication and division. (For example, $4 \times 5 = 20$, and so $20 \div 5 = 4$ and $20 \div 4 = 5$.) Fact Triangles can also serve as flash cards. You can use the triangles to quiz your child on the basic facts and test your child's progress.

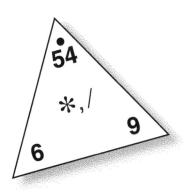

In this unit, alternative symbols for multiplication and division are introduced. An asterisk ($*$) may be substituted for the traditional $\times$ symbol, as in $4 * 5 = 20$. A slash ($/$) may be used in place of the traditional $\div$ symbol, as in $20/4 = 5$.

In Unit 3, the class will continue the World Tour, a yearlong project in which the students travel to a number of different countries. Their first flight will take them to Cairo, Egypt. These travels serve as background for many interesting activities in which students look up numerical information, analyze this information, and solve problems.

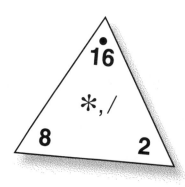

Finally, the class will have its first formal introduction to solving equations in algebra. (Informal activities with missing numbers in number stories have been built into the program since first grade.) Formal introduction to algebra in fourth grade may surprise you, since algebra is usually regarded as a high school subject. However, an early start in algebra is integral to the *Everyday Mathematics* philosophy.

Please keep this Family Letter for reference as your child works through Unit 3.

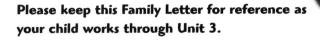

Vocabulary

Important terms in Unit 3:

change diagram A diagram used in *Everyday Mathematics* to represent situations in which quantities are increased or decreased.

Start	Change	End
14	−5	9

comparison diagram A diagram used in *Everyday Mathematics* to represent situations in which two quantities are compared.

Quantity
12

Quantity	Difference
9	?

dividend In division, the number that is being divided. For example, in 35 ÷ 5 = 7, the dividend is 35.

divisor In division, the number that divides another number. For example, in 35 ÷ 5 = 7, the divisor is 5.

Fact Triangle A triangular flash card labeled with the numbers of a fact family that students can use to practice addition/subtraction or multiplication/division facts.

factor One of two or more numbers that are multiplied to give a product. The numbers multiplied are called *factors* of the *product*. For example, 4 and 3 are factors of 12, because 4 * 3 = 12.

number sentence A sentence that is made up of at least two numbers or expressions and a relation symbol (=, >, <, ≥, ≤, or ≠). Most number sentences also contain at least one operation symbol (+, −, ×, *, ·, ÷, /). Number sentences may also have grouping symbols, such as parentheses.

open sentence A *number sentence* in which one or more *variables* hold the places of missing numbers. For example, 5 + x = 13 is an open sentence.

parts-and-total diagram A diagram used in *Everyday Mathematics* to represent situations in which two or more quantities are combined.

Total		
?		
Part	Part	Part
9	10	9

Total	
30	
Part	Part
12	18

product The result of multiplying two numbers called *factors*. For example, in 4 * 3 = 12, the product is 12.

percent Per hundred, or out of a hundred. For example, "48% of the students in the school are boys" means that 48 out of every 100 students in the school are boys.

quotient The result of dividing one number by another. For example, in 35 ÷ 5 = 7, the quotient is 7.

square number A number that is the product of a whole number multiplied by itself. For example, 25 is a square number because 25 = 5 * 5. The square numbers are 1, 4, 9, 16, 25, and so on.

variable A letter or other symbol that represents a number. A variable can represent one specific number or it can stand for many different numbers.

Use with Lesson 2.10.

Do-Anytime Activities

To work with your child on the concepts taught in this unit, try these interesting and rewarding activities:

1 Continue work on multiplication and division facts by using Fact Triangles and fact families or by playing games described in the *Student Reference Book*.

2 As the class proceeds through the unit, give your child multidigit addition and subtraction problems related to the lessons covered, such as $348 + 29$, $427 + 234$, $72 - 35$, and $815 - 377$.

3 Help your child recognize and identify real-world examples of right angles, such as the corner of a book, and examples of parallel lines, such as railroad tracks.

Building Skills through Games

Baseball Multiplication   *See Student Reference Book, pages 186 and 187.*
Two players will need 4 regular dice, 4 pennies, and a calculator to play this game. Practicing the multiplication facts for 1–12 and strengthening mental arithmetic skills are the goals of *Baseball Multiplication*.

Beat the Calculator   *See Student Reference Book, page 188.*
This game involves 3 players and requires a calculator and a deck of number cards with 4 each of the numbers 1 through 10. Playing *Beat the Calculator* helps your child review basic multiplication facts.

Broken Calculator   *See Student Reference Book, page 189.*
This game reinforces skills in using the four operations as your child tries to display a given number on a calculator without the use of a "broken" key.

Division Arrays   *See Student Reference Book, page 194.*
Materials for this game include number cards, 1 each of the numbers 6 through 18; a regular (6-sided) die; 18 counters; and paper and pencil. This game, involving 2 to 4 players, reinforces the idea of dividing objects into equal groups.

Multiplication Top-It   *See Student Reference Book, page 208.*
The game can be played with 2 to 4 players and requires a deck of cards with 4 each of the numbers 1 through 10. This game helps your child review basic multiplication facts.

Name That Number   *See Student Reference Book, page 203.*
Played with 2 or 3 players, this game requires a complete deck of number cards and paper and pencil. Your child tries to name a target number by adding, subtracting, multiplying, and dividing the numbers on as many of the cards as possible.

Use with Lesson 2.10.

As You Help Your Child with Homework

As your child brings assignments home, you may want to go over the instructions together, clarifying them as necessary. The answers listed below will guide you through some of the Study Links in this unit.

Study Link 3.2

1. 24   **2.** 54   **3.** 28

4. 16   **5.** 45   **6.** 18

7. 40   **8.** 25   **9.** 48

Study Link 3.3

1. 6   **2.** 8   **3.** 6   **4.** 3

6. 20; 5   **7.** 18; 6   **8.** 49; 7   **9.** 9; 2

10. 7; 5   **11.** 7; 4   **12.** 3; 9   **13.** 6; 6

Study Link 3.4

1. 5   **2.** 7   **3.** 72   **4.** 10

5. 32   Answers vary for Problems 6–14.

Study Link 3.5

1. 4   **2.** 3,360   **3.** Answers vary.

4. a. less   **b.** less   **5.** false

6. 134,950

Study Link 3.6

Cities	Measurement on Map (inches)	Real Distance (miles)
Cape Town and Durban	4 inches	800 miles
Durban and Pretoria	$1\frac{3}{4}$ inches	350 miles
Cape Town and Johannesburg	4 inches	800 miles
Johannesburg and Queenstown	2 inches	400 miles
East London and Upington	$2\frac{1}{2}$ inches	500 miles
_____ and _____	Answers vary.	

Study Link 3.7

1. $659 - 457 = 202$

2. $1,545 + 2,489 = 4,034$

3. $700 - 227 = 473$

4. $939 + 2,657 = 3,596$

5. $624 + 470 + 336 = 1,430$

Study Link 3.8

1. F   **2.** F   **3.** T   **4.** T

5. F   **6.** T   **7.** T   **8.** ?

9. Sample answers: $25 / 5 = 5$; $150 + 250 > 300$

10. Sample answers: $25 + 20 < 30$; $158 - 52 = 100$

11. a. There is not a relation symbol such as =, >, or <.

     b. Sample answer: $7 * 8 = 56$

     c. Sample answer: $7 * 8 = 49$

Study Link 3.9

1. 33   **2.** 27   **3.** 1   **4.** 24

5. 37   **6.** 8   **7.** $3 * (6 + 4) = 30$

8. $15 = (20 - 7) + 2$ **9.** $7 + (7 * 3) = 4 * 7$

10. $9 * 6 = (25 * 2) + 4$ **11.** $72 / 9 = (2 * 3) + 18 / 9$

12. $35 / (42 / 6) = (10 - 6) + 1$

13. T   **14.** ?   **15.** F

16. F   **17.** T   **18.** ?

Study Link 3.11

1. Logic Grid

	Red	Yellow	Blue
Rafael	✔	✗	✗
Adena	✗	✗	✔
Jordana	✗	✔	✗

Rafael: red   Adena: blue   Jordana: yellow

2. Logic Grid

	Pizza	Hamburger	Hot Dog	Macaroni and Cheese
Mike	✔	✗	✗	✗
Laura	✗	✔	✗	✗
Fred	✗	✗	✔	✗
Liz	✗	✗	✗	✔

Mike: pizza   Laura: hamburger
Fred: hot dog   Liz: macaroni and cheese

Multiplication Facts

Complete the Multiplication/Division Facts Table below.

*,/	1	2	3	4	5	6	7	8	9	10
1						6				
2										
3	3		9							
4		8								
5										
6										
7		14								
8										
9										
10										

Fact Triangles

Complete these Multiplication/Division Fact Triangles.

1.

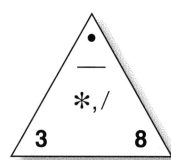

2.

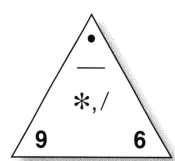

3.

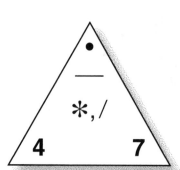

4.

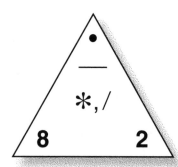

5.

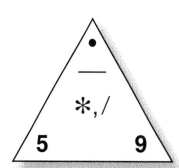

6.

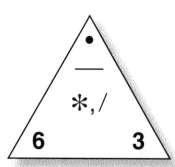

7.

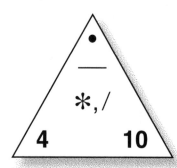

8.

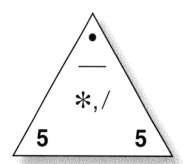

9.

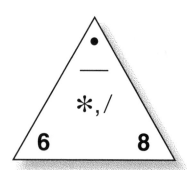

Use with Lesson 3.2.

Mystery Numbers

Find the mystery numbers.

1. I am thinking of a mystery number. If I multiply it
by 4, the answer is 24. What is the mystery number?   _____

2. I am thinking of another number. If I multiply it
by 3, the answer is 24. What is the number?   _____

3. I multiplied a number by itself and got 36.
What number did I multiply by itself?   _____

4. If I multiply 7 by a number, I get 21.
What number did I use?   _____

Write your own mystery number problem.

5. _____

_____

_____

Fill in the missing numbers.

6. $4 * 5 =$ _____   _____ $* 4 = 20$

7. _____ $= 6 * 3$ $18 =$ _____ $* 3$

8. $7 * 7 =$ _____   _____ $* 7 = 49$

9. _____ $* 2 = 18$ $18 =$ _____ $* 9$

10. $35 =$ _____ $* 5$ _____ $* 7 = 35$

11. $28 =$ _____ $* 4$ _____ $* 7 = 28$

12. _____ $* 9 = 27$ $27 =$ _____ $* 3$

13. _____ $* 6 = 36$ $6 *$ _____ $= 36$

Missing Numbers

Equivalents				
3 * 4	12 / 3	12 ÷ 3	3 < 5	(< means "is less than")
3 × 4	$\frac{12}{3}$	3)‾12‾	5 > 3	(> means "is greater than")

Complete each fact by filling in the missing numbers.
Use the Multiplication/Division Facts Table to help you.

1. 30 / 6 = _____

2. 21 / _____ = 3

3. 9 = _____ ÷ 8

4. 100 / _____ = 10

5. _____ / 4 = 8

6. 25 ÷ _____ = _____

7. _____ = 42 / _____

8. 8 / _____ = _____

9. 4 = _____ / _____

10. _____ ÷ _____ = 1

11. _____ / 2 = _____

12. 10 * _____ = _____

Challenge

13. 5 * _____ * _____ = 30   **14.** 54 = _____ * _____ * _____

*,/	1	2	3	4	5	6	7	8	9	10
1	1	2	3	4	5	6	7	8	9	10
2	2	4	6	8	10	12	14	16	18	20
3	3	6	9	12	15	18	21	24	27	30
4	4	8	12	16	20	24	28	32	36	40
5	5	10	15	20	25	30	35	40	45	50
6	6	12	18	24	30	36	42	48	54	60
7	7	14	21	28	35	42	49	56	63	70
8	8	16	24	32	40	48	56	64	72	80
9	9	18	27	36	45	54	63	72	81	90
10	10	20	30	40	50	60	70	80	90	100

     Use with Lesson 3.4.

Number Stories about Egypt

1. The area of Egypt is about 386,700 square miles. The area of Wyoming is about 97,818 square miles. About how many times larger is Egypt than Wyoming?

   About _____ times larger

2. The Nile is the longest river in the world. It is about 4,160 miles long. The Huang River is the fourth longest river in the world. It is about 800 miles shorter than the Nile. About how long is the Huang River?

   About _____ miles

3. The Suez Canal links the Mediterranean and Red Seas. It is 103 miles long and was opened in 1869. For how many years has the Suez Canal been open?

   _____ years

4. **a.** Aswan, Egypt, is the driest inhabited place in the world. The average annual rainfall is 0.02 inch. Is this more or less than $\frac{1}{4}$ inch per year?

   _____

   b. Minya el Qamn, Egypt, is the sixth driest inhabited place in the world. The average annual rainfall is 0.20 inch. Is this more or less than $\frac{1}{4}$ inch per year?

   _____

5. The population of Cairo, Egypt, is about 6,789,000. Lagos, Nigeria, is the most populated city in Africa, with 10,287,000 people. True or false: There are about 5 million more people living in Lagos than in Cairo.

   _____

6. There are about 2,950 miles of railroad in Egypt. There are about 137,900 miles of railroad in the United States. About how many fewer miles of railroad are there in Egypt than in the United States?

   About _____ miles

Map Scale

Here is a map of South Africa. Use a ruler to measure the shortest distance between cities. Use the map scale to convert these measurements to real distances.

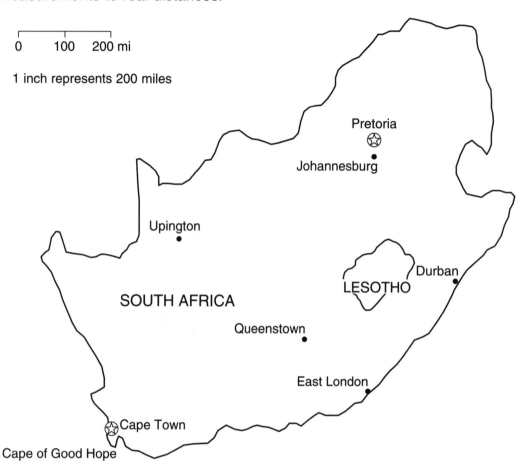

0   100   200 mi

1 inch represents 200 miles

Pretoria

Johannesburg

Upington

Durban

LESOTHO

SOUTH AFRICA

Queenstown

East London

Cape Town

Cape of Good Hope

Cities	Measurement on Map (inches)	Real Distance (miles)
Cape Town and Durban		
Durban and Pretoria		
Cape Town and Johannesburg		
Johannesburg and Queenstown		
East London and Upington		
_____ and _____		

Addition and Subtraction Number Stories
Study Link 3.7

1. In 1896, the United Kingdom had the largest navy in the world with 659 ships. France had the second-largest navy with 457 ships. The United States was tenth with only 95 ships. How many more ships did the United Kingdom have than France?

   _____
   (number model)

   Answer: _____ more ships

2. Rhode Island, the smallest state in the United States, has an area of 1,545 square miles. The area of the second-smallest state, Delaware, is 2,489 square miles. What is the combined area of these two states?

   _____
   (number model)

   Answer: _____ square miles

3. A polar bear can weigh as much as 700 kilograms. An American black bear can weigh as much as 227 kilograms. How much more can a polar bear weigh than an American black bear?

   _____
   (number model)

   Answer: _____ kilograms more

4. The Cat Fancier's Association registered 939 Burmese cats and 2,657 Siamese cats in 1997. How many Burmese and Siamese cats were registered?

   _____
   (number model)

   Answer: _____ cats

5. According to the National Register of Historic Places, New York City has the greatest number of historic places in the United States with 624 sites. Philadelphia is second with 470 sites and Washington, D.C., is third with 336 sites. In all, how many historic sites are there in the top three cities?

   _____
   (number model)

   Answer: _____ historic sites

True, False, and "Can't Tell" Number Sentences

Next to each number sentence, write "T" if it is true, "F" if it is false, or "?" if you can't tell.

1. $20 - 12 = 8 * 3$ _____

2. $7 = 14 * 2$ _____

3. $497 < 500$ _____

4. $16 / 4 = 4$ _____

5. $15 + 10 = 5$ _____

6. $24 > 11 + 11$ _____

7. $100 - 5 = 95$ _____

8. $33 - 4$ _____

9. Write two true number sentences.

_____

_____

10. Write two false number sentences.

_____

_____

11. a. Explain why $7 * 8$ is not a number sentence.

_____

_____

_____

   b. How could you change $7 * 8$ to make a true number sentence?

_____

   c. How could you change $7 * 8$ to make a false number sentence?

_____

Parentheses in Number Sentences

Make each of the following a true sentence by filling in the missing number.

1. 9 + (4 * 6) = _____

2. (45 / 5) * 3 = _____

3. (20 / 4) / 5 = _____

4. _____ = (33 − 25) * 3

5. _____ = (25 / 5) + (8 * 4)

6. (33 + 7) / (3 + 2) = _____

Make each of the following a true sentence by inserting parentheses.

7. 3 * 6 + 4 = 30

8. 15 = 20 − 7 + 2

9. 7 + 7 * 3 = 4 * 7

10. 9 * 6 = 25 * 2 + 4

11. 72 / 9 = 2 * 3 + 18 / 9

12. 35 / 42 / 6 = 10 − 6 + 1

For each of the following, write "T" if it is true, "F" if it is false, or "?" if you can't tell.

13. (4 * 6) + 13 = 47 − 10 _____

14. (3 * 7) / (15 − 12) _____

15. 15 > (7 * 6) * (10 − 9) _____

16. 30 = 1 + (4 * 6) _____

17. 20 < (64 / 8) * (12 / 4) _____

18. (6 * 5) / 3 _____

Review

Solve the problems. When you've finished, show them to someone at home or to a classmate. The answers to some of the problems are given at the bottom of the page for you to check yourself.

Equivalents			
3 * 4	12 / 3	12 ÷ 3	3 < 5 (< means "is less than")
3 × 4	$\frac{12}{3}$	3)¯12¯	5 > 3 (> means "is greater than")

Tell whether the number sentence is true or false.

1. $35 = 7 * 5$ _____

2. $43 > 34$ _____

3. $25 + 25 < 50$ _____

4. $49 - (7 \times 7) = 0$ _____

Make a true number sentence by filling in the missing number.

5. _____ $= 12 / (3 + 3)$

6. $(60 - 28) / 4 =$ _____

7. $(3 \times 8) ÷ 6 =$ _____

8. $30 - (4 + 6) =$ _____

Make a true number sentence by inserting parentheses.

9. $4 * 2 + 10 = 18$

10. $16 = 16 - 8 * 2$

11. $27 / 9 / 3 = 1$

12. $27 / 9 / 3 = 9$

Find the solution of each open sentence below. Write a number sentence with the solution in place of the variable. Check to see whether the number sentence is true.

Example: $6 + x = 14$ *Solution:* 8   *Number sentence:* $6 + 8 = 14$

Open sentence	**Solution**	**Number sentence**
13. $12 + x = 32$	_____	_____
14. $s = 200 - 3$	_____	_____
15. $5 * y = 40$	_____	_____
16. $7 = x / 4$	_____	_____

1. true   **3.** false   **5.** 2   **7.** 4   **9.** $(4 * 2) + 10 = 18$ **11.** $(27 / 9) / 3 = 1$ **13.** 20   **15.** 8

Use with Lesson 3.10.

Logic Problems

1. Rafael, Adena, and Jordana each have a different favorite color.

- Rafael's favorite color can be mixed with blue to make purple.

- Adena doesn't like colors that can be found on traffic lights.

- Jordana likes to eat bananas because they are her favorite color.

Logic Grid			
	Red	**Yellow**	**Blue**
Rafael			
Adena			
Jordana			

What is each person's favorite color?

Rafael _____   Adena _____   Jordana _____

2. Fred, Laura, Mike, and Liz all have a favorite type of food. Each one has a different favorite food.

- Laura's favorite food usually comes with a bun.

- Fred does not like food with cheese.

- Fred's favorite food comes in a foot-long size, and he puts mustard and catsup on it.

- Mike likes cheese, sausage, and pepperoni toppings on his favorite food.

Logic Grid				
	Pizza	**Hamburger**	**Hot Dog**	**Macaroni and Cheese**
Mike				
Laura				
Fred				
Liz				

What is each person's favorite food?

Mike _____   Laura _____

Fred _____   Liz _____

Family Letter

Unit 4: Decimals and Their Uses

In previous grades, your child had many experiences with amounts of money written in decimal notation. In the next unit, the class will learn about other uses of decimals.

Decimals are needed because numerical information often cannot be expressed by a whole number—it may be a quantity between two whole numbers.

The class will focus on a number of examples of uses of decimals in everyday life. For example, a small thermometer for taking body temperatures usually has marks that are spaced $\frac{2}{10}$ of a degree apart. This allows for very accurate measurements of body temperature.

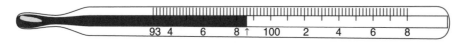

Normal body temperature is about 98.6 °F.

Students will explore how decimals are used in measuring distances, times, and gasoline mileage. If you have a car, your child will also calculate the average number of miles your car can travel on 1 gallon of gasoline. Your assistance will be needed to complete this project.

We will also begin a yearlong measurement routine. Students will find their very own "personal references," which they will use to estimate lengths, heights, and distances in metric units. For example, your child might discover that the distance from the base of his or her thumb to the tip of his or her index finger is about 10 centimeters and then use this fact to estimate the width of this page to be about 20 centimeters.

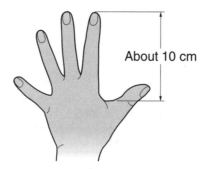

About 10 cm

The World Tour will continue. Small groups of students will work together to gather information about different countries in Africa and then share what they have learned with the rest of the class. This will provide an opportunity for students to compare and interpret data for a large number of countries from the same region.

Please keep this Family Letter for reference as your child works through Unit 4.

Vocabulary

Important terms in Unit 4:

centimeter (cm) In the metric system, a unit of length equivalent to $\frac{1}{100}$ of a meter; 10 millimeters; $\frac{1}{10}$ of a decimeter.

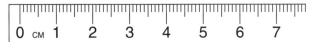

decimeter (dm) In the metric system, a unit of length equivalent to $\frac{1}{10}$ of a meter; 10 centimeters.

hundredths The place-value position in which a digit has a value equal to $\frac{1}{100}$ of itself; the second digit to the right of the decimal point.

meter (m) In the metric system, the fundamental unit of length from which other units of length are derived. One meter is the distance light will travel in a vacuum (empty space) in $\frac{1}{299,792,458}$ second.

millimeter (mm) In the metric system, a unit of length equivalent to $\frac{1}{1,000}$ of a meter; $\frac{1}{10}$ of a centimeter.

ONE Same as whole. See *whole.*

ones The place-value position in which a digit has a value equal to the digit itself.

personal measurement reference A convenient approximation for a standard unit of measurement. For example, many people have thumbs that are approximately one inch wide.

place value A system that values a digit according to its position *or place* in a number. Each place has a value ten times that of the place to its right and one-tenth of the value of the place to its left. For example, in the number 456, the 4 is in the hundreds place and has a value of 400.

1,000s	100s	10s	1s	.	0.1s	0.01s	0.001s
Thousands	Hundreds	Tens	Ones	.	Tenths	Hundredths	Thousandths

tens The place-value position in which a digit has a value equal to ten times itself.

tenths The place-value position in which a digit has a value equal to $\frac{1}{10}$ of itself; the first digit to the right of the decimal point.

thousandths The place-value position in which a digit has a value equal to $\frac{1}{1,000}$ of itself; the third digit to the right of the decimal point.

whole (or ONE or unit) The entire object, collection of objects, or quantity being considered; the ONE; the unit; 100%.

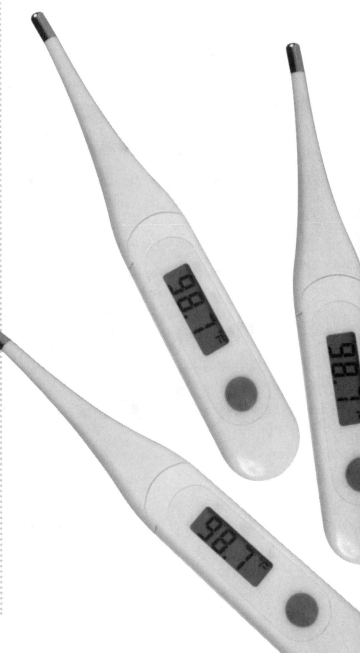

Use with Lesson 3.12.

Do-Anytime Activities

To work with your child on the concepts taught in this unit, try these interesting and rewarding activities:

1 Have your child track the sports statistics of a favorite athlete. Discuss the use of decimals in the statistics he or she finds.

2 Have your child compare prices of items in the supermarket.

3 Help your child create and use new personal reference measures.

4 Together, find statistics about countries in the World Tour. Look in newspapers and almanacs.

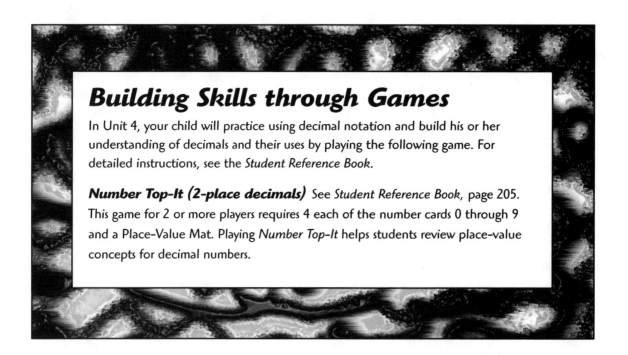

Building Skills through Games

In Unit 4, your child will practice using decimal notation and build his or her understanding of decimals and their uses by playing the following game. For detailed instructions, see the *Student Reference Book.*

Number Top-It (2-place decimals) See *Student Reference Book,* page 205. This game for 2 or more players requires 4 each of the number cards 0 through 9 and a Place-Value Mat. Playing *Number Top-It* helps students review place-value concepts for decimal numbers.

Use with Lesson 3.12.

As You Help Your Child with Homework

As your child brings assignments home, you may want to go over the instructions together, clarifying them as necessary. The answers listed below will guide you through some of the Study Links in this unit.

Study Link 4.2

1. | S | L | I | P | P | E | R | S |

2. | B | O | B | | H | O | P |

3. | T | H | E | | L | E | T | T | E | R | | M |

Study Link 4.3

1. Seikan and Channel Tunnel
2. Between 90 and 120 miles
3. About 20 miles
4. About 12 miles
5. About 8 miles

Study Link 4.4

1. 5.18
2. 0.03
3. 120.41
4. 1.46
5. >
6. <
7. >
8. >
9. $7.37
10. $6.48

Study Link 4.5

1. a. $0.76   b. $2.43   c. $4.64   d. $2.95
2. $16.40   3. $2.57   4. $7.32
5. $18.10   6. $10.78

Study Link 4.6

1. $\frac{335}{1,000}$ 0.335
2. $\frac{301}{1,000}$ 0.301
3. $\frac{7}{100}$ 0.07
4. $1\frac{5}{100}$ 1.05
5. 0.346
6. 0.092
7. 0.003
8. 2.7
9. 0.536
10. 0.23
11. 7.008
12. 0.4
13. >   14. >   15. <   16. <

Study Link 4.7

1. About 7 cm; 0.07 m   2. About 12 cm; 0.12 m
3. About 4 cm; 0.04 m   4. About 6 cm; 0.06 m
5. About 2 cm; 0.02 m   6. About 14 cm; 0.14 m

Study Link 4.8

1. Answers vary.   2. 180   3. 4
4. 3,000   5. 400   6. 7
7. 460   8. 794   9. 4.5
10. 0.23   11. 60

Study Link 4.9

2. 64.8 mm   6.48 cm
3. 0.5 mm   0.05 cm
4. 19.0 mm   1.9 cm
5. 18.5 mm   1.85 cm
6. 5.0 mm   0.5 cm

Study Link 4.10

1. six thousand, eight hundred fifty-four

1,000s	100s	10s	1s
6	8	5	4

2. two and nine hundred fifty-nine thousandths

100s	10s	1s		0.1s	0.01s	0.001s
		2	.	9	5	9

3. seventy-three and four thousandths

10s	1s		0.1s	0.01s	0.001s
7	3	.	0	0	4

Use with Lesson 3.12.

Decimals All Around

SRB
24

Find examples of decimals in newspapers, in magazines, in books, or on food packages. Ask people in your family for examples.

Write your numbers below or, if an adult says you may, cut them out and tape them on this page. Be sure to write what the numbers mean. For example: "The body temperature of a hibernating dormouse may go down to 35.6°F."

_____

_____

_____

_____

_____

_____

_____

_____

_____

_____

_____

_____

_____

_____

_____

_____

_____

_____

_____

_____

Use with Lesson 4.1.

Silly Decimal Riddles

Put the letters in the correct boxes to answer the riddles.

Example In Problem 1, the letter L goes with 0.33. Since 0.33 is between 0.25 and 0.5, put the letter L in the second box.

1. What kind of clothing can you make out of banana peels?

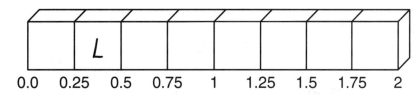

L	0.33	P	1.01	S	0.1
R	1.6	S	1.99	P	0.8
I	0.7	E	1.33		

2. What frog was a famous comedian?

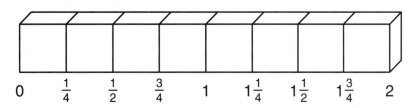

P	1.66	O	1.3
H	1.01	B	0.60
O	0.3	B	0.01

3. What's once in every minute, twice in every moment, but not once in a thousand years?

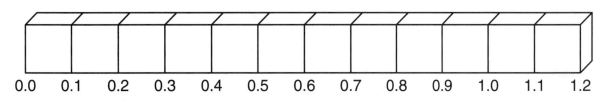

T	0.67	R	0.99	E	0.55
T	0.05	M	1.15	E	0.88
T	$\frac{3}{4}$	E	$\frac{1}{4}$		
L	0.49	H	0.101		

Railroad Tunnel Lengths

The table below shows the five longest railroad tunnels in the world.

Tunnel	Location	Year Completed	Length in Miles
Seikan	Japan	1988	33.49
Channel Tunnel	France/England	1994	31.03
Moscow Metro	Russia	1979	19.07
London Underground	United Kingdom	1939	17.30
Dai-Shimizu	Japan	1982	13.78

Source: The Top Ten of Everything 2000

Use estimation to answer the following questions. Do not work the problems on paper or with a calculator.

1. Which two tunnels have a combined length of about 60 miles?

_____

2. Circle the best estimate for the combined length of all five tunnels.

   a. Less than 90 miles   **b.** Between 90 and 120 miles

   c. Between 120 and 150 miles   **d.** More than 150 miles

3. About how many miles longer is the Seikan tunnel than the Dai-Shimizu tunnel?

   About _____ miles

4. About how many miles longer is the Channel Tunnel than the Moscow Metro tunnel?

   About _____ miles

Challenge

5. The Cascade tunnel in Washington state is the longest railroad tunnel in the United States. It is about $\frac{1}{4}$ the length of the Seikan. About how long is the Cascade tunnel?

   About _____ miles

Addition and Subtraction of Decimals

Add or subtract.

1. 9.87 − 4.69 = _____

2. 0.4 − 0.37 = _____

3. 96.45 + 23.96 = _____

4. 1.06 + 0.4 = _____

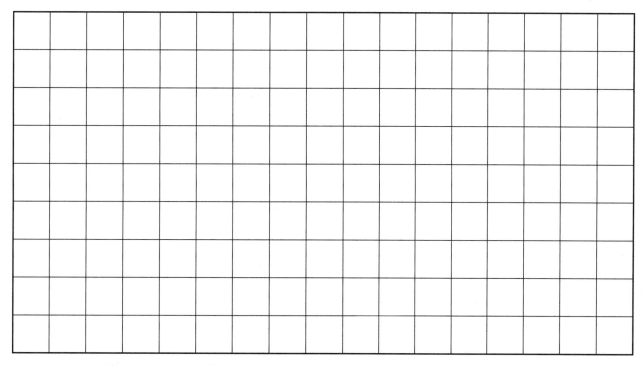

Write <, >, or = to make each statement true.

5. 2.78 + 9.1 _____ 3.36 + 8.49

6. 0.08 + 0.97 _____ 1.04 + 0.03

7. 13.62 − 4.9 _____ 9.4 − 1.33

8. 9.4 − 5.6 _____ 8.3 − 4.7

Solve.

9. Cleo went to the store to buy school supplies. She bought a notebook for $2.39, a pen for $0.99, and a set of markers for $3.99. How much money did she spend in all?

_____

10. Nicholas went to the store with a $20 bill. His groceries cost $13.52. How much change did he get?

_____

Grocery Prices—Now and Future

The table below shows some USDA grocery prices for the year 2000 and estimates of grocery prices for the year 2025.

Grocery Item	Price in 2000	Estimated Price in 2025
dozen eggs	$1.02	$1.78
loaf of white bread	$0.88	$3.31
pound of butter	$2.72	$7.36
gallon of milk	$2.70	$5.65

1. How much more is each item predicted to cost in 2025?

    a. eggs _____

    b. bread _____

    c. butter _____

    d. milk _____

2. The year is 2000. You buy bread and butter. You hand the cashier a $20 bill. How much change should you receive?

_____

3. The year is 2025. You buy eggs and milk. You hand the cashier a $10 bill. How much change should you receive?

_____

4. The year is 2000. You buy all 4 items. What is the total cost? _____

5. The year is 2025. You buy all 4 items. What is the total cost? _____

6. If the predictions are correct, how much more will you pay in 2025 for the 4 items than you paid in 2000?

_____

Tenths, Hundredths, and Thousandths

Complete the table. The big cube is the ONE.

Base-10 Blocks	Fraction Notation	Decimal Notation
1. ☐☐☐ ⫴		
2. ☐☐☐ .		
3. ⦀⦀ ⫴		
4. ☐☐ ⦀⦀⦀		

Write each number in decimal notation.

5. $\dfrac{346}{1,000}$ _____

6. $\dfrac{92}{1,000}$ _____

7. $\dfrac{3}{1,000}$ _____

8. $2\dfrac{7}{10}$ _____

Write each of the following in decimal notation.

9. 536 thousandths _____

10. 23 hundredths _____

11. 7 and 8 thousandths _____

12. 4 tenths _____

Write < or >.

13. 0.407 _____ 0.074

14. 0.65 _____ 0.437

15. 0.672 _____ 0.7

16. 2.38 _____ 2.4

Measuring in Centimeters

Measure each line segment to the nearest centimeter. Record the measurement in centimeters and meters.

Example

About _____5_____ centimeters   About _0.05_ meter

1.

About _____ centimeters   About _____ meter

2.

About _____ centimeters   About _____ meter

3.

About _____ centimeters   About _____ meter

4.

About _____ centimeters   About _____ meter

5.

About _____ centimeters   About _____ meter

6.

About _____ centimeters   About _____ meter

Metric Measurements

1. Use your personal references to estimate the lengths of 4 objects in metric units. Then measure each object. Record your estimates and measurements.

Object	Estimated Length	Actual Length

Complete.

2. 18 cm = _____ mm

3. _____ cm = 40 mm

4. 3 m = _____ mm

5. 4 m = _____ cm

6. _____ m = 700 cm

7. 4.6 m = _____ cm

8. 7.94 m = _____ cm

9. _____ m = 450 cm

10. _____ m = 23 cm

11. 0.6 m = _____ cm

The Invention of the Meter

In 1790, the meter was defined as $\frac{1}{10,000,000}$ (one ten-millionth) of the distance from the North Pole to the equator along the meridian near Dunkerque, France, and Barcelona, Spain. The true distance along the meridian from the North Pole to the equator has been found to be 10,002,000 meters—only a 0.02% difference from the 200-year-old measurement.

Source: World Book Encyclopedia

Rainfall Measurements

The table below shows the average annual rainfall for the 10 driest inhabited places in the world.

1. Fill in the missing measurements in the table.

Location	Average Annual Rainfall (mm)	Average Annual Rainfall (cm)
Aswan, Egypt	0.5	0.05
Luxor, Egypt	0.7	
Arica, Chile	1.1	
Ica, Peru	2.3	
Antofagasta, Chile	4.9	
Minya el Qamn, Egypt		0.51
Asyut, Egypt	5.2	
Callao, Peru	12.0	
Trujillo, Peru		1.4
Fayyum, Egypt	19.0	

Source: The Top Ten of Everything 2000

For each of the questions below, record the measurement in both millimeters and centimeters.

2. What is the total annual rainfall of the 10 driest places? _____ mm _____ cm

3. What is the minimum average annual rainfall? _____ mm _____ cm

4. What is the maximum average annual rainfall? _____ mm _____ cm

5. What is the range of average annual rainfall? _____ mm _____ cm

6. What is the median average rainfall? _____ mm _____ cm

Place-Value Puzzles

Study Link 4.10

Use the clues to write the digits in the boxes and find each number. Then write the number in words on the line below the problem. For example, for 345, you would write *three hundred forty-five*.

SRB
28 29

1. • Write 5 in the tens place.

• Find $\frac{1}{2}$ of 24. Subtract 4. Write the result in the hundreds place.

• Add 7 to the digit in the tens place. Divide by 2. Write the result in the thousands place.

• In the ones place, write an even number greater than 2 that has not been used yet.

1,000s	100s	10s	1s

Answer (in words): _____

2. • Divide 15 by 3. Write the result in the hundredths place.

• Multiply 2 by 10. Divide by 10. Write the result in the ones place.

• Write a digit in the tenths place that is 4 more than the digit in the hundredths place.

• Add 7 to the digit in the ones place. Write the result in the thousandths place.

100s	10s	1s	0.1s	0.01s	0.001s
		.			

Answer (in words): _____

3. • Write the result of 6 * 9 divided by 18 in the ones place.

• Double 8. Divide by 4. Write the result in the thousandths place.

• Add 3 to the digit in the thousandths place. Write the result in the tens place.

• Write the same digit in the tenths and hundredths places so that the sum of all the digits is 14.

10s	1s	0.1s	0.01s	0.001s
	.			

Answer (in words): _____

© 2002 Everyday Learning Corporation

Family Letter

Unit 5: Big Numbers, Estimation, and Computation

In this unit, your child will begin to multiply 1- and 2-digit numbers using what we call the **partial-products method.** In preparation for this, students will learn to play the game *Multiplication Wrestling.* Ask your child to explain the rules to you and play an occasional game together. While students are expected to learn the partial-products method, they will also investigate the **lattice multiplication method,** which students have often enjoyed in the past.

If your child is having trouble with multiplication facts, give short (five-minute) reviews at home, concentrating on the facts he or she finds difficult.

Another important focus in this unit is on reading and writing big numbers. Big numbers are part of our everyday lives. Students will use big numbers to solve problems and make reasonable estimates.

Sometimes it is helpful to write big numbers in an abbreviated form so that they are easier to work with. One way is to use **exponents,** which tell how many times a number is a factor. For example, 100,000 is equal to $10 * 10 * 10 * 10 * 10$. So 100,000 can be written as 10^5. The small raised 5 is called an exponent, and 10^5 is read as "10 to the fifth power." This will be most students' first experience with exponents, which will be studied in depth during fifth and sixth grades. Help your child locate big numbers in newspapers and other sources and ask your child to read them to you. Or, you can read the numbers and have your child write them.

The class is well into the World Tour. Students are beginning to see how numerical information about a country helps them get a better understanding of the country—of its size, climate, location, and population distribution—and how these characteristics affect the way people live. The next stop on the World Tour will be Budapest, Hungary, the starting point for an exploration of European countries. Encourage your child to bring to school materials about Europe, such as articles in the travel section of your newspaper, magazine articles, and travel brochures.

Please keep this Family Letter for reference as your child works through Unit 5.

Vocabulary

Important terms in Unit 5:

billion 1,000,000,000, or 10^9; 1,000 million.

estimate A close, rather than exact, answer; an approximate answer to a computation; a number close to another number.

exponent See *exponential notation*.

exponential notation A way to show repeated multiplication by the same factor. For example, 2^3 is exponential notation for $2 * 2 * 2$. The small, raised 3, is the *exponent*. It tells how many times the number 2, called the *base*, is used as a *factor*.

$2^3 \leftarrow$ exponent
$\quad \llcorner$ base

extended multiplication fact A multiplication fact involving multiples of 10, 100, and so on. In an extended multiplication fact, each factor has only one digit that is not 0. For example, $400 * 6 = 2,400$ and $20 * 30 = 600$ are extended multiplication facts.

lattice multiplication A very old way to multiply multidigit numbers. The steps below show how to find the product $46 * 73$ using lattice multiplication.

Step 1: Write the factors on the outside of the lattice.

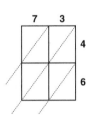

Step 2: Multiply each digit in one factor by each digit in the other factor.

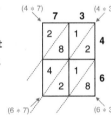

Step 3: Add the numbers inside the lattice along each diagonal.

$46 * 73 = 3,358$

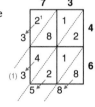

magnitude estimate A very rough estimate. A magnitude estimate tells whether an answer should be in the 1s, 10s, 100s, 1,000s, and so on.

million 1,000,000, or 10^6; 1,000 thousand.

partial-products method A way to multiply in which the value of each digit in one factor is multiplied by the value of each digit in the other factor. The final product is the sum of the several partial products.

Partial–Products Method
Multiply each part of one factor by each part of the other factor. Then add the partial products.

$$
\begin{array}{rl}
& 73 \\
* & 46 \\
\hline
40 * 70 \rightarrow & 2800 \\
40 * 3 \rightarrow & 120 \\
6 * 70 \rightarrow & 420 \\
6 * 3 \rightarrow + & 18 \\
\hline
& 3,358
\end{array}
$$

power of 10 A whole number that can be written as a product using only 10s as factors. For example, 100 is equal to $10 * 10$, or 10^2; it is 10 to the second power.

rough estimate An estimate that is probably not very close to the exact answer. Rough estimates are often good enough for practical purposes.

round a number To replace a number with a nearby number that is easier to work with or better reflects the precision of the data. Often, numbers are rounded to the nearest multiple of 10, 100, 1,000, and so on. For example, 12,964 rounded to the nearest thousand is 13,000.

Do-Anytime Activities

To work with your child on concepts taught in this unit, try these interesting and rewarding activities:

1 To facilitate your child's ease in handling big numbers, have him or her look up the distances from Earth to some of the planets in the solar system, such as the distance from Earth to Mars, to Jupiter, to Saturn, and so on.

2 Have your child look up the box-office gross of one or more favorite movies.

3 Help your child look up the populations and land areas of the state and city in which you live and compare them with the populations and areas of other states and cities.

4 Have your child locate big numbers in newspapers and other sources and ask him or her to read them to you. Or, you can read the numbers and have your child write them.

Building Skills through Games

In Unit 5, your child will practice multiplication skills and build his or her understanding of multidigit numbers by playing the following games. For detailed instructions, see the *Student Reference Book*.

Multiplication Wrestling See *Student Reference Book* page 202.

This is a game for 2 players and requires 4 each of the number cards 0 through 9. The game reinforces understanding of the partial-products method for mulitiplication.

High-Number Toss See *Student Reference Book* page 201.

This is a game for 2 players and requires 1 six-sided die and paper and pencil. The game reinforces understanding of place value.

Number Top-It See *Student Reference Book* page 204.

This is a game for 2 to 5 players and requires a place-value mat and 4 each of the number cards 0 through 9. The game strengthens understanding of place value.

Use with Lesson 4.11.

As You Help Your Child with Homework

As your child brings assignments home, you may want to go over the instructions together, clarifying them as necessary. The answers listed below will guide you through some of the Study Links in this unit.

Study Link 5.1

1. 1,104
2. 1,200
3. 832
4. 3,008
5. 1,854
6. 6,450

Study Link 5.2

Mike:

$(50) * (20) = 1,000$
$(50) * (6) = 300$
$(2) * (20) = 40$
$(2) * (6) = 12$
Score: 1,352

Kara:

$38 * 32 = (30 + 8) *$
$(30 + 2)$
$(30) * (30) = 900$
$(30) * (2) = 60$
$(8) * (30) = 240$
$(8) * (2) = 16$
Score: 1,216

Jenny:

$19 * 68 = (10 + 9) *$
$(60 + 8)$
$(10) * (60) = 600$
$(10) * (8) = 80$
$(9) * (60) = 540$
$(9) * (8) = 72$
Score: 1,292

Larry:

$13 * 99 = (10 + 3) *$
$(90 * 9)$
$(10) * (90) = 900$
$(10) * (9) = 90$
$(3) * (90) = 270$
$(3) * (9) = 27$
Score: 1,287

Study Link 5.3

Sample answers:

1. Estimate: $400 + 1,000 + 500 = 1,900$; 1,824
2. Estimate: $400 + 700 = 1,100$; 1,126
3. Estimate: $600 + 600 + 400 = 1,600$; 1,595
4. Estimate: $800 + 700 = 1,500$; 1,547
5. Estimate: $300 + 300 + 500 = 1,100$; 1,107

Study Link 5.4

Sample answers:

1. Number model: $20 * 400 = 8,000$; 1,000s
2. Number model: $10 * 20 = 200$; 100s
3. Number model: $6,000 * 20 = 120,000$; 100,000s
4. Number model: $10,000 * 50 = 500,000$; 100,000s
5. Number model: $10 * 500,000 = 5,000,000$; 1,000,000s

Study Link 5.5

1. a. 392
   b. 2,200
   c. 11,916
2. a. 36   b. 216
   c. 1,296   d. 1,554

Study Link 5.6

1. 1,680   2. 486
3. 3,266   4. 17,000
5. 4,074   6. 3,133

Study Link 5.7

7. 6,552

```
  7  8
 ⌐5¹⌐6¹
6 ⌐6 ⌐4 8
 ⌐2 ⌐3
5 ⌐8 ⌐2 4
  5  2
```

```
    84
  * 78
  5600
   280
   640
 +  32
  6552
```

Study Link 5.8

92,106,354,879

92 billion, 106 million, 354 thousand, 879

Study Link 5.10

1. 19,000; 24,000; 22,000; 18,000;
   19,000; 20,000; 20,000; 17,000
2. Boston Celtics and Milwaukee Bucks;
   New Jersey Nets and New York Knicks
3. 123,000,000; 151,000,000; 203,000,000;
   249,000,000

Partial-Sums Addition

Example   2,000 + 280 + 300 + 42 = ?

$$
\begin{array}{r}
2000 \\
280 \\
300 \\
+\quad 42 \\
\end{array}
$$

Add the thousands:	2000	
Add the hundreds:	500	(200 + 300)
Add the tens:	120	(80 + 40)
Add the ones:	2	
Find the total:	2622	

Solve each problem.

1. 800 + 120 + 160 + 24 = _____   **2.** 700 + 420 + 50 + 30 = _____

3. _____ = 600 + 180 + 40 + 12   **4.** _____ = 2,400 + 160 + 420 + 28

5. _____ = 1,500 + 90 + 240 + 24   **6.** 5,600 + 420 + 400 + 30 = _____

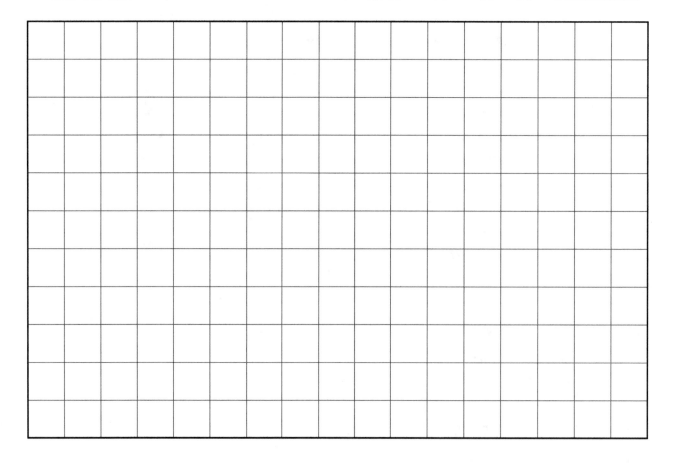

Use with Lesson 5.1.

Multiplication Wrestling

Mike, Kara, Jenny, and Larry played a game of *Multiplication Wrestling.*

Who do you think got the highest score? _____

To check your estimate, fill in the blanks. Then find each player's score.

Were you correct? _____

Mike: 52 * 26

$52 * 26 = (50 + 2) * (20 + 6)$

(____) * (____) = _____

(____) * (____) = _____

(____) * (____) = _____

(____) * (____) = _____

Score: _____

Kara: 38 * 32

$38 * 32 = ($ ____ $+$ ____ $) * ($ ____ $+$ ____ $)$

(____) * (____) = _____

(____) * (____) = _____

(____) * (____) = _____

(____) * (____) = _____

Score: _____

Jenny: 19 * 68

$19 * 68 = ($ ____ $+$ ____ $) * ($ ____ $+$ ____ $)$

(____) * (____) = _____

(____) * (____) = _____

(____) * (____) = _____

(____) * (____) = _____

Score: _____

Larry: 13 * 99

$13 * 99 = ($ ____ $+$ ____ $) * ($ ____ $+$ ____ $)$

(____) * (____) = _____

(____) * (____) = _____

(____) * (____) = _____

(____) * (____) = _____

Score: _____

Estimating Sums

For each problem, write a number model to estimate the sum.

- If the estimate is greater than or equal to 1,500, find the exact sum.

- If the estimate is less than 1,500, **do not** solve the problem.

Example 867 + 734 = _____

Estimate: _900 + 700 = 1,600_

$$
\begin{array}{r}
867 \\
+\ 734 \\
\hline
1500 \\
90 \\
+\ \ 11 \\
\hline
1601
\end{array}
$$

1. 374 + 962 + 488 = _____

Estimate: _____

2. 382 + 744 = _____

Estimate: _____

3. 581 + 648 + 366 = _____

Estimate: _____

4. 845 + 702 = _____

Estimate: _____

5. 318 + 296 + 493 = _____

Estimate: _____

Name _____   Date _____   Time _____

Estimating Products

Study Link
5.4

Estimate whether the answer will be in the tens, hundreds, thousands, or more. Write a number model to show how you estimated. Then circle the box that shows your estimate.

1. A koala sleeps an average of 22 hours each day. About how many hours does a koala sleep in a year?

Number model _____

10s	100s	1,000s	10,000s	100,000s	1,000,000s

2. A prairie vole (a mouselike rodent) has an average of 9 babies per litter. If it has 17 litters in a season, how many babies are produced?

Number model _____

10s	100s	1,000s	10,000s	100,000s	1,000,000s

3. In the next three seconds, Americans will eat approximately 6,000 eggs. About how many eggs will they eat in the next minute?

Number model _____

10s	100s	1,000s	10,000s	100,000s	1,000,000s

4. In the next hour, French people will save 12,000 trees by recycling paper. About how many trees will they save in two days?

Number model _____

10s	100s	1,000s	10,000s	100,000s	1,000,000s

5. The average American consumes 11 pounds of chocolate each year. The population of Wyoming is about 500,000 people. About how many pounds of chocolate are consumed each year in Wyoming?

Number model _____

10s	100s	1,000s	10,000s	100,000s	1,000,000s

© 2002 Everyday Learning Corporation

Use with Lesson 5.4.

Multiplication

1. Solve the problems. Show your work in the grid below.

   a. 56 * 7 = _____   **b.** 8 * 275 = _____   **c.** _____ = 1,324 * 9

2. An old puzzle begins: "A man has 6 houses. In each house he keeps 6 cats. Each cat has 6 whiskers. And on each whisker sit 6 fleas."

   a. How many cats are there?   _____

   b. How many whiskers are there on all the cats?   _____

   c. How many fleas sit on all the cats' whiskers?   _____

   d. Answer the last line of the puzzle: "Houses,
   cats, whiskers, fleas—how many are there in all?"   _____

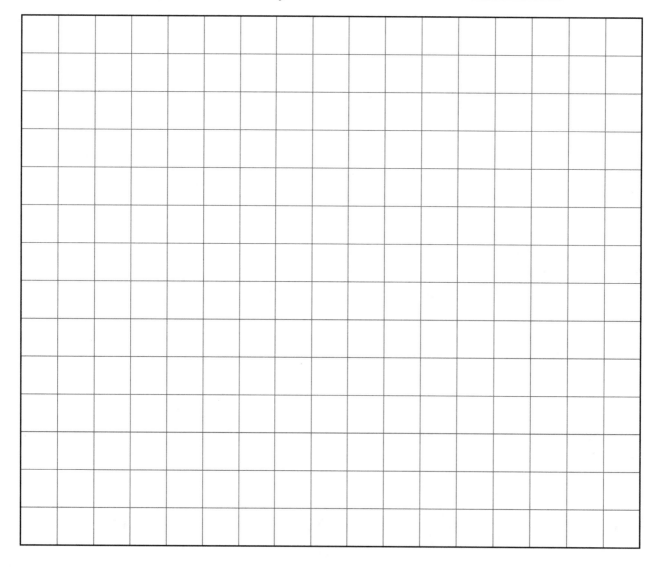

More Multiplication

Multiply. Show your work in the grid below and on the back of this page.

1. 56 * 30 = _____

2. _____ = 27 * 18

3. _____ = 46 * 71

4. 340 * 50 = _____

5. 582 * 7 = _____

Example 38 * 72 = ?

1,000s	100s	10s	1s	
		7	2	
	*	3	8	
2	1	0	0	← 30 [70s]
		6	0	← 30 [2s]
	5	6	0	← 8 [70s]
+		1	6	← 8 [2s]
2	7	3	6	

Challenge

6. _____ = 241 * 13

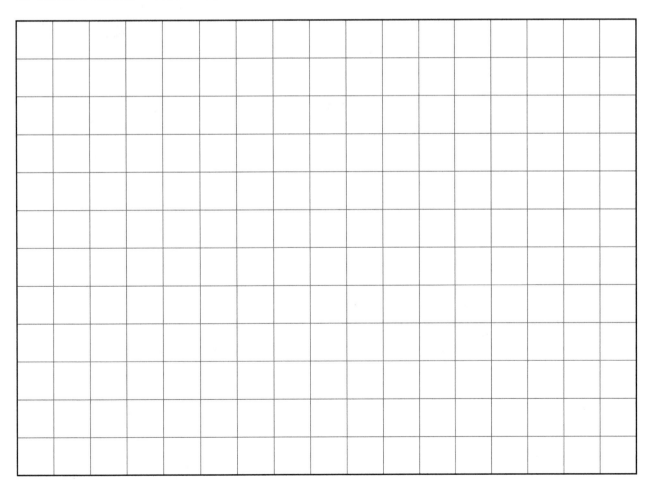

Lattice Multiplication

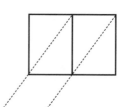

Use the lattice method to find the following products.

1. 5 * 46 = _____

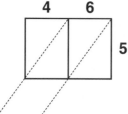

2. 8 * 67 = _____

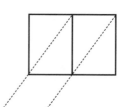

3. 7 * 836 = _____

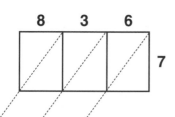

4. 4 * 329 = _____

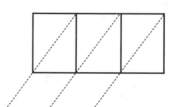

5. 25 * 31 = _____

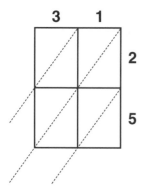

6. 49 * 52 = _____

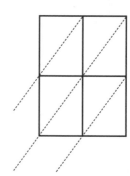

7. Use the lattice method and the partial-products method to find the product.

84 * 78 = _____

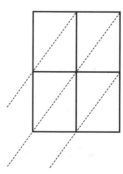

Use with Lesson 5.7.

Place-Value Puzzle

Use the clues below to fill in the place-value chart.

Billions				Millions				Thousands				Ones		
100 B	10 B	1 B	,	100 M	10 M	1 M	,	100 Th	10 Th	1 Th	,	100	10	1

Clues:

1. Find $\frac{1}{2}$ of 24. Subtract 4. Write the result in the hundreds place.

2. Find $\frac{1}{2}$ of 30. Divide the result by 3. Write the answer in the ten-thousands place.

3. Find $\frac{1}{10}$ of 30. Double the result and write it in the one-millions place.

4. Find $\frac{3}{4}$ of 12 and write it in the ones place.

5. Find $9 * 8$. Reverse the digits in the result and divide by 9. Write the answer in the hundred-thousands place.

6. Double 8. Divide the result by 4. Write the answer in the one-thousands place.

7. In the one-billions place, write the even number greater than 0 that has not been used yet.

8. Write $\frac{5}{5}$ as a whole number in the hundred-millions place.

9. In the tens place, write the odd number that has not been used yet.

10. Find the sum of all the digits in the chart so far. Divide the result by 5 and write it in the ten-billions place.

11. Write 0 in the empty column whose place value is less than billions.

Write the number in words. For example, 17,450,206 would be written as "17 million, 450 thousand, 206."

_____

_____

Estimating the Sizes of Numbers

For each item in the table below, estimate the size of the number and make an X in the appropriate column.

Example Most new cars cost at least $10,000. This means that the cost of a new car is in the ten-thousands.

Item	Hundred-Thousands	Ten-Thousands	Thousands	Hundreds	Tens	Ones
Cost of a new car (in dollars)		X				
Amount of food eaten by a person per day (in pounds)						
Distance from New York to Los Angeles (in miles)						
Distance around Earth at the equator (in miles)						
Speed of a car (in miles per hour)						
Speed of a jet plane (in miles per hour)						
Weight of an African elephant (in pounds)						
Height of the tallest tree in the world (in feet)						
Number of seats in a major-league baseball stadium						
Number of steps to the top of the Empire State Building, which has 102 floors						

Use with Lesson 5.9.

Rounding

SRB
156 157

1. Round the seating capacities in the table to the nearest thousand.

National Basketball Association Seating Capacity of Home Courts		
Team	Seating Capacity	Seating Capacity Rounded to the Nearest 1,000
Boston Celtics	18,624	
Charlotte Hornets	24,042	
Chicago Bulls	21,711	
Indiana Pacers	18,400	
Milwaukee Bucks	18,717	
New Jersey Nets	20,049	
New York Knicks	19,763	
Seattle Supersonics	17,072	

Source: 1999 World Almanac

2. Look at your rounded numbers. Which teams' stadiums have about the same capacity?

_____

_____

3. Round the population figures in the table to the nearest million.

U.S. Population by Official Census from 1930 to 1990		
Year	Population	Rounded to the Nearest Million
1930	123,202,624	
1950	151,325,798	
1970	203,302,031	
1990	248,718,301	

Source: The World Almanac and Book of Facts 1997

Use with Lesson 5.10.

Comparing Data

The table below shows the number of gallons of cow's milk produced by certain countries in 1997. Read each of these numbers aloud to a friend or a family member.

Country	Gallons of Milk
Brazil	4,898,768,000
France	6,406,870,400
Germany	7,373,800,000
India	8,848,560,000
Netherlands	2,869,498,240
Poland	2,923,872,000
Russia	8,720,320,000
Ukraine	3,924,144,000
United Kingdom	3,798,032,784
United States	18,228,546,560

1 gallon of milk contains
16 cups of milk.

1. Which country produced the most milk in 1997? _____

2. Which country produced the least amount of milk in 1997? _____

For each pair, circle the country that produced more milk.

3. Brazil   Germany

4. United States   France

5. India   Russia

6. Ukraine   United Kingdom

7. Netherlands   Poland

Family Letter

Unit 6: Division; Map Reference Frames; Measures of Angles

The first four lessons of Unit 6 focus on understanding the division operation, developing a method for dividing whole numbers, and solving division number stories.

Although most adults will reach for a calculator to do a long-division problem, it is useful to know a paper-and-pencil procedure for computations such as $567 \div 6$ and $15\overline{)235}$. Fortunately, there is a method that is similar to the one most of us learned in school but is much easier to understand and use. The method is presented in this unit.

Students have had considerable practice with extended division facts, such as $420 \div 7 = 60$, and questions such as "About how many 12s are in 150?" Using the "low stress" method called the partial-quotients method, your child will apply these skills to build up partial quotients until the exact quotient and remainder are determined.

The second focus in this unit is on numbers in map coordinate systems. For maps of relatively small areas, rectangular coordinate grids are used. For world maps and the world globe, the system of latitude and longitude is used to locate places.

Since this global system is based on angle measures, the class will practice measuring and drawing angles with circular (360°) and half-circle (180°) protractors. If you have a protractor, ask your child to show you how to use this tool.

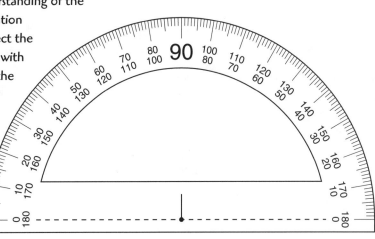

Circular (360°) protractor

The class is well into the World Tour. Students have visited Africa and are now traveling in Europe. They are beginning to see how numerical information about a country helps them get a better understanding of the country—its size, climate, location, and population distribution—and how these characteristics affect the way people live. Your child may want to share with you information about some of the countries the class has visited. Encourage your child to take materials about Europe to school, such as magazine articles, travel brochures, and articles in the travel section of your newspaper.

Half-circle (180°) protractor

Please keep this Family Letter for reference as your child works through Unit 6.

Vocabulary

Important terms in Unit 6:

acute angle An angle with a measure greater than 0° and less than 90°.

acute angle

coordinate grid A device for locating points in a plane using *ordered number pairs,* or *coordinates.*

equal-groups notation A way to denote a number of equal-sized groups. The size of the groups is written inside square brackets and the number of groups is written in front of the brackets. For example, 3[6s] means 3 groups with 6 in each group.

index of locations A list of places together with a system for locating them on a map. For example, "Billings D3," indicates that Billings can be found within the rectangle where column 3 and row D meet on the map.

meridian bar A device on a globe that shows degrees of latitude north and south of the equator.

multiplication/division diagram A diagram used for problems in which there are several equal groups. The diagram has three parts: a number of groups, a number in each group, and a total number.

rows	chairs per row	chairs
6	4	24

obtuse angle An angle with a measure greater than 90° and less than 180°.

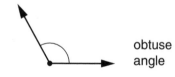

obtuse angle

ordered number pair Two numbers that are used to locate a point on a *coordinate grid.* The first number gives the position along the horizontal axis, and the second number gives the position along the vertical axis. The numbers in an ordered pair are called *coordinates.* Ordered pairs are usually written within parentheses: (2,3).

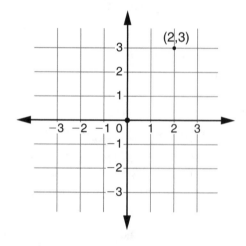

protractor A tool for measuring or drawing angles. A half-circle protractor can be used to measure and draw angles up to 180°; a full-circle protractor can be used to measure and draw angles up to 360°.

quotient The result of dividing one number by another number. For example, in 35 ÷ 5 = 7, the quotient is 7.

reflex angle An angle with a measure greater than 180° and less than 360°.

straight angle An angle with a measure of 180°.

vertex The point at which the rays of an angle, the sides of a polygon, or the edges of a polyhedron meet.

Use with Lesson 5.12.

To work with your child on concepts taught in this unit, try these interesting and rewarding activities:

1 Help your child practice division by solving problems for everyday situations.

2 Name places on the world globe and ask your child to give the latitude and longitude for each.

3 Encourage your child to identify and classify acute, right, obtuse, straight, and reflex angles in buildings, bridges, and other structures.

4 Work together with your child to construct a map, coordinate system, and index of locations for your neighborhood.

Building Skills through Games

In Unit 6, your child will practice using division and reference frames by playing the following games. For detailed instructions, see the *Student Reference Book.*

Division Dash See *Student Reference Book*, page 195.

This is a game for one or two players. Each player will need a calculator. The game helps students practice division and mental calculation.

Grid Search See *Student Reference Book*, pages 199 and 200.

This is a game for two players, and each player will require *two* playing grids. The game helps students practice using a letter–number coordinate system and developing a search strategy.

Robot

One player is the Controller, and the other is the Robot. The Controller picks a destination, giving the Robot directions for the amount of each turn and number of steps until the Robot reaches the destination. The amount of each turn may be given as a fraction of a full turn or as a degree measure.

Example: "Make a half turn and go forward 5 steps. Now turn clockwise 90 degrees and go back 3 steps."

As You Help Your Child with Homework

As your child brings assignments home, you may want to go over the instructions together, clarifying them as necessary. The answers listed below will guide you through some of this unit's Study Links.

Study Link 6.1

1. 38 6-packs   **2.** 38 tables

3. 37 R6   **4.** 47 R1

5. 23 teams   **6.** 72 bags

Study Link 6.2

1. 53 R3

2. 184 R3

3. 46 R10

4. Answer: 11 shelves

Number model: 165 ÷ 15 = 11

Study Link 6.3

1.

pages	cards per page	cards in all
?	6	744

Answer: 124 pages
Number model: 744 ÷ 6 = 124

2.

porcupines	quills per porcupine	quills in all
4	30,000	?

Answer: About 120,000 quills
Number model: 4 * 30,000 = 120,000

3.

boxes	calculators per box	calculators in all
?	14	364

Answer: 26 boxes
Number model: 364 ÷ 14 = 26

Study Link 6.4

1. 21 sets   **2.** 9 shelves

3. 14 batches   **4.** 5 strawberries

Study Link 6.7

1. 90°; 180°; 270°; 360°

2. a. Angle *D*   **b.** Angle *C*

    c. Angle *B*   **d.** Angle *A*

Study Link 6.8

1. 60°   **2.** 150°   **3.** 84°

4. 105°   **5.** 32°   **6.** 300°

Study Link 6.10

1. *B*   **2.** *C*   **3.** *D*

Study Link 6.6

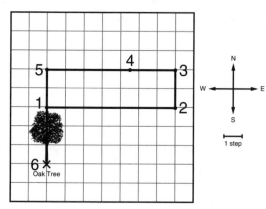

Study Link 6.9

1.

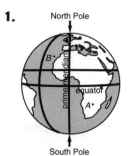

2. Eastern Hemisphere

3. water

Use with Lesson 5.12.

A Multiples-of-10 Strategy for Division   **Study Link 6.1**

For Problems 1–4, fill in the multiples-of-10 list. Use the completed list to help answer the question. Write a number model.

1. The community center bought 228 cans of soda for the picnic. How many 6-packs is that?

10 [6s] = _____

20 [6s] = _____

30 [6s] = _____

40 [6s] = _____

50 [6s] = _____

Answer: _____ 6-packs

Number model: 228 ÷ 6 = _____

2. We have tables that each seat 5 people. How many tables are needed to seat 190 people?

10 [5s] = _____

20 [5s] = _____

30 [5s] = _____

40 [5s] = _____

50 [5s] = _____

Answer: _____ tables

Number model: _____ ÷ ____ = _____

3. How many 7s are in 265?

10 [7s] = _____

20 [7s] = _____

30 [7s] = _____

40 [7s] = _____

50 [7s] = _____

Answer: _____

Number model: 7)‾265‾

4. How many 3s are in 142?

10 [3s] = _____

20 [3s] = _____

30 [3s] = _____

40 [3s] = _____

50 [3s] = _____

Answer: _____

Number model: ___)‾‾‾‾

5. There are 8 girls on each team in the basketball league. There are 184 girls in the league. How many teams are there?

Answer: _____ teams

Number model: 184 ÷ 8 = _____

6. José's class baked 290 cookies for the school bake sale. Students put 4 cookies in each bag. How many bags of 4 cookies did they make?

Answer: _____ bags

Number model: ___)‾‾‾‾

Division

> These notations for division are equivalent:
>
> $12\overline{)246}$ $246 \div 12$ $246 / 12$ $\dfrac{246}{12}$

Here is a method for dividing 246 by 9.

$9\overline{)246}$		How many 9s in 246? At least 20.
$-\ 180$	20	Use 20 as the first partial quotient. 20 * 9 = 180
66		Subtract. At least 7 [9s] are left.
$-\ 63$	7	Use 7 as the second partial quotient. 7 * 9 = 63
3	27	Subtract. Add the partial quotients. 20 + 7 = 27
↑	↑	

Remainder **Quotient** **Answer: 27 R3**

Now do these problems using this method—or one of your own.

1. $8\overline{)427}$ Answer: _____   **2.** $5\overline{)923}$ Answer: _____

3. $700 \div 15$ Answer: _____

4. Adena has 165 stuffed bears. 15 bears will fit on a shelf. How many shelves does Adena need to display her bears?

Answer: _____ shelves

Number model: _____ ÷ _____ = _____

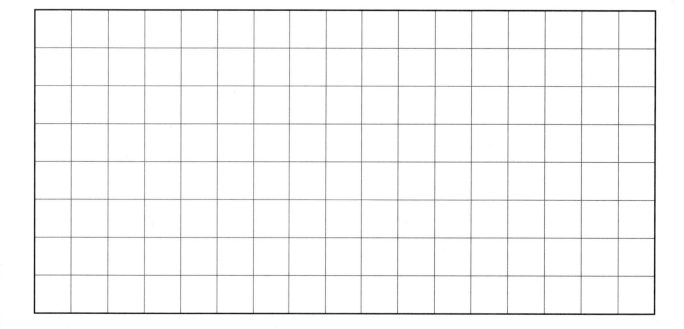

Use with Lesson 6.2.

Multiplication and Division Stories

Study Link 6.3

Fill in each Multiplication/Division Diagram. Then solve the problem and write a number model.

1. Trung's collection of 744 baseball cards is in an album. There are 6 cards on each page. How many pages of baseball cards are in the album?

pages	cards per page	cards in all

Answer: _____

Number model: _____

2. An average porcupine has about 30,000 quills. About how many quills would 4 porcupines have?

porcupines	quills per porcupine	quills in all

Answer: _____

Number model: _____

3. There are 364 calculators for the students at Madison School. A box holds 14 calculators. How many boxes are needed to hold all of the calculators?

boxes	calculators per box	calculators in all

Answer: _____

Number model: _____

Rewriting and Interpreting Remainders

Solve. For each problem, think carefully about what to do with the remainder.

1. Ms. Chew has a can of buttons. She asks Maurice to divide the buttons into sets of 16 buttons each. There are 348 buttons in the can. How many sets of 16 can Maurice make?

_____ sets

2. Emma has 75 CDs. Each shelf holds 9 CDs. How many shelves does she need to hold her entire collection?

_____ shelves

3. Jake wants to make at least 160 brownies for the bake sale. Each batch makes about 12 brownies. He plans to charge 35 cents per brownie. How many batches does he have to make?

at least

_____ batches

4. Mrs. Zis brought a box of 125 strawberries to the party. She wants to divide the strawberries evenly among 24 people. How many whole strawberries does each person get?

_____ strawberries

© 2002 Everyday Learning Corporation

Use with Lesson 6.4.

Grid Art

Plot the following points onto the grid below. After you plot each point, draw a line segment to connect it to the last one you plotted. *Remember to use your straightedge!*

(10,2); (4,2); (2,7); (4,12); (7,13); (13,13); (15,8); (13,3); (10,2); (12,7); (10,12); (4,12)

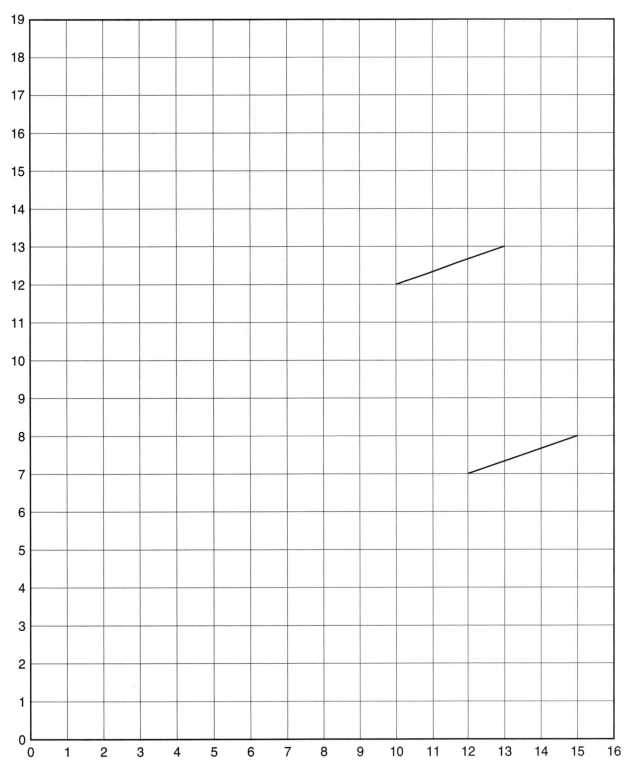

Nice work! You have just drawn a **hexagonal prism.**

Treasure Hunt

Marge and her friends are playing Treasure Hunt. Help them find the treasure. Follow the directions. Draw the path from the oak tree to the treasure. Mark the spot where the treasure is buried.

1. Start at the dot under the oak tree; face north. Walk 3 steps.

2. Make a quarter turn, clockwise. Walk 7 steps.

3. Make a quarter turn, counterclockwise. Walk 2 steps.

4. Make a $\frac{3}{4}$ turn, clockwise. Walk $2\frac{1}{2}$ steps.

5. Make a full turn. Walk $4\frac{1}{2}$ steps.

6. Make a quarter turn, counterclockwise. Walk 5 steps.

7. Make an X to mark the spot where you end.

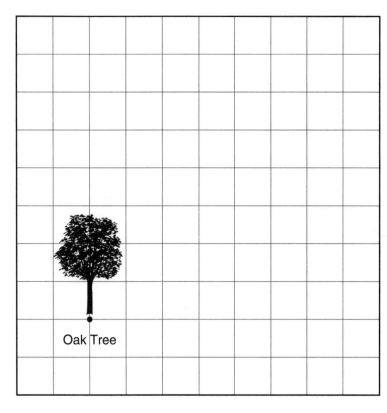

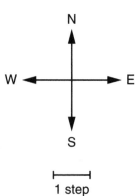

       Use with Lesson 6.6.

Estimating Angle Measures

1. Complete the table.

Fill in the exact degree measure.

Rotation	Degree Measure
$\frac{1}{4}$ turn	
$\frac{1}{2}$ turn	
$\frac{3}{4}$ turn	
full turn	

2. Estimate which angle below shows a rotation

a. between 180° and 270°.   Angle ____

b. between 0° and 90°.   Angle ____

c. between 270° and 360°.   Angle ____

d. between 90° and 180°.   Angle ____

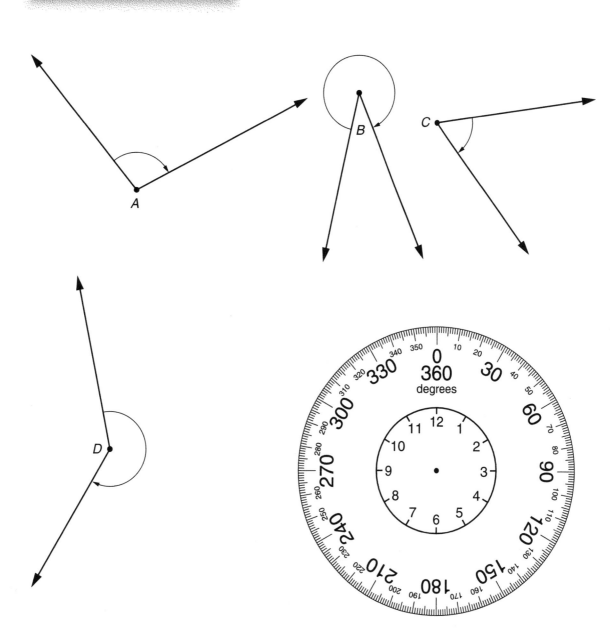

Measuring Angles with a Protractor

Use a half-circle protractor. If you don't have one, cut out the protractor at the bottom of the page. Use a pencil to make a hole in the bottom of the protractor where the dot is.

Measure each angle as accurately as you can.

1. ∠A: _____°

2. ∠B: _____°

3. ∠C: _____°

4. ∠QRS: _____°

5. ∠NOP: _____°

6. ∠KLM: _____°

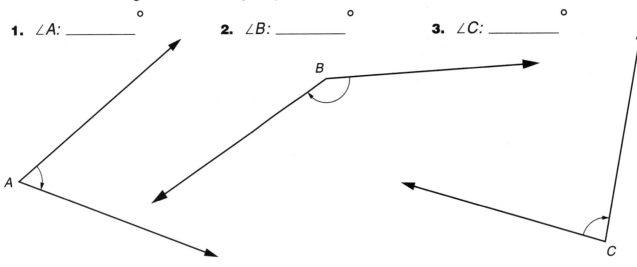

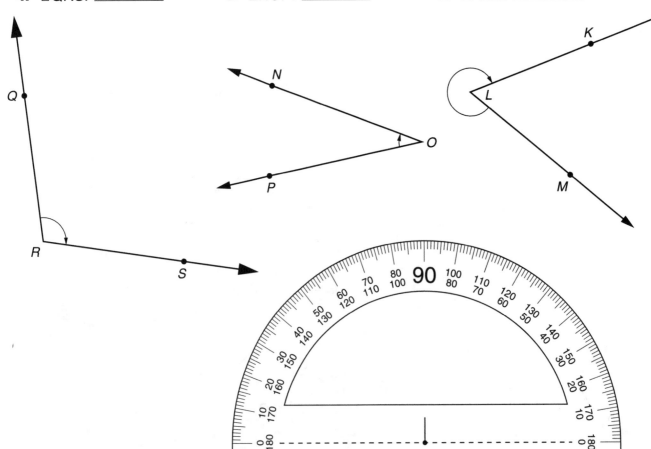

The World Globe

You need your *Student Reference Book* to complete this Study Link.

Read pages 216 and 217. Read the examples and study the figures.

1. Do the following on the picture of the world globe.

    a. Draw and label the equator.

    b. Label the prime meridian.

    c. Label the North Pole.

    d. Label the South Pole.

    e. Draw a line of latitude that is
north of the equator.

    f. Draw a line of longitude that is
west of the prime meridian.

    g. Mark a point that is in the Southern
Hemisphere and also in the Eastern
Hemisphere. Label the point *A.*

    h. Mark a point that is in the Northern
Hemisphere and also in the Western
Hemisphere. Label the point *B.*

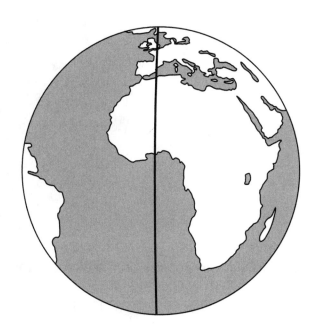

2. All of the continent of Africa is shown in the figure above. Is Africa
mostly in the Western Hemisphere or in the Eastern Hemisphere?

_____

3. Do the equator and prime meridian meet over water or over land?

_____

Latitude and Longitude

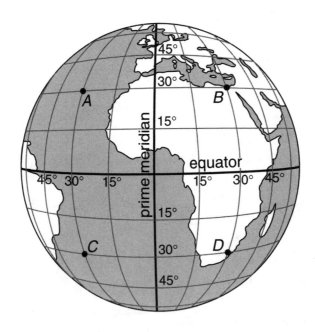

Find the following points on the picture of the globe. Write the letter of each point.

1. 30° North latitude and 30° East longitude _____

2. 30°S and 30°W _____

3. 30°S and 30°E _____

Mark the following points on the picture of the globe.

4. Point *E* at 15° South latitude and 45° East longitude

5. Point *F* at 45°N and 30°W

6. Point *G* at 30°N and 0°E

Family Letter

Unit 7: Fractions and Their Uses; Chance and Probability

In the unit just completed, your child practiced locating places on the globe using degrees of latitude and longitude with relation to the equator and the prime meridian. If you have a world globe or atlas, ask your child to show you how to use latitude and longitude to describe the locations of your hometown and other places of interest.

One of the most important ideas in mathematics is the concept that a number can be named in many different ways. For example, a store might advertise an item at $\frac{1}{2}$ off its original price or at a 50% discount—both mean the same thing. Much of the mathematics your child will learn involves finding equivalent names for numbers.

A few weeks ago, the class studied decimals as a way of naming numbers between whole numbers. Fractions serve the same purpose. After reviewing the meaning and uses of fractions, students will explore equivalent fractions—fractions that have the same value, such as $\frac{1}{2}$, $\frac{2}{4}$, $\frac{3}{6}$, and so on. As in past work with fractions, students will handle concrete objects and look at pictures, because they first need to "see" fractions in order to understand what fractions mean.

Fractions are also used to express the chance that an event will occur. For example, if we flip a coin, we say that it will land heads-up about $\frac{1}{2}$ of the time. The branch of mathematics that deals with chance events is called **probability.** Your child will begin to study probability by performing simple experiments.

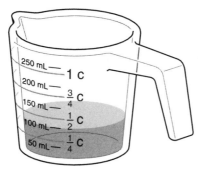

A measuring cup showing fractional increments

Please keep this Family Letter for reference as your child works through Unit 7.

Vocabulary

Important terms in Unit 7:

denominator The number below the line in a fraction. In a fraction where the whole is divided into equal parts, the denominator represents the number of equal parts into which the whole (or ONE or unit) is divided. In the fraction $\frac{a}{b}$, b is the denominator.

$$\frac{5}{9} \qquad 5/9$$
denominator

equal chance or equally likely When each of the possible outcomes for some situation has the same chance of occurring, the outcomes are said to have an equal chance or to be equally likely. For example, in tossing a coin there is an equal chance of getting heads or tails. Heads and tails are equally likely outcomes.

equivalent fractions Fractions that have different denominators but name the same amount. For example, $\frac{1}{2}$ and $\frac{4}{8}$ are equivalent fractions.

fair (coin, die, or spinner) A device that is free from bias. Each side of a fair die or coin will come up about equally often. Each section of a fair spinner will come up in proportion to its area.

A die has six faces. If the die is fair, each face has the same chance of coming up.

fair game A game in which every player has the same chance of winning.

mixed number A number that is written using both a whole number and a fraction. For example, $2\frac{1}{4}$ is a mixed number equal to $2 + \frac{1}{4}$.

numerator The number above the line in a fraction. In a fraction where the whole is divided into a number of equal parts, the numerator represents the number of equal parts being considered. In the fraction $\frac{a}{b}$, a is the numerator.

numerator
$$\frac{5}{9} \qquad 5/9$$

probability A number from 0 to 1 that tells the chance that an event will happen. The closer a probability is to 1, the more likely the event is to happen.

whole (or ONE or unit) The entire object, collection of objects, or quantity being considered; the ONE; the unit; 100%.

"whole" box A box in which students write the name of the whole (or ONE or unit).

Whole
24 pennies

Use with Lesson 6.11.

Do-Anytime Activities

To work with your child on concepts taught in this unit, try these interesting and rewarding activities:

1 Have your child look for everyday uses of fractions in grocery items, clothing sizes, cookbooks, measuring cups and spoons, and statistics in newspapers and on television.

2 Encourage your child to express numbers, quantities, and measures, such as a quarter of an hour, a quart of orange juice, a dozen eggs, and a pint of milk.

3 While grocery shopping, help your child compare prices by looking at shelf labels or calculating unit prices. Help your child make decisions about the "better buy." If a calculator is available, have your child take it to the store.

4 Have your child look for everyday uses of probabilities in games, sports, and weather reports. Ask your child to make a list of events that could never happen, might happen, and are sure to happen.

Building Skills through Games

In this unit, your child will work on his or her understanding of numbers and fractions by playing the following games. For detailed instructions, see the *Student Reference Book.*

Name That Number See *Student Reference Book,* page 203.

This is a game for 2 or 3 players and requires a complete deck of number cards. The game helps students review operations with whole numbers.

Fraction Top-It See *Student Reference Book,* page 197.

This is a game for 2 to 4 players and requires one set of 32 Fraction Cards. The game develops skill in comparing fractions.

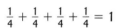

Family Letter, continued

As You Help Your Child with Homework

As your child brings assignments home, you may want to go over the instructions together, clarifying them as necessary. The answers listed below will guide you through some of the Study Links in this unit.

Study Link 7.2

1. **a.** 15 nickels   **c.** $0.30
2. **a.** 4   **b.** 12   **c.** 8   **3.** 6
4. 12   **5.** 7   **6.** 28
7. 10   **8.** 30   **9.** 10
10. 12   **11.** 12   **12.** $2\frac{1}{2}$

Study Link 7.3

3. 8 cans

Study Link 7.4

1. Less than $1.00
2. $3\frac{3}{4}$ inches
3. $\frac{1}{6}$
4. $2\frac{3}{8}$
5. Sample answers:

$\frac{1}{4} + \frac{1}{4} + \frac{1}{4} + \frac{1}{4} = 1$ $\frac{1}{4} + \frac{3}{12} + \frac{3}{6} = 1$

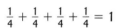

$\frac{2}{4} + \frac{3}{6} = 1$

Study Link 7.5

1. $\frac{5}{12}$ **2.** $\frac{1}{6}$ **3.** $\frac{1}{4}$

4.   **5.**   **6.**

7. $\frac{3}{4}$ **8.** $\frac{1}{4}$ **9.** $\frac{1}{3}$

10. no; Sample answer: It took more than 1 hour to drive, because $\frac{1}{2} + \frac{1}{2}$ is 1 hour, and $\frac{3}{4}$ is larger than $\frac{1}{2}$; or $\frac{1}{2} + \frac{3}{4} = \frac{15}{12}$.

Study Link 7.6

1. C, F, I   **2.** B, D
3. E, H   **4.** A, G

Study Link 7.7

1. =   **2.** ≠   **3.** =
4. =   **5.** =   **6.** ≠
7. ≠   **8.** =   **9.** ≠
10. 8   **11.** 3   **12.** 10
13. 18   **14.** 12   **15.** 12

16. Sample answer: You could tell her that the Equivalent Fractions Rule states that you will get an equivalent fraction if you multiply by (not add) the same number in the numerator and denominator. Or you could draw a picture to show that $\frac{1}{4}$ is not equal to $\frac{3}{6}$.

Study Link 7.8

Sample answers:

1. $\frac{2}{10}, \frac{1}{5}, \frac{20}{100}$ **2.** $\frac{6}{10}, \frac{3}{5}, \frac{60}{100}$
3. $\frac{5}{10}, \frac{1}{2}, \frac{50}{100}$ **4.** $\frac{3}{4}, \frac{30}{40}, \frac{75}{100}$

Sample answers:

5. 0.3   **6.** 0.63
7. 0.7   **8.** 0.4
9. 0.70; $\frac{70}{100}$ **10.** 0.2; $\frac{2}{10}$

Study Link 7.9

1. >   **2.** <   **3.** =
4. =   **5.** <   **6.** >
7. Answers vary. **8.** Answers vary. **9.** $\frac{1}{4}, \frac{4}{10}, \frac{3}{7}, \frac{24}{50}$
10. $\frac{1}{50}, \frac{1}{20}, \frac{1}{5}, \frac{1}{3}, \frac{1}{2}$ **11.** $\frac{4}{100}, \frac{4}{12}, \frac{4}{8}, \frac{4}{5}, \frac{4}{4}$ **12.** $\frac{1}{12}, \frac{3}{12}, \frac{7}{12}, \frac{8}{12}, \frac{11}{12}$

Study Link 7.10

3. 28   **4.** 27   **5.** 8
6. 30   **7.** 10   **8.** 36

    Use with Lesson 6.11.

Fractions

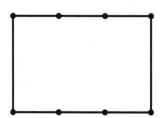

1. Divide the circle into 6 equal parts.
Color $\frac{5}{6}$ of the circle.

Whole
circle

2. Divide the rectangle into 3 equal parts.
Shade $\frac{2}{3}$ of the rectangle.

Whole
rectangle

3. Divide each square into fourths.
Color $1\frac{3}{4}$ of the squares.

Whole
square

Fill in the missing numbers on the number lines.

4.

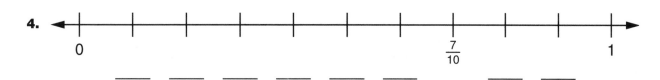

5.

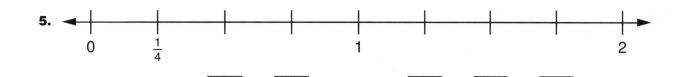

"Fraction-of" Problems

1. a. Fill in the "whole" box.

   b. Circle $\frac{2}{5}$ of the nickels.

   c. How much money is that? _____

Whole

2. Theresa had 24 cookies. She gave $\frac{1}{6}$ to her sister and $\frac{3}{6}$ to her mother.

   a. How many cookies did she give to her sister? _____ cookies

   b. How many did she give to her mother? _____ cookies

   c. How many did she have left? _____ cookies

Solve.

3. $\frac{1}{3}$ of 18 = _____

4. $\frac{2}{3}$ of 18 = _____

5. $\frac{1}{5}$ of 35 = _____

6. $\frac{4}{5}$ of 35 = _____

7. $\frac{1}{4}$ of 40 = _____

8. $\frac{3}{4}$ of 40 = _____

9. $\frac{5}{8}$ of 16 = _____

10. $\frac{4}{9}$ of 27 = _____

11. $\frac{3}{5}$ of 20 = _____

12. What is $\frac{1}{4}$ of 10? _____ Explain.

_____

_____

Use with Lesson 7.2.

Dividing Squares

Use a straightedge and the dots below to help you divide each of the squares into equal parts.

Example Squares A, B, C, and D are each divided in half in a different way.

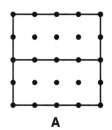
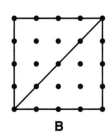
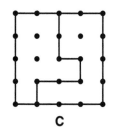
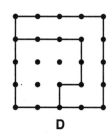

A   B   C   D

1. Square E is divided into fourths. Divide squares F, G, and H into fourths, each in a different way.

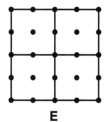
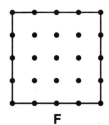
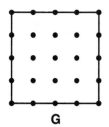
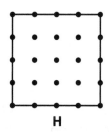

E   F   G   H

2. Square I is divided into eighths. Divide squares J, K, and L into eighths, each in a different way.

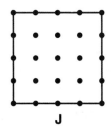
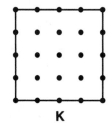
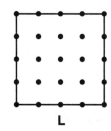

I   J   K   L

3. Rosa has 15 quarters and 10 nickels. She buys juice from a vending machine for herself and her friends. The juice costs 35 cents a can. She puts $\frac{2}{3}$ of the quarters and $\frac{3}{5}$ of the nickels in the machine and gets no change back.

How many cans of juice did she buy? _____ cans

Show your work on the back of this paper.

Fractions

1. Jake has $\frac{3}{4}$ of a dollar. Maxwell has $\frac{1}{10}$ of a dollar.
Do they have more or less than $1.00 in all? _____

2. Jillian draws a line segment $2\frac{1}{4}$ inches long. Then she makes the
line segment $1\frac{1}{2}$ inches longer. How long is the line segment now? _____ inches

$2\frac{1}{4}$ in. $1\frac{1}{2}$ in.

3. A pizza was cut into 6 slices. Benjamin ate $\frac{1}{3}$ of the
pizza and Dana ate $\frac{1}{2}$. What fraction of the pizza was left? _____

4. Rafael drew a line segment $2\frac{7}{8}$ inches long.
Then he erased $\frac{1}{2}$ inch. How long is the line segment now? _____ inches

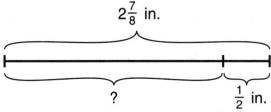

$2\frac{7}{8}$ in.

? $\frac{1}{2}$ in.

5. Two hexagons together are one whole. Draw line segments to divide each
whole into trapezoids, rhombuses, and triangles. Write a number model for
each way you divided the whole.

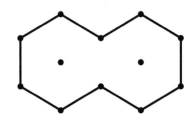

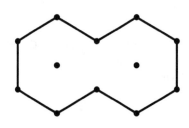

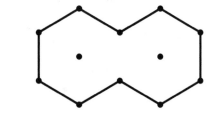

_____   _____   _____

Use with Lesson 7.4.

Clock Fractions

Write the fraction represented by each clock face.

1.
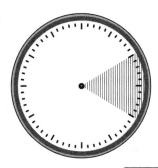
_____

2.

_____

3.

_____

Shade each clock face to show the fraction. Start shading at the line segment.

4. $\frac{3}{4}$
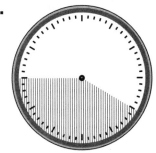

5. $\frac{2}{3}$

6. $\frac{11}{12}$
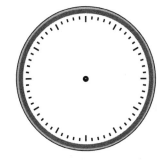

Use the clock faces below to help you solve these problems.

7. $\frac{2}{3} + \frac{1}{12} =$ _____

8. $\frac{11}{12} - \frac{2}{3} =$ _____

9. $\frac{3}{4} - \frac{5}{12} =$ _____

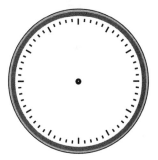

10. It took Denise $\frac{3}{4}$ of an hour to drive from Zion to Platt, and $\frac{1}{2}$ hour to drive from Platt to Rome. To figure out her total driving time, Denise wrote the following number model: $\frac{3}{4} + \frac{1}{2} = \frac{4}{6}$

Do you agree that it took her about $\frac{4}{6}$ of an hour? _____

Explain. _____

_____

_____

Many Names for Fractions

Write the letters of the pictures that represent each fraction.

1. $\frac{1}{2}$ *C,* _____

2. $\frac{3}{4}$ _____

3. $\frac{4}{5}$ _____

4. $\frac{2}{3}$ _____

A

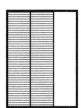

B

C

D

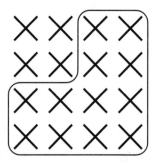

E

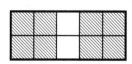

F

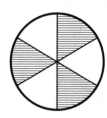

G

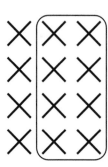

H

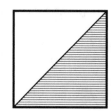

I

Use with Lesson 7.6.

Equivalent Fractions

For each pair of fractions below, ask yourself: "If I multiply both the numerator and denominator of one fraction by the same number, will I get the other fraction?"

- If the answer is *yes,* the fractions are equivalent. Write = in the blank.

- If the answer is *no,* the fractions are not equivalent. Write ≠ in the blank.
  (≠ means "not equal to")

1. $\frac{1}{3}$ —— $\frac{4}{12}$ **2.** $\frac{1}{4}$ —— $\frac{5}{12}$ **3.** $\frac{2}{3}$ —— $\frac{4}{6}$

4. $\frac{6}{8}$ —— $\frac{3}{4}$ **5.** $\frac{1}{2}$ —— $\frac{6}{12}$ **6.** $\frac{3}{6}$ —— $\frac{2}{3}$

7. $\frac{2}{5}$ —— $\frac{6}{10}$ **8.** $\frac{2}{3}$ —— $\frac{6}{9}$ **9.** $\frac{2}{6}$ —— $\frac{6}{12}$

In each box, write a number to make a fraction that is equivalent to the given fraction.

10. $\frac{4}{5} = \frac{\boxed{}}{10}$ **11.** $\frac{30}{40} = \frac{\boxed{}}{4}$ **12.** $\frac{15}{50} = \frac{3}{\boxed{}}$

13. $\frac{2}{3} = \frac{12}{\boxed{}}$ **14.** $\frac{8}{\boxed{}} = \frac{2}{3}$ **15.** $\frac{\boxed{}}{20} = \frac{3}{5}$

16. Margot says the value of a fraction doesn't change if you do the same thing to the numerator and denominator. Margot says that she added 2 to both the numerator and denominator in $\frac{1}{4}$ and got $\frac{3}{6}$.

$$\frac{1+2}{4+2} = \frac{3}{6}$$

Therefore, she says that $\frac{1}{4} = \frac{3}{6}$. How could you explain or show Margot that she is wrong?

_____

_____

_____

_____

Fractions and Decimals

Write 3 equivalent fractions for each decimal.

Example

0.8 $\dfrac{8}{10}$ $\dfrac{4}{5}$ $\dfrac{80}{100}$

1. 0.20   _____   _____   _____

2. 0.6   _____   _____   _____

3. 0.50   _____   _____   _____

4. 0.75   _____   _____   _____

Write an equivalent decimal for each fraction.

5. $\dfrac{3}{10}$ _____   **6.** $\dfrac{63}{100}$ _____

7. $\dfrac{7}{10}$ _____   **8.** $\dfrac{2}{5}$ _____

9. Shade more than $\dfrac{53}{100}$ of the square and less than $\dfrac{8}{10}$ of the square. Write the value of the shaded part as a decimal and a fraction.

Decimal: _____

Fraction: _____

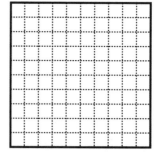

10. Shade more than $\dfrac{11}{100}$ of the square and less than $\dfrac{1}{4}$ of the square. Write the value of the shaded part as a decimal and a fraction.

Decimal: _____

Fraction: _____

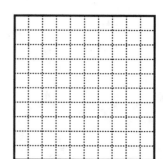

Compare and Order Fractions

Write <, >, or = to make each number sentence true.

> < is less than
> > is greater than
> = is equal to

1. $\dfrac{5}{6}$ _____ $\dfrac{1}{6}$

2. $\dfrac{3}{10}$ _____ $\dfrac{3}{4}$

3. $\dfrac{2}{3}$ _____ $\dfrac{10}{15}$

4. $\dfrac{10}{40}$ _____ $\dfrac{4}{16}$

5. $\dfrac{4}{9}$ _____ $\dfrac{7}{9}$

6. $\dfrac{5}{6}$ _____ $\dfrac{5}{8}$

7. Explain how you solved Problem 1.

_____

_____

8. Explain how you solved Problem 2.

_____

_____

9. Circle each fraction that is less than $\dfrac{1}{2}$.

$\dfrac{7}{8}$ $\dfrac{1}{4}$ $\dfrac{4}{10}$ $\dfrac{7}{12}$ $\dfrac{5}{9}$ $\dfrac{3}{7}$ $\dfrac{24}{50}$ $\dfrac{67}{100}$

Write the fractions in order from smallest to largest.

10. $\dfrac{1}{5}, \quad \dfrac{1}{3}, \quad \dfrac{1}{20}, \quad \dfrac{1}{2}, \quad \dfrac{1}{50}$

_____ _____ _____ _____ _____
smallest   largest

11. $\dfrac{4}{5}, \quad \dfrac{4}{100}, \quad \dfrac{4}{4}, \quad \dfrac{4}{8}, \quad \dfrac{4}{12}$

_____ _____ _____ _____ _____
smallest   largest

12. $\dfrac{3}{12}, \quad \dfrac{7}{12}, \quad \dfrac{1}{12}, \quad \dfrac{11}{12}, \quad \dfrac{8}{12}$

_____ _____ _____ _____ _____
smallest   largest

What Is the ONE?

For Problems 1 and 2, use your Geometry Template or sketch the shapes.

1. Suppose is $\frac{1}{4}$. Draw each of the following:

Example $\frac{3}{4}$ **a.** 1   **b.** $1\frac{1}{2}$ **c.** 2

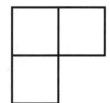

2. Suppose ◇ is $\frac{2}{3}$. Draw each of the following:

a. $\frac{1}{3}$ **b.** 1   **c.** $\frac{4}{3}$ **d.** 2

Solve.

3. If 14 counters are $\frac{1}{2}$, then what is the ONE? _____ counters

4. If 9 counters are $\frac{1}{3}$, then what is the ONE? _____ counters

5. If 6 counters are $\frac{3}{4}$, then what is the ONE? _____ counters

6. If 12 counters are $\frac{2}{5}$, then what is the ONE? _____ counters

7. If 8 counters are $\frac{4}{5}$, then what is the ONE? _____ counters

8. If 16 counters are $\frac{4}{9}$, then what is the ONE? _____ counters

Spinners and Fractions

Design your own spinner. Use as many colors as you wish.

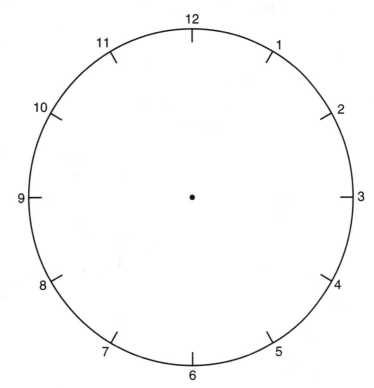

Describe your spinner. Tell the chance of the paper clip landing on each of the colors. Use sentences *like the following:*

• The chances of the paper clip landing on blue are 1 out of 3.

• The paper clip has a $\frac{3}{4}$ chance of landing on green.

• It is very unlikely to land on yellow.

• It is 3 times as likely to land on red as on blue.

• It has the same chance of landing on black as on white.

_____

_____

_____

_____

_____

Layout of a Kitchen

Study Link 7.11

Pages 322 and 323 will be needed to do Lesson 8.1 in the next unit. Please complete the pages and return them to class.

Every kitchen needs a stove, a sink, and a refrigerator. Notice how the stove, sink, and refrigerator are arranged in the kitchen below. The triangle shows the work path in the kitchen. Walking from the stove to the sink and to the refrigerator forms an invisible "triangle" on the floor.

Front View of Kitchen

Bird's-Eye View of Kitchen
(looking down at appliances
and countertops)

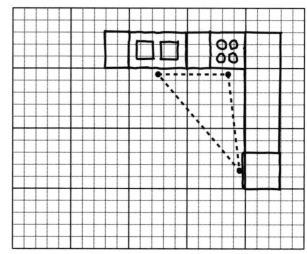

The side of a square represents 1 foot.

1. Put one coin or other marker on the floor in front of your sink, one in front of your stove, and one in front of your refrigerator.

2. Measure the distance between each pair of markers. Use feet and inches and record your measurements below.

Distance between

  a. stove and refrigerator   About _____ feet _____ inches

  b. refrigerator and sink   About _____ feet _____ inches

  c. sink and stove   About _____ feet _____ inches

Use with Lesson 7.11.

Layout of a Kitchen (cont.)

3. On the grid below, make a sketch that shows how the stove, sink, and refrigerator are arranged in your kitchen.

Your sketch should show a bird's-eye view of these 3 appliances (including all countertops).

If your oven is separate from your stove, sketch the stove top only.

Use the following symbols in your sketch:

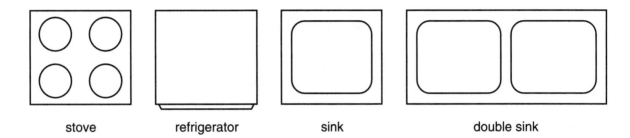

| stove | refrigerator | sink | double sink |

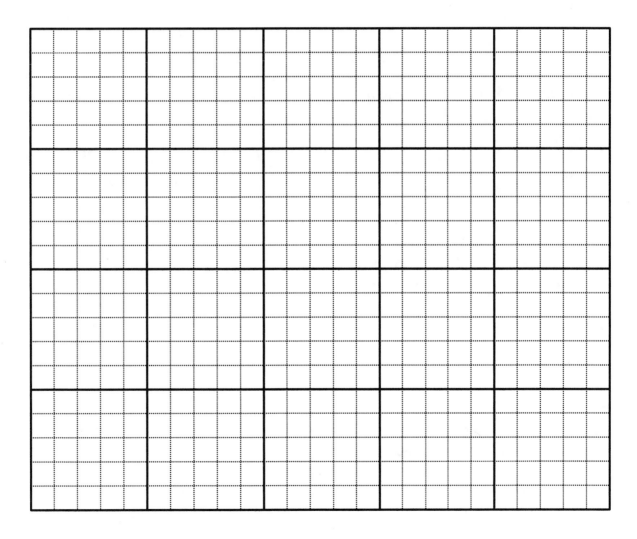

Chances Are ...

SRB
71

1. You are going to toss 2 pennies 20 times. Make a prediction. How many times do you think the 2 pennies will come up as

   a. 2 heads? _____ times

   b. 2 tails? _____ times

   c. 1 head and 1 tail? _____ times

2. Now toss 2 pennies together 20 times. Record the results in the table.

A Penny Toss

Results	Number of Times
2 heads	
2 tails	
1 head and 1 tail	

3. What fraction of the tosses came up as

   a. 2 heads? _____

   b. 2 tails? _____

   c. 1 head and 1 tail? _____

4. Suppose you were to flip the coins 1,000 times. What fraction do you think would come up as

   a. 2 heads? _____

   b. 2 tails? _____

   c. 1 head and 1 tail? _____

5. Explain how you got your answers for Problem 4.

   _____

   _____

Use with Lesson 7.12.

Family Letter

Unit 8: Perimeter and Area

In previous grades, your child studied the *perimeter* (distance around) and the *area* (amount of surface) of various geometric figures. This next unit will extend your child's understanding of geometry by developing and applying formulas for the areas of figures such as rectangles, parallelograms, and triangles.

Area of a Rectangle

Area = base * height (or length * width)

$A = b * h$ (or $l * w$)

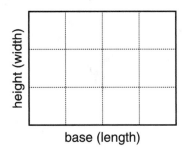

base (length)

Area of a Parallelogram

Area = base * height

$A = b * h$

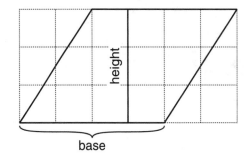

base

Area of a Triangle

Area = $\frac{1}{2}$ of (base * height)

$A = \frac{1}{2} * b * h$

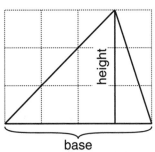

base

Students will learn how to make scale drawings and apply their knowledge of perimeter, area, and scale drawing by analyzing the arrangement of the appliances in their kitchens and the furniture in their bedrooms.

Students will also calculate the area of the skin that covers the entire body. A rule of thumb is that the area of a person's skin is about 100 times the area of one side of that person's hand. Ask your child to show you how to calculate the area of your own skin.

At the beginning of the year, the class learned to draw certain geometric figures using only a compass and straightedge. In this unit, your child will practice several new compass-and-straightedge constructions.

The World Tour will continue. Students will examine how geographical areas are measured, and difficulties in making accurate measurements. They will compare areas for South American countries by using division to calculate the ratio of areas.

Please keep this Family Letter for reference as your child works through Unit 8.

Vocabulary

Important terms in Unit 8:

area The amount of surface inside a closed boundary. Area is measured in *square units,* such as square inches or square centimeters.

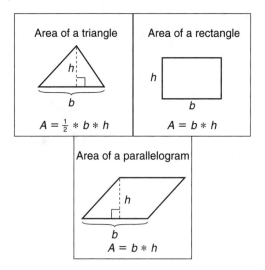

Area of a triangle
$A = \frac{1}{2} * b * h$

Area of a rectangle
$A = b * h$

Area of a parallelogram
$A = b * h$

formula A general rule for finding the value of something. A formula is often written using letters, called *variables,* that stand for the quantities involved.

length The measurement of something along its greatest dimension. The length of a rectangle is usually the longer dimension of the rectangle.

perimeter The distance around a closed 2-dimensional shape. The perimeter of a circle is called its *circumference.* The perimeter of a polygon is the sum of the lengths of its sides.

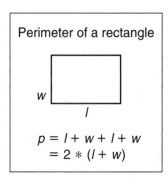

Perimeter of a rectangle

$$p = l + w + l + w$$
$$= 2 * (l + w)$$

perpendicular Meeting at right angles. Lines, rays, line segments, and planes that meet at right angles are perpendicular. The symbol $\perp$ is read "is perpendicular to," as in "line *CD* $\perp$ line *AB*." The symbol $\llcorner$ indicates a right angle.

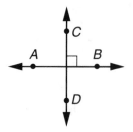

Perpendicular lines

scale The ratio of the distance on a map, globe, drawing, or model to an actual distance.

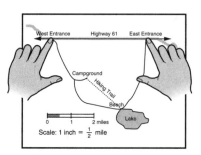

scale drawing A drawing of an object or region in which all parts are drawn to the same scale. Architects and builders often use scale drawings.

square unit A unit used in measuring area. For example, a square that measures one inch on each side has an area of one square inch.

variable A letter or other symbol that represents a number. A variable can represent one specific number or it can stand for many different numbers.

width The measurement of something along its shortest dimension. The width of a rectangle is usually the shorter dimension of the rectangle.

Use with Lesson 7.13.

Do-Anytime Activities

To work with your child on concepts taught in this unit, try these interesting and rewarding activities:

1 Have your child pretend that he or she is a carpenter whose job is to redesign a room—for example, a bedroom, the kitchen, or the living room. Have him or her make a rough estimate of the area of the room. Then help your child check the estimate by finding the actual area using a tape measure or, if possible, blueprints.

2 Have your child pretend that he or she is an architect. Give him or her some dimensions and space requirements to work with. Then have your child design a "dream house," "dream bedroom," or sports stadium, and make a scale drawing for that design.

3 Work with your child to make a scale drawing of your neighborhood. Or have your child make a scale drawing of the floor plan of your house or apartment.

4 Have your child compare the areas of continents, countries, states, or major cities.

As You Help Your Child with Homework

As your child brings assignments home, you may want to go over the instructions together, clarifying them as necessary. The answers listed below will guide you through this unit's Study Links.

Study Link 8.1

1a. Perimeter = 19 feet 6 inches

1b. Perimeter = 20 feet 2 inches

2. Distance = 9 feet 3 inches; no

Study Link 8.2

1. **a.** 52

    b. 117

    c. $32\frac{1}{2}$

    d. $175\frac{1}{2}$

3.

Rectangle	Height in Drawing	Actual Height
Rectangle A	$\frac{1}{2}$ in.	12 ft
Rectangle B	$1\frac{1}{4}$ in.	30 ft
Rectangle C	2 in.	48 ft
Rectangle D	$1\frac{3}{4}$ in.	42 ft
Rectangle E	1 in.	24 ft

Study Link 8.3

1. 24

2. 24

Study Link 8.4

1. 85,000

2. 17,500

Study Link 8.5

1. 78 ft

2. 27 ft

3. 2,106 sq ft

4. 2,808 sq ft

5. Sample answer: In a singles game, each player covers $\frac{1}{2}$ of 2,106 sq ft, or 1,053 sq ft. In a doubles game, each player covers $\frac{1}{4}$ of 2,808 sq ft, or 702 sq ft.

Study Link 8.6

1. 36

2. $29\frac{1}{4}$

3. 24

4. 46.8

5. 13

6. 8.5

Study Link 8.7

1. 16

2. 30

3. 12.75, or $12\frac{3}{4}$

4. 11.25, or $11\frac{1}{4}$

5. 3

6. 6

Study Link 8.8

1. Russia and Mexico and Brazil

2. Pakistan and Argentina

3. 5

4. 10, or 11

5. $\frac{1}{2}$

6. 9 or 10

Use with Lesson 7.13.

Work Triangles

Recommended distances between appliances:

Between stove and refrigerator: 4 feet to 9 feet

Between refrigerator and sink: 4 feet to 7 feet

Between sink and stove: 4 feet to 6 feet

1. Find the perimeter of each of the work triangles below. Convert measures of 12 inches or more to feet and inches. (For example, 15 feet 16 inches = 16 feet 4 inches.) Circle the triangle whose sides are within the recommended range.

a.

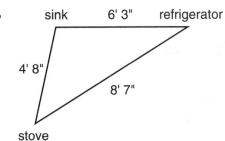

Perimeter = _____ feet _____ inches

b.

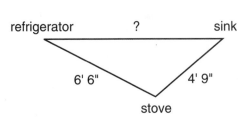

Perimeter = _____ feet _____ inches

2. The perimeter of the work triangle below is 20 feet 6 inches.

a. What is the distance between the refrigerator and the sink?

_____ feet _____ inches

refrigerator   ?   sink

6' 6"   4' 9"

stove

b. Does this kitchen meet the recommendations? _____

Scale

1. If 1 inch on a map represents 13 miles, then

   a. 4 inches represent _____ miles.

   b. 9 inches represent _____ miles.

   c. $2\frac{1}{2}$ inches represent _____ miles.

   d. $13\frac{1}{2}$ inches represent _____ miles.

2. The scale for a drawing is 1 centimeter : 5 meters. Make a scale drawing of a rectangle that measures 20 meters by 15 meters.

   SRB
   125

3. Scale: $\frac{1}{4}$ inch represents 6 feet. Measure the height of each rectangle to the nearest $\frac{1}{4}$ inch. Complete the table.

   A

   B

   C

   D

   E

Rectangle	Height in Drawing	Actual Height
A		
B		
C		
D		
E		

Use with Lesson 8.2.

Exploring Area

1. Rectangle A at the right is drawn on a 1-centimeter grid. Find its area.

Area = _____ cm^2

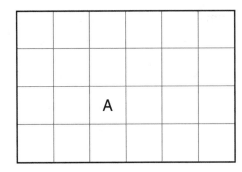

2. Rectangle B has the same area as Rectangle A. Cut out Rectangle B. Then cut it into 5 pieces, any way you want.

Rearrange the pieces into a new shape that is not a rectangle. Then tape the pieces together in the space below. What is the area of the new shape?

Area of new shape = _____ cm^2

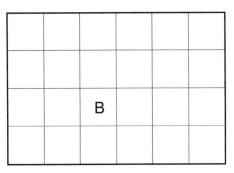

Areas of Irregular Figures

1. Here is a map of São Paulo State in Brazil. Each grid square represents 2,500 square miles. Estimate the area of São Paulo State.

The area is about _____ square miles.

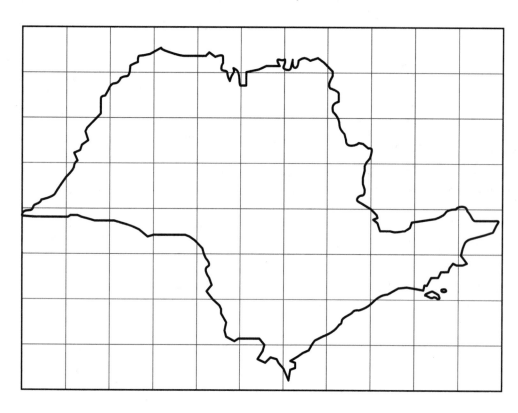

2. Here is a map of Rio de Janeiro State in Brazil. Each grid square represents 2,500 square miles. Estimate the area of Rio de Janeiro State.

The area is about _____ square miles.

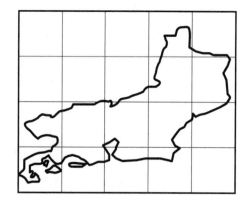

Use with Lesson 8.4.

The Tennis Court

SRB
114

> Area of rectangle = length * width

Tennis can be played either by 2 people or by 4 people. When 2 people play, it is called a game of singles. When 4 people play, it is called a game of doubles.

Here is a diagram of a tennis court. The net divides the court in half.

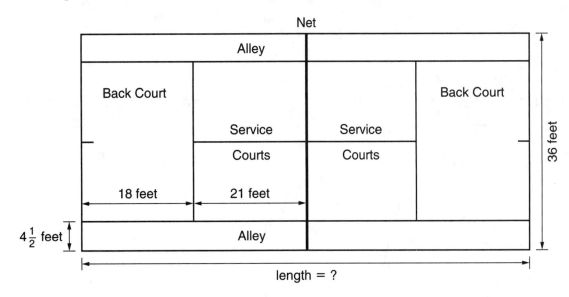

The two *alleys* are used only in doubles. They are never used in singles.

1. What is the total length of a tennis court? _____

2. The court used in a game of doubles is 36 feet wide. Each alley is $4\frac{1}{2}$ feet wide. What is the width of the court used in a game of singles? _____

3. What is the **area** of a singles court? _____

4. What is the **area** of a doubles court? _____

5. Do you think a player needs to cover more court in a game of singles or in a game of doubles? Explain.

_____

_____

_____

_____

Areas of Parallelograms

Find the area of each parallelogram.

1.

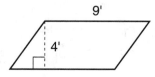

9'

4'

Area = _____ square feet

2.

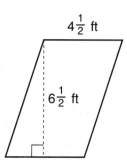

$4\frac{1}{2}$ ft

$6\frac{1}{2}$ ft

Area = _____ square feet

3.

3 cm

8 cm

Area = _____ square centimeters

4.

6.5 m

7.2 m

Area = _____ square meters

The area of each parallelogram is given. Find the length of the base.

5.

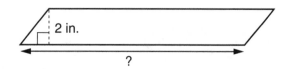

2 in.

?

Area = 26 square inches

base = _____ inches

6.

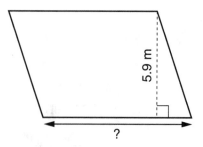

5.9 m

?

Area = 50.15 square meters

base = _____ meters

Percents in My World

Percent means *per hundred* or *out of a hundred.* "1 percent" means $\frac{1}{100}$ or 0.01.

SRB
38

"48 percent of the students in our school are boys" means that out of every 100 students in the school, 48 are boys.

Percents are written in two ways: with the word *percent,* as in the sentence above, and with the symbol %.

Collect examples of percents. Look in newspapers, magazines, books, almanacs, and encyclopedias. Ask people at home to help. Write the examples below. Also tell where you found them. If an adult says you may, cut out examples and paste them on the back of this page.

Encyclopedia: 91% of the area of New Jersey is land, and 9% is covered by water.

Newspaper: 76 percent of the seniors in Southport High School say they plan to attend college next year.

Areas of Triangles

Find the area of each triangle.

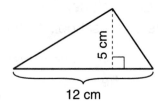

1.

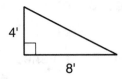

4'

8'

Area = _____ square feet

2.

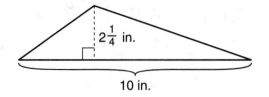

5 cm

12 cm

Area = _____ square centimeters

3.

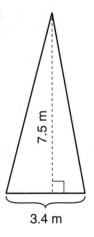

7.5 m

3.4 m

Area = _____ square meters

4.

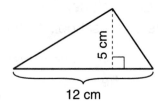

$2\frac{1}{4}$ in.

10 in.

Area = _____ square inches

The area of each triangle is given. Find the length of the base.

5.

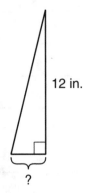

12 in.

?

Area = 18 square inches

base = _____ inches

6.

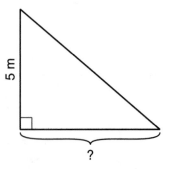

5 m

?

Area = 15 square meters

base = _____ meters

Use with Lesson 8.7.

Daily Newspapers

Use the information in the table below to estimate the answers
to the questions.

Country	Number of Daily Newspapers
India	1,802
United States	1,533
Germany	406
Turkey	400
Brazil	320
Mexico	310
Russia	292
Pakistan	223
Argentina	190
Greece	168

Source: The Top 10 of Everything 1999

1. India has about 6 times as many daily newspapers as which three countries?

_____ , _____ and _____

2. Which two countries have about $\frac{1}{2}$ as many daily newspapers as Germany?

_____ and _____

3. The United States has about _____ times as many daily newspapers as Mexico.

4. India has about _____ times as many daily newspapers as Greece.

5. Greece has about _____ as many daily newspapers as Brazil.

6. India has about _____ times as many daily newspapers as Argentina.

Unit 9: Percents

In Unit 9, we will be studying percents and their uses in everyday situations. Your child should begin finding examples of percents in newspapers and magazines, on food packages, on clothing labels, and so on, and bring them to class. Students' collections will be used to illustrate a variety of percent applications.

As we study percents, your child will learn equivalent values for percents, fractions, and decimals. For example, 50% is equivalent to the fraction $\frac{1}{2}$ and to the decimal 0.5. The class will develop the understanding that **percent** always refers to a **part out of 100.**

Converting "easy" fractions, such as $\frac{1}{2}$, $\frac{1}{3}$, $\frac{1}{10}$, and $\frac{3}{4}$, to decimal and percent equivalents should become automatic for your child. Such fractions are common in percent situations and are helpful with "more difficult" fractions, decimals, and percents. To aid in memorizing the "easy" fraction/percent equivalencies, your child will play *Fraction/Percent Concentration*.

"Easy" Fractions	Decimals	Percents
$\frac{1}{2}$	0.50	50%
$\frac{1}{4}$	0.25	25%
$\frac{3}{4}$	0.75	75%
$\frac{2}{5}$	0.40	40%
$\frac{7}{10}$	0.70	70%
$\frac{2}{2}$	1.00	100%

Throughout the unit, your child will use a calculator to convert fractions to percents and will learn how to use the percent key ⬚%⬚ to calculate discounts, sale prices, and percents of discount.

As part of the World Tour, your child will explore population data, such as literacy rates and percents of people who live in rural and urban areas.

Finally, the class will begin to apply the multiplication and division algorithms to problems that contain decimals. The approach used in *Everyday Mathematics* is quite simple: Students solve the problems as if the numbers were whole numbers. Then they estimate the answers to help them locate the decimal point in the exact answer. In this unit, we begin with fairly simple problems. Your child will solve progressively more difficult problems in *Fifth* and *Sixth Grade Everyday Mathematics*.

Please keep this Family Letter for reference as your child works through Unit 9.

Use with Lesson 8.9.

Vocabulary

Important terms in Unit 9:

discount The amount by which the regular price of an item is reduced.

life expectancy The average number of years a person may be expected to live.

literate and illiterate A literate person can read and write; an illiterate person cannot read and write.

100% box The entire object, the entire collection of objects, or the entire quantity being considered.

100% box
24 books

"24 books = 100%, the Whole, the ONE"

percent (%) Per hundred or out of a hundred. 1% equals $\frac{1}{100}$ or 0.01. For example, "48% of the students in the school are boys" means that 48 out of 100 students in the school are boys.

percent of literacy The percent of the total population that is literate; the number of people out of 100 who are able to read and write. For example, 90% of the population in Mexico is literate—this means that 90 out of 100 people can read and write.

percent or fraction discount The percent or fraction of the regular price that you save. See example under *regular price*.

rank To put in order by size; to sort from smallest to largest or vice versa.

Countries Ranked from Smallest to Largest Percent of Population, Ages 0-14	
1. Japan	15%
2. Russia	19%
3. Australia	21%
4. Thailand	24%
5. China	26%
6. Turkey	30%
7. Vietnam	33%
8. India	34%
9. Iran	36%
10. Bangladesh	38%

regular price or list price The price of an item without a discount.

Regular Price	Sale!	Sale Price	You Saved
$19.95	25% OFF	$14.96	$4.99

rural Living in the country.

sale price The amount you pay after subtracting the discount from the regular price. See example under *regular price*.

urban Living in the city.

Use with Lesson 8.9.

Do-Anytime Activities

To work with your child on the concepts taught in this unit, try these interesting and rewarding activities:

1 Help your child compile a percent portfolio that includes examples of the many ways percents are used in everyday life.

2 Encourage your child to incorporate such terms as "whole," "halves," "thirds," and "fourths" into his or her everyday vocabulary.

3 Practice renaming fractions as percents, and vice versa, in everyday situations. For example, when preparing a meal, quiz your child on what percent $\frac{3}{4}$ of a cup would be.

4 Look through advertisements of sales and discounts. If the original price of an item and the percent of discount are given, have your child calculate the amount of discount and the sale price. If the original price and sale price are given, have your child calculate the amount and percent of discount.

Building Skills through Games

In this unit, your child will work on matching fractions to equivalent percents, and vice versa, by playing the following game:

Fraction/Percent Concentration See *Student Reference Book*, page 196.

Two or three players need 1 set of Fraction/Percent Tiles and a calculator to play this game. Playing *Fraction/Percent Concentration* helps students recognize fractions and percents that are equivalent.

Use with Lesson 8.9.

As You Help Your Child with Homework

As your child brings assignments home, you may want to go over the instructions together, clarifying them as necessary. The answers listed below will guide you through this unit's Study Links.

Study Link 9.1

1. $\frac{53}{100}$; 53%
2. $\frac{4}{100}$; 4%
3. $\frac{90}{100}$; 90%
4. $\frac{25}{100}$; 0.25
5. $\frac{7}{100}$; 0.07
6. $\frac{60}{100}$; 0.60
7. 0.75; 75%
8. 0.06; 6%
9. 0.50; 50%

Study Link 9.2

1. 100; $\frac{1}{100}$; 0.01; 1%
2. 20; $\frac{1}{20}$; 0.05; 5%
3. 10; $\frac{1}{10}$; 0.10; 10%
4. 4; $\frac{1}{4}$; 0.25; 25%
5. 2; $\frac{1}{2}$; 0.50; 50%
6. 0.75; 75%
7. 0.20; 20%

Study Link 9.3

1.

$\frac{1}{2}$	0	.	5					
$\frac{1}{3}$	0	.	3	3	3	3	3	3
$\frac{1}{4}$	0	.	2	5				
$\frac{1}{5}$	0	.	2					
$\frac{1}{6}$	0	.	1	6	6	6	6	6
$\frac{1}{7}$	0	.	1	4	2	8	5	7
$\frac{1}{8}$	0	.	1	2	5			
$\frac{1}{9}$	0	.	1	1	1	1	1	1
$\frac{1}{10}$	0	.	1					
$\frac{1}{11}$	0	.	0	9	0	9	0	9
$\frac{1}{12}$	0	.	0	8	3	3	3	3
$\frac{1}{13}$	0	.	0	7	6	9	2	3
$\frac{1}{14}$	0	.	0	7	1	4	2	8
$\frac{1}{15}$	0	.	0	6	6	6	6	6
$\frac{1}{16}$	0	.	0	6	2	5		
$\frac{1}{17}$	0	.	0	5	8	8	2	3
$\frac{1}{18}$	0	.	0	5	5	5	5	5
$\frac{1}{19}$	0	.	0	5	2	6	3	1
$\frac{1}{20}$	0	.	0	5				
$\frac{1}{21}$	0	.	0	4	7	6	1	9
$\frac{1}{22}$	0	.	0	4	5	4	5	4
$\frac{1}{23}$	0	.	0	4	3	4	7	8
$\frac{1}{24}$	0	.	0	4	1	6	6	6
$\frac{1}{25}$	0	.	0	4				

Study Link 9.4

1. 34%
2. 67%
3. 84%
4. 52%
5. 85%
6. 20%
7. 25%
8. 30%
9. 62.5%
10. 70%
11. 15%
12. 37.5%
13. Sample answer: I divided the numerator by the denominator and then multiplied by 100.
14. 86%
15. 3%
16. 14%
17. 83.5%

Study Link 9.5

1. 7%; 6%; 7%; 10%; 10%; 10%; 10%; 10%; 10%; 7%; 8%
2. Sample answer: I divided the first three digits of the number by 2,342 and multiplied the answer by 100. Then I rounded to the nearest percent.
3. No; Sample answer: Because each percentage was rounded to the nearest whole percent

Study Link 9.6

2. #2: 11; $\frac{5}{11}$; 45%   #3: 3; $\frac{3}{3}$; 100%
   #4: 11; $\frac{9}{11}$; 82%   #5: 7; $\frac{4}{7}$; 57%
   #6: 16; $\frac{11}{16}$; 69%   #7: 10; $\frac{6}{10}$; 60%
   #8: 2; $\frac{1}{2}$; 50%
3. Sample answer: I would choose player #4, who has taken 11 shots and made 82% of her shots. Player #3 has a higher percent of shots made (100%), but she has taken only 3 shots.

Study Link 9.7

1. 54,000
2. 64,140
3. $\frac{1}{3}$
4. 50%
5. 64,000
6. 152,000
7. 17%

Study Link 9.8

1. 25.8
2. 489.6
3. 45.12
4. 112.64
5. 82878.6
6. 5.6
7. Sample answer: I estimated that the answer should be about 5 * 20 = 100.
8. 212.4
9. 38.64
10. 382.13

Study Link 9.9

1. 14.8
2. .2700
3. 24.96
4. .860
5. 23.4
6. 58.32
7. Sample answer: I estimated that the answer should be about 100 / 4 = 25.
8. 4.2
9. 38.7
10. 0.65

Fractions, Decimals, and Percents

SRB 59 25 60

Study Link 9.1

Rename each decimal as a fraction and a percent.

1. $0.53 = \dfrac{\boxed{}}{100} = $ ____%

2. $0.04 = \dfrac{\boxed{}}{100} = $ ____%

3. $0.90 = \dfrac{\boxed{}}{100} = $ ____%

Rename each percent as a fraction and a decimal.

4. $25\% = \dfrac{\boxed{}}{100} = $ ___.____

5. $7\% = \dfrac{\boxed{}}{100} = $ ___.____

6. $60\% = \dfrac{\boxed{}}{100} = $ ___.____

Rename each fraction as a decimal and a percent.

7. $\dfrac{75}{100} = $ ___.____ $= $ ____%

8. $\dfrac{6}{100} = $ ___.____ $= $ ____%

9. $\dfrac{50}{100} = $ ___.____ $= $ ____%

10. Shade more than 25% and less than 60% of the square.
Write the value of the shaded part as a decimal and a fraction.

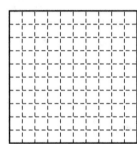

Decimal: _____

Fraction: $\dfrac{\boxed{}}{100}$

11. Shade more than $\dfrac{10}{100}$ and less than $\dfrac{30}{100}$ of the square.
Write the value of the shaded part as a decimal and a percent.

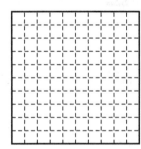

Decimal: _____

Percent: _____

12. Shade more than 0.65 and less than 0.85 of the square.
Write the value of the shaded part as a fraction and a percent.

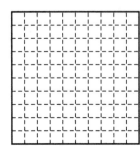

Fraction: $\dfrac{\boxed{}}{100}$

Percent: _____

Trivia Survey

Conduct the survey below. The results won't be needed until Lesson 9.6.

Ask at least 5 people the following questions. You can ask family members, relatives, neighbors, and friends. You can ask the questions in person or by telephone.

Record each answer with a tally mark in the "Yes" or "No" column.

BE CAREFUL! You will not ask everyone every question. Pay attention to the instructions that go with each question.

Question	Yes	No
1. Is Monday your favorite day? (Ask everyone younger than 20.)		
2. Have you gone to the movies in the last month? (Ask everyone older than 8.)		
3. Did you eat breakfast today? (Ask everyone over 25.)		
4. Do you keep a map in your car? (Ask everyone who owns a car.)		
5. Did you eat at a fast-food restaurant yesterday? (Ask everyone.)		
6. Did you read a book during the last month? (Ask everyone over 20.)		
7. Are you more than 1 meter tall? (Ask everyone over 20.)		
8. Do you like liver? (Ask everyone.)		

Coins as Percents of $1

1. How many pennies in $1? _____

What fraction of $1 is 1 penny? _____

Write the decimal that shows what part of $1 is 1 penny. _____

What percent of $1 is 1 penny? _____%

2. How many nickels in $1? _____ What fraction of $1 is 1 nickel? _____

Write the decimal that shows what part of $1 is 1 nickel. _____

What percent of $1 is 1 nickel? _____%

3. How many dimes in $1? _____ What fraction of $1 is 1 dime? _____

Write the decimal that shows what part of $1 is 1 dime. _____

What percent of $1 is 1 dime? _____%

4. How many quarters in $1? _____ What fraction of $1 is 1 quarter? _____

Write the decimal that shows what part of $1 is 1 quarter. _____

What percent of $1 is 1 quarter? _____%

5. How many half-dollars in $1? _____ What fraction of $1 is 1 half-dollar? _____

Write the decimal that shows what part of $1 is 1 half-dollar. _____

What percent of $1 is 1 half-dollar? _____%

6. Three quarters (75¢) is $\frac{3}{4}$ of $1.

Write the decimal. _____

What percent of $1 is 3 quarters? _____%

7. Two dimes (20¢) is $\frac{2}{10}$ of $1.

Write the decimal. _____

What percent of $1 is 2 dimes? _____%

Calculator Decimals

1. Use your calculator to rename each fraction below as a decimal.

$\frac{1}{2}$	0	.	5				
$\frac{1}{3}$	0	.	3	3	3	3	3	3
$\frac{1}{4}$							
$\frac{1}{5}$							
$\frac{1}{6}$							
$\frac{1}{7}$							
$\frac{1}{8}$							
$\frac{1}{9}$							
$\frac{1}{10}$							
$\frac{1}{11}$							
$\frac{1}{12}$							
$\frac{1}{13}$							

$\frac{1}{14}$							
$\frac{1}{15}$							
$\frac{1}{16}$							
$\frac{1}{17}$							
$\frac{1}{18}$							
$\frac{1}{19}$							
$\frac{1}{20}$							
$\frac{1}{21}$							
$\frac{1}{22}$							
$\frac{1}{23}$							
$\frac{1}{24}$							
$\frac{1}{25}$							

2. Make up some of your own.

$\frac{1}{73}$	0	.	0	1	3	6	9	8
$\frac{1}{}$								
$\frac{1}{}$								
$\frac{1}{}$								
$\frac{1}{}$								

$\frac{1}{}$							
$\frac{1}{}$							
$\frac{1}{}$							
$\frac{1}{}$							
$\frac{1}{}$							

Fractions and Decimals to Percents

Do **not** use a calculator to convert these fractions to percents.
Show your work for Problems 3–6.

1. $\dfrac{34}{100} =$ _____%

2. $\dfrac{67}{100} =$ _____%

3. $\dfrac{42}{50} =$ _____%

4. $\dfrac{13}{25} =$ _____%

5. $\dfrac{17}{20} =$ _____%

6. $\dfrac{25}{125} =$ _____%

Use a calculator to convert these fractions to percents.

7. $\dfrac{23}{92} =$ _____%

8. $\dfrac{12}{40} =$ _____%

9. $\dfrac{20}{32} =$ _____%

10. $\dfrac{49}{70} =$ _____%

11. $\dfrac{60}{400} =$ _____%

12. $\dfrac{21}{56} =$ _____%

13. Describe how you used your calculator to convert the fractions
in Problems 7–12 to percents.

_____

_____

_____

Do **not** use a calculator to convert these decimals to percents.

14. 0.86 = _____%

15. 0.03 = _____%

16. 0.140 = _____%

17. 0.835 = _____%

Use with Lesson 9.4.

Renaming Fractions as Percents

In 1996, there were about 2,342,000 marriages in the United States.
The table below shows the approximate number of marriages each month.

1. Use a calculator to find the percent of the total number of marriages that occurred each month. Round the answers to the nearest whole percent.

Month	Approximate Number of Marriages	Approximate Percent of Total Marriages
January	100,000	4%
February	155,000	
March	147,000	
April	172,000	
May	241,000	
June	242,000	
July	235,000	
August	239,000	
September	225,000	
October	231,000	
November	171,000	
December	184,000	

Source: The Top 10 of Everything 1999

2. Describe how you used your calculator to calculate the percent for each month.

_____

_____

_____

3. Do the percents in the table add up to 100%? _____ Explain why or why not.

_____

_____

Using Percents to Compare Fractions

SRB
60 169

1. The girls' varsity basketball team won 8 of the 10 games it played. The junior varsity team won 6 of 8 games. Which team has the better record? Explain your reasoning.

_____

_____

2. The record keeper for the varsity team kept a record of the shots taken by each player (not including free throws) during the most recent game. Complete the table. Calculate the percent of shots made to the nearest whole percent.

Player	Shots Made	Shots Missed	Total Shots	$\dfrac{\text{Shots Made}}{\text{Total Shots}}$	% of Shots Made
#1	5	12	17	$\dfrac{5}{17}$	29%
#2	5	6			
#3	3	0			
#4	9	2			
#5	4	3			
#6	11	5			
#7	6	4			
#8	1	1			

3. The basketball game is tied. Your team has the ball. There is only enough time for one more shot. Based only on the information in the table, which player would you choose to take the shot? Why?

_____

_____

_____

_____

Least Populated Countries

The table below shows the approximate population for the
10 least populated countries in the world.

Country	Approximate Population
Vatican City	860
Nauru	11,000
Tuvalu	11,000
San Marino	25,000
Monaco	32,000
Liechtenstein	32,000
Dominica	65,000
Marshall Islands	66,000
Seychelles	79,000
Kiribati	86,000

Use the data in the table to complete the statements.

1. There are about _____ more people living in Kiribati than Monaco.

2. The difference in population between Vatican City and Dominica

is about _____ people.

3. The population of San Marino is about $\dfrac{\boxed{}}{\boxed{}}$ the population of Seychelles.

4. The combined population of Monaco and Liechtenstein is about _____ people.

5. The population of Liechtenstein is about _____% of the population
of Dominica.

6. The combined population of Kiribati and the Marshall Islands

is about _____ people.

7. The population of Tuvalu is about _____% of the population of the Marshall Islands.

Multiplying Decimals

For each problem below, the multiplication has been done correctly, but the decimal point is missing in the answer. Correctly place the decimal point in the answer.

1. 6 * 4.3 = 2 5 8

2. 72 * 6.8 = 4 8 9 6

3. 0.96 * 47 = 4 5 1 2

4. 5.12 * 22 = 1 1 2 6 4

5. 8,457 * 9.8 = 8 2 8 7 8 6

6. 0.04 * 140 = 5 6

7. Explain how you decided where to place the decimal point in Problem 4.

_____

_____

_____

Multiply. Show your work.

8. 5.9 * 36 = _____	**9.** 0.46 * 84 = _____	**10.** _____ = 7.21 * 53

Use with Lesson 9.8.

Dividing Decimals

For each problem below, the division has been done correctly, but the decimal point is missing in the answer. Correctly place the decimal point in the answer.

1. 88.8 / 6 = **1 4 8**

2. 1.35 / 5 = **2 7 0 0**

3. 99.84 / 4 = **2 4 9 6**

4. 2.58 / 3 = **8 6 0**

5. 163.8 / 7 = **2 3 4**

6. 233.28 / 4 = **5 8 3 2**

7. Explain how you decided where to place the decimal point in Problem 3.

_____

_____

_____

Divide. Show your work.

8. 6)25.2	**9.** 4)154.8	**10.** 9)5.85
Answer: _____	Answer: _____	Answer: _____

Family Letter

Unit 10: Reflections and Symmetry

In this unit, your child will take another look at geometry, with an emphasis on symmetry. Many objects in nature are symmetric: flowers, insects, and the human body, to name just a few. Symmetry is all around—in buildings, furniture, clothing, paintings, and so on.

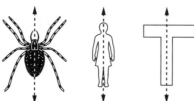

The class will focus on **reflectional symmetry,** also called **line symmetry** or **mirror symmetry,** in which half of a figure is the mirror image of the other half. Encourage your child to look for symmetric objects, and if possible, to collect pictures of symmetric objects from magazines and newspapers. For example, the right half of the printed letter T is the mirror image of the left half. If you have a small hand mirror, have your child check letters, numbers, and other objects to see whether they have line symmetry. The class will use a device called a **transparent mirror,** which is pictured below. Students will use it to see and trace the mirror image of an object.

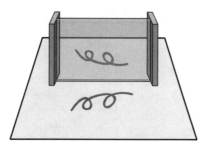

Geometry is not only the study of figures (such as lines, rectangles, and circles), but also the study of transformations or "motions" of figures. These motions include **reflections** (flips), **rotations** (turns), and **translations** (slides). Your child will use these motions to create pictures like the ones below, called **frieze patterns.**

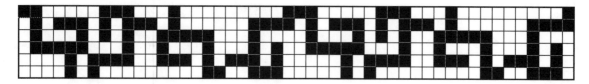

Students will also work with positive and negative numbers, looking at them as reflections of each other across zero on a number line. They will develop skills of adding positive and negative numbers by thinking in terms of credits and debits for a new company, and they will practice these skills in the *Credits/Debits Game.*

Please keep this Family Letter for reference as your child works through Unit 10.

© 2002 Everyday Learning Corporation

Vocabulary

Important terms in Unit 10:

frieze pattern A geometric design in a long strip in which an element is repeated over and over. Frieze patterns are often found on the walls of buildings, on the borders of rugs and tiled floors, and on clothing.

image A figure that is produced by a transformation of another figure. See *preimage* below.

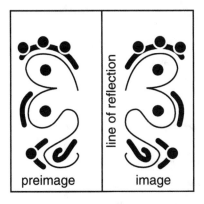

line of reflection A line halfway between a figure (preimage) and *its* reflected image.

line of symmetry A line drawn through a figure that divides the figure into two parts that look exactly alike but are facing in opposite directions.

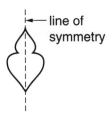

negative number A number that is less than zero; a number to the left of zero on a horizontal number line or below zero on a vertical number line.

preimage A geometric figure that is somehow changed (by a *reflection*, a *rotation*, or a *translation*, for example) to produce another figure. See *image* above.

reflection (flip) The "flipping" of a figure over a line (the *line of reflection*) so that its image is the mirror image of the original (preimage).

reflection

rotation (turn) A movement of a figure around a fixed point or axis.

symmetry Having the same size and shape across a dividing line or around a point.

transformation An operation on a geometric figure that produces a new figure (the image) from the original figure (the preimage).

translation (slide) The motion of "sliding" an object or picture along a line segment.

translation

Do-Anytime Activities

To work with your child on concepts taught in this unit, try these interesting and rewarding activities:

1 Have your child look for frieze patterns on buildings, rugs, floors, and clothing. If possible, have your child bring pictures to school or make sketches of friezes that he or she sees.

2 Encourage your child to study the mathematical qualities of the patterns of musical notes and rhythms. Composers of even the simplest of tunes use reflections and translations of notes and chords (groups of notes).

3 Encourage your child to incorporate transformation vocabulary—**symmetric, reflected, rotated,** and **translated**—into his or her everyday vocabulary.

Building Skills through Games

In this unit, your child will develop his or her understanding of addition and subtraction of positive and negative numbers by playing the following game. For detailed instructions, see the *Student Reference Book.*

Credits/Debits Game See *Student Reference Book,* page 192.
Two players need 1 complete deck of number cards and a recording sheet to play this game. Playing the *Credits/Debits Game* offers students practice adding and subtracting positive and negative numbers.

Use with Lesson 9.10.

As You Help Your Child with Homework

As your child brings assignments home, you may want to go over the instructions together, clarifying them as necessary. The answers listed below will guide you through some of the Study Links in this unit.

Study Link 10.2

1.

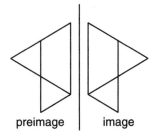

preimage | image

3. preimage

image

5.

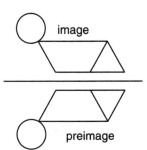

Study Link 10.3

1. preimage   image

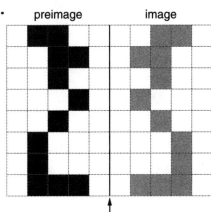

line of reflection

3. image   preimage

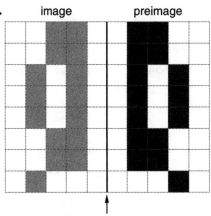

line of reflection

Study Link 10.4

2. A H I M O T U V W X Y

3. B C D E H I K O X

4. H I O X

5. O

6. Sample answers:

horizontal	vertical
BOX	TAX
KID	YOU
BOOK	MAT
KICK	HIM

Study Link 10.6

1. <   **2.** <

3. >   **4.** <

5. >   **6.** >

7. -8, -3.4, $-\frac{1}{4}$, $\frac{1}{2}$, 1.7, 5

8. -43, -3, 0, $\frac{14}{7}$, 5, 22

9. Sample answers: 0.3, 0.95, $\frac{8}{8}$, 1.99

10. Sample answers: -2.4, $-\frac{18}{9}$, -1.67, -0.4

11. 13   **12.** 2

13. -20 **14.** -2

15. 19   **16.** 7

17. -5 **18.** -22

Use with Lesson 9.10.

A Reflected Image

There is a simple design in the box in the middle of this page. It is the **preimage.**

Hold this page in front of a mirror, with the printed side facing the mirror. On a blank piece of paper, sketch what the design looks like in the mirror—the **image.**

Compare your sketch (image) with the design on the Study Link page (preimage). Bring both the preimage and image to school tomorrow.

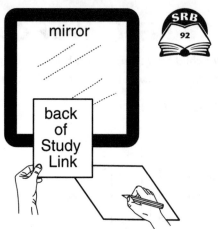

Sketch the design as it looks in the mirror.

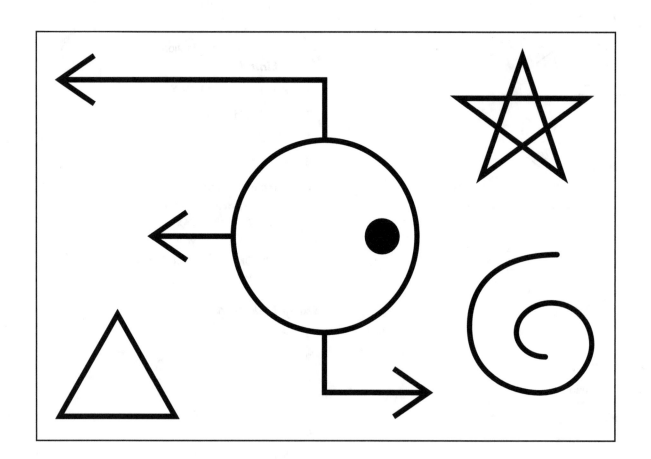

Use with Lesson 10.1.

Lines of Reflection

For each preimage and image, draw the line of reflection.

1.

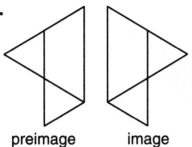

preimage   image

2.

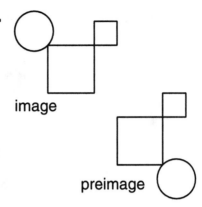

image

preimage

3. preimage

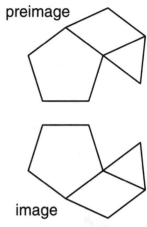

image

For each preimage, use your Geometry Template to draw the image on the other side of the line of reflection.

4.

preimage

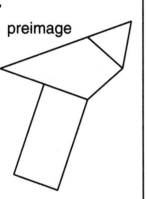

5.

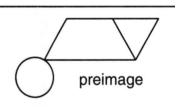

preimage

6.

preimage

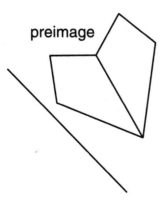

Reflections

Shade squares to create the reflected image of each preimage.

1.   preimage   image

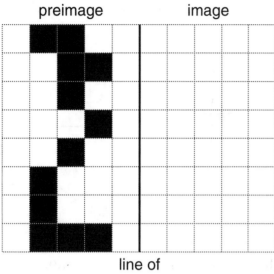

line of
reflection

2.   preimage   image

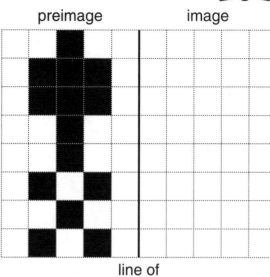

line of
reflection

3.   image   preimage

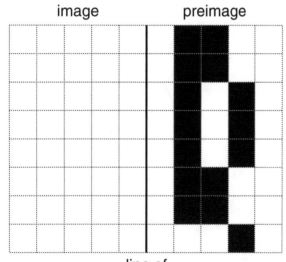

line of
reflection

4.   image   preimage

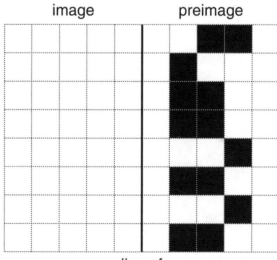

line of
reflection

Use with Lesson 10.3.

Line Symmetry in the Alphabet

1. Write the 26 CAPITAL letters of the alphabet below.

— —

2. The capital letter A has a vertical line of symmetry. A

Name the other capital letters of the alphabet that have a vertical line of symmetry.

A _ _ _ _ _ _ _ _ _ _

3. The capital letter B has a horizontal line of symmetry. B

Name the other capital letters of the alphabet that have a horizontal line of symmetry.

B _ _ _ _ _ _ _ _

4. Which capital letters have both a vertical and a horizontal line of symmetry?
(*Hint:* Find the letters that appear as answers in both Problem 2 and Problem 3.)

— — — —

5. Which capital letter has an infinite (unlimited) number of lines of symmetry?

—

6. The word BED has a horizontal line of symmetry. BED

The word HIT has a vertical line of symmetry.

Use capital letters to list words that have horizontal or vertical line symmetry.

horizontal	vertical
_____	_____
_____	_____
_____	_____
_____	_____

Geometric Patterns

1. Continue each pattern. Then tell if you continued the pattern by using a reflection, rotation, or translation of the original design.

a.

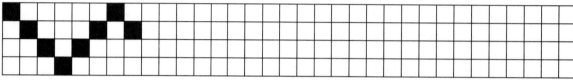

_____

b.

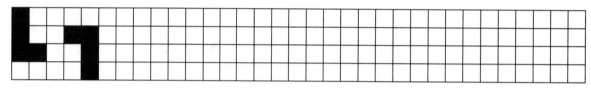

_____

c.

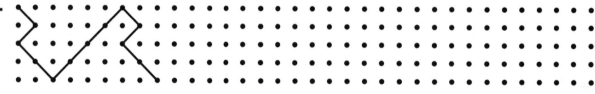

_____

2. Make up your own patterns.

a.

b.

Positive and Negative Numbers

Write < or > to make a true number sentence.

1. −7 _____ 7

2. 3 _____ 14

3. −8 _____ −10

4. 19 _____ 20

5. 8 _____ 0

6. 0 _____ −4

List the numbers in order from least to greatest.

7. 5, −8, $\frac{1}{2}$, −$\frac{1}{4}$, 1.7, −3.4

_____, _____, _____, _____, _____, _____
least   greatest

8. −43, 22, $\frac{14}{7}$, 5, −3, 0

_____, _____, _____, _____, _____, _____
least   greatest

9. Name four positive numbers less than 2.

_____   _____   _____   _____

10. Name four negative numbers greater than −3.

_____   _____   _____   _____

Add.

11. 4 + 9 = _____

12. 5 + (−3) = _____

13. _____ = −8 + (−12)

14. _____ = 7 + (−9)

15. 13 + 6 = _____

16. (−4) + 11 = _____

17. _____ = (−13) + 8

18. _____ = −9 + (−13)

Family Letter

Unit 11: 3-Dimensional Shapes, Weight, Volume, and Capacity

Our next unit introduces several new topics, as well as reviewing some of the work with geometric solids from previous grades and some of the main ideas your child has been studying this past year.

We begin with a lesson on weight, focusing on grams and ounces. Students handle and weigh a variety of objects, trying to develop "weight sense" so that they can estimate weights effectively.

As part of a review of the properties of 3-dimensional shapes (prisms, pyramids, cylinders, and cones), your child will construct models of geometric solids using straws and paper patterns. The class will also search for 3-dimensional objects that look like geometric shapes to put into a Shapes Museum. For example, someone might bring a can of soup to represent a cylinder. You might want to help your child find such objects.

By experimenting with cubes, the class will develop and apply a formula for finding the volumes of rectangular prisms (solids that look like boxes).

We will consider familiar units of capacity (cups, pints, quarts, gallons) and the relationships among them.

Your child will also explore subtraction of positive and negative numbers by playing a variation of the *Credits/Debits Game* introduced in Unit 10.

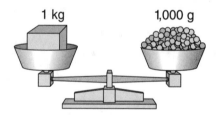

1 kg   1,000 g

In Lesson 11.1, a pan balance is used to measure weight in grams.

Please keep this Family Letter for reference as your child works through Unit 11.

Vocabulary

Important terms in Unit 11:

capacity The amount a container can hold. Also, the heaviest weight a scale can measure.

cone A 3-dimensional shape that has a circular *base*, a curved surface, and one vertex, which is called the *apex*. The points on the curved surface of a cone are on straight lines connecting the apex and the circumference of the base.

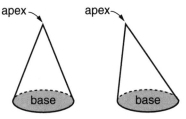

cubic unit A unit used in measuring volume, such as cubic centimeters or cubic feet.

curved surface A surface that is not flat.

cylinder A 3-dimensional shape that has two circular or elliptical bases that are parallel and congruent and are connected by a curved surface. The points on the curved surface of a cylinder are on straight lines connecting corresponding points on the bases. A can is shaped like a cylinder.

dimension A property of space; extension in a given direction. A straight line has one dimension, a square has two dimensions, and a rectangular prism has three dimensions.

formula A general rule for finding the value of something. A formula is often written using letters, called variables, that stand for the quantities involved. For example, the formula for the area of a rectangle may be written as $A = l * w$, where A represents the area of the rectangle, l represents its length, and w represents its width.

geometric solid A 3-dimensional shape, such as a prism, cylinder, cone, or sphere. Despite its name, a geometric solid is hollow; it does not contain the points in its interior.

pan balance A tool used to weigh objects or compare their weights.

prism A solid with two parallel *faces*, called *bases*, that are congruent polygons, and other *faces* that are all parallelograms. The points on the lateral faces of a prism are all on lines connecting corresponding points on the bases. A prism is named for the shape of its base.

triangular   rectangular   hexagonal
prism   prism   prism

pyramid A solid in which one face, the *base*, is any polygon and all the other *faces* are triangles that come together at a point called the *vertex* or *apex*. A pyramid is named for the shape of its base.

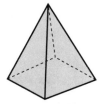

hexagonal   rectangular
pyramid   pyramid

3-dimensional (3-D) Solid objects that take up volume. 3-dimensional objects have length, width, and thickness.

volume The amount of space inside a 3-dimensional object. Volume is usually measured in cubic units, such as cubic centimeters or cubic inches. Sometimes volume is measured in units of capacity, such as gallons or liters.

weight A measure of the force of gravity on an object. Weight is measured in metric units such as grams, kilograms, and milligrams; and in U.S. customary units such as pounds and ounces.

Use with Lesson 10.7.

Do-Anytime Activities

To work with your child on the concepts taught in this unit, try these interesting and rewarding activities:

1 Have your child compile a list of the world's heaviest objects or things. For example, which animal has the heaviest baby? What is the world's heaviest man-made structure? What is the greatest amount of weight ever hoisted by a person?

2 Have your child compile a portfolio of 3-dimensional shapes. Images can be taken from newspapers, magazines, photographs, and so on.

3 Encourage your child to create his or her own mnemonics and/or sayings for converting between units of capacity and weight. One such example is the old English saying, "A pint's a pound the world around." (1 pint = 16 oz = 1 lb)

Building Skills through Games

In this unit, your child will work on his or her understanding of operations with positive and negative numbers by playing the following games. For detailed instructions, see the *Student Reference Book*.

Credits/Debits Game See *Student Reference Book*, page 192.

This is a game for 2 players. Game materials include 1 complete deck of number cards and a recording sheet. The *Credits/Debits Game* helps students to practice addition of positive and negative integers.

Credits/Debits Game **(Advanced Version)** See *Student Reference Book*, page 193.

This game is similar to the *Credits/Debits Game* and helps students to practice both addition and subtraction of positive and negative integers.

Use with Lesson 10.7.

As You Help Your Child with Homework

As your child brings assignments home, you may want to go over the instructions together, clarifying them as necessary. The answers listed below will guide you through this unit's Study Links.

Study Link 11.1

Answers vary.

Study Link 11.2

1. **a.** square pyramid **b.** cone
   c. sphere **d.** cylinder
   e. rectangular prism **f.** triangular prism

2.

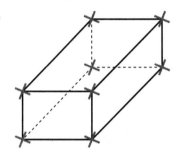

3. 6

Study Link 11.3

1. cone
2. square pyramid
3. hexagonal prism
4. octahedron

Study Link 11.4

Answers vary.

Study Link 11.5

1. **a.** 39 cm³ **b.** 30 cm³
2. **a.** 54 cm³ **b.** 97 cm³
3. **a.** 133 cubes **b.** 137 cubes

Study Link 11.6

1. <   2. <
3. >   4. >
5. >   6. >

7. $-14, -2.5, -0.7, \frac{30}{6}, 5.6, 8$

8. $-7, -\frac{24}{6}, -\frac{3}{5}, 0.02, 0.46, 4$

9. Sample answers:
   $4 - 12 = -8$ $-20 - (-12) = -8$

10. Sample answers:
    $-50 + 20 = -30$ $-15 + (-15) = -30$

11. -110
12. -8
13. -8
14. 15
15. 14
16. -19
17. -70
18. 18

Study Link 11.7

Answers vary for Problems 1–4.

5. 4
6. 48
7. 2
8. 3
9. 3
10. 10

Use with Lesson 10.7.

Weighing Objects

Study Link
11.1

Find a scale or balance around your house or borrow one from a neighbor.

Estimate the weight of 10 objects. Then use the scale or balance to weigh each object. This activity will help you improve your estimation skills.

Be sure to include units in all your estimates and measures.

Object	Estimated Weight	Measured Weight

Use with Lesson 11.1.

Solids

1. The pictures below show objects that are shaped approximately like geometric solids. Identify each object as one of the following: **cylinder, cone, sphere, triangular prism, square pyramid,** or **rectangular prism.**

a.

Type: _____

_____

b.

Type: _____

_____

c.

Type: _____

_____

d.

Type: _____

_____

e.

Type: _____

_____

f.

Type: _____

_____

2. Mark Xs on the vertices of the rectangular prism.

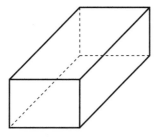

3. How many edges does the tetrahedron have? _____ edges

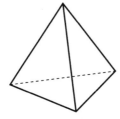

Geometry Riddles

Answer the following riddles.

1. I am a geometric solid.
I have two surfaces.
One of my surfaces is formed by a circle.
The other surface is curved.

What am I? _____

2. I am a geometric solid.
I have one square base.
I have four triangular faces.
Some Egyptian pharaohs were buried in tombs
shaped like me.

What am I? _____

3. I am a polyhedron.
I am a prism.
My two bases are hexagons.
My other faces are rectangles.

What am I? _____

4. I am a polyhedron.
All of my faces are the same.
All of my faces are equilateral triangles.
I have eight faces.

What am I? _____

Use with Lesson 11.3.

Volume

Cut out the pattern below and tape it together to form an open box.

1. Find and record two items in your home that have volumes equal to
about $\frac{1}{2}$ of the volume of the open box.

_____

_____

2. Find and record two items in your home that have about the same volume
as the open box.

_____

_____

3. Find and record two items in your home that have volumes equal to
about 2 times the volume of the open box.

_____

_____

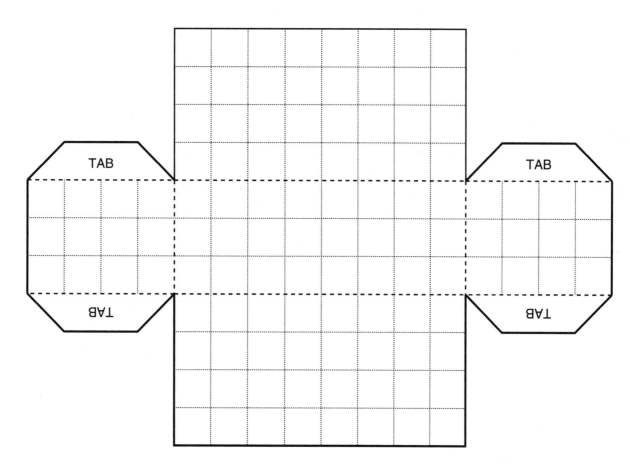

Volume

1. Find the volume of each stack of centimeter cubes.

a.

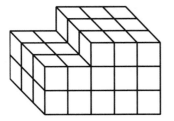

Volume = _____ cm^3

b.

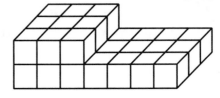

Volume = _____ cm^3

2. Calculate the volume.

a.

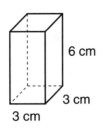

6 cm

3 cm

3 cm

Volume = _____ cm^3

b.

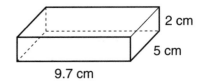

2 cm

5 cm

9.7 cm

Volume = _____ cm^3

3. How many more cubes are needed to completely fill each box?

a.

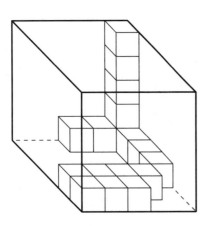

_____ more cubes

b.

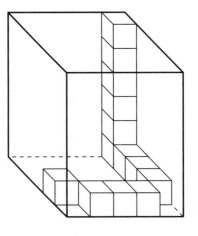

_____ more cubes

Positive and Negative Numbers

Write < or > to make a true number sentence.

1. $0 - 7$ _____ -6

2. -11 _____ $-13 - (-5)$

3. $7 + (-2)$ _____ -8

4. $18 + (-8)$ _____ -18

5. $26 - (-14)$ _____ $27 + (-16)$

6. $9 - (-11)$ _____ $0 + (-20)$

List the numbers in order from least to greatest.

7. $\frac{30}{6}$,   8, -14, -0.7,   5.6, -2.5

_____ , _____ , _____ , _____ , _____ , _____
least   greatest

8. 0.02, $-\frac{3}{5}$, -7,   4,   0.46, $-\frac{24}{6}$

_____ , _____ , _____ , _____ , _____ , _____
least   greatest

9. Write two subtraction problems with an answer of -8.

_____ $-$ _____ $= -8$ _____ $-$ _____ $= -8$

10. Write two addition problems with an answer of -30.

_____ $+$ _____ $= -30$ _____ $+$ _____ $= -30$

Add or subtract.

11. $-40 + (-70) =$ _____

12. $12 - 20 =$ _____

13. _____ $= -14 - (-6)$

14. _____ $= 10 - (-5)$

15. $15 + (-1) =$ _____

16. $-12 - 7 =$ _____

17. _____ $= 60 + (-130)$

18. _____ $= -2 - (-20)$

Capacity

Find at least one container that holds each of the amounts listed below.
Describe each container and record all the **capacity** measurements on the label.

1. Less than 1 Pint

Container	Capacity Measurements on Label
bottle of hot chili sesame oil	*5 fl oz, 148 mL*

2. 1 Pint

Container	Capacity Measurements on Label
bottle of cooking oil	*16 fl oz, 473 mL*

3. 1 Quart

Container	Capacity Measurements on Label

4. More than 1 Quart

Container	Capacity Measurements on Label

Solve.

5. 2 quarts = _____ pints

6. 3 gallons = _____ cups

7. _____ pints = 4 cups

8. _____ quarts = 12 cups

9. 6 pints = _____ quarts

10. _____ quarts = $2\frac{1}{2}$ gallons

Use with Lesson 11.7.

Unit 12: Rates

For the next two or three weeks, your child will be studying rates. Rates are among the most common applications of mathematics in daily life.

A rate is a comparison involving two different units. Familiar examples come from working (dollars per hour), driving (miles per hour), eating (calories per serving), reading (pages per day), and so on.

Our exploration of rates will begin with students collecting data on the rate at which their classmates blink their eyes. The class will try to answer the question, "Does a person's eye-blinking rate depend on what the person is doing?"

During this unit, students will collect many examples of rates to display in a Rates Museum. Then they will use these examples to make up rate problems, such as the following:

1. If cereal costs $2.98 per box, what will 4 boxes cost?

2. If a car's gas mileage is about 20 miles per gallon, how far can the car travel on a full tank of gas (16 gallons)?

3. If I make $6.25 per hour, how long must I work to earn enough to buy shoes that cost $35?

Then the class will work together to develop strategies for solving rate problems.

The unit emphasizes the importance of mathematics to smart consumers. Your child will learn about unit-pricing labels on supermarket shelves and how to use these labels to decide which of two items is the better buy. Your child will see that comparing prices is only *part* of being a smart consumer. Other factors to consider include quality, the need for the product, and, perhaps, the product's effect on the environment.

This unit provides a great opportunity for your child to help with the family shopping. Have your child help you decide whether the largest size is necessarily the best buy. Is an item on sale necessarily a better buy than a similar product that is not on sale?

Finally, students will look back on their experiences in the yearlong World Tour and share them with one another.

Nutrition Facts	
Serving Size 1 link (45 g)	
Servings per Container 10	
Amount per Serving	
Calories 150 Calories from Fat 120	
	% Daily Value
Total Fat 13 g	20%
Total Carbohydrate 1 g	<1%
Protein 7 g	

Please keep this Family Letter for reference as your child works through Unit 12.

Vocabulary

Important terms in Unit 12:

comparison shopping Comparing prices and collecting other information needed to make good decisions about which of several competing products or services to buy.

consumer A person who acquires products or uses services.

per *In each* or *for each,* as in ten chairs per row or six tickets per family.

rate A comparison by division of two quantities with unlike units. For example, a speed such as 55 miles per hour is a rate that compares distance with time.

rate table A way of displaying *rate* information.

Miles	35	70	105	140	175	210
Gallons	1	2	3	4	5	6

Rate Table

unit price The price for one item or unit of measure. For example, if a 5-ounce package of something costs $2.50, then $0.50 per ounce is the unit price.

unit rate A *rate* with 1 in the denominator. For example, 600 calories per 3 servings $\left(\frac{600\ \text{calories}}{3\ \text{servings}}\right)$ is not a unit rate, but 200 calories per serving $\left(\frac{200\ \text{calories}}{1\ \text{serving}}\right)$ is a unit rate.

Use with Lesson 11.8.

Do-Anytime Activities

To work with your child on concepts taught in this unit, try these interesting and rewarding activities:

1 Have your child examine the Nutrition Facts labels on various cans and packages of food. The label lists the number of servings in the container and the number of calories per serving. Have your child use this information to calculate the total number of calories in the full container or food. *For example:*

> A can of soup has 2.5 servings.
> There are 80 calories per serving.
> So the full can has $2.5 * 80 = 200$ calories.

2 Have your child point out rates in everyday situations. *For example:*

> store price rates: cost per dozen, cost per 6-pack, cost per ounce
> rent payments: dollars per month, or dollars per year
> fuel efficiency: miles per gallon
> wages: dollars per hour
> sleep: hours per night
> telephone rates: cents per minute
> copy machine rates: copies per minute

3 Use supermarket visits to compare prices for different brands of an item, and for different sizes of the same item. Have your child calculate unit prices and discuss best buys.

Building Skills through Games

In this unit, your child will extend his or her understanding of addition and subtraction of positive and negative numbers by playing the following game. For detailed instructions, see the *Student Reference Book,* page 193.

Credits/Debits Game **(Advanced Version)** This game for 2 players simulates bookkeeping for a small business. A deck of number cards represents "credits" and "debits." Transactions are entered by the players on recording sheets that are easily drawn. The game offers practice in addition and subtraction of positive and negative integers.

As You Help Your Child with Homework

As your child brings assignments home, you may want to go over the instructions together, clarifying them as necessary. The answers listed below will guide you through this unit's Study Links.

Study Link 12.1

Answers vary.

Study Link 12.2

1. $315

2. $12

3. 14 hours

Hours	2	4	6	8	10	12	14
Days	1	2	3	4	5	6	7

4. **a.** 364   **b.** 156

Minutes	52	104	156	208	260	312	364
Days	1	2	3	4	5	6	7

Study Link 12.3

1.

Gallons	20	140	600	7,300
Days	1	7	30	365

7,300 gallons per year

2.

Gallons	300	2,100	9,000	109,500
Days	1	7	30	365

109,500 gallons per year

3.

Gallons	3	21	90	1,095
Days	1	7	30	365

90 gallons per month

4. 195,000 gallons

Study Link 12.4

Answers vary.

Study Link 12.5

1. $0.63

2. $0.37

3. $0.15

4. $0.15

5. $0.94

6. Sample answer: The 8-ounce cup costs $0.09 per ounce, and the 6-ounce cup costs $0.10 per ounce, so the 8-ounce cup is the better buy.

Study Link 12.6

1. 1,245

2. 9

3. **a.** 70

   b. 50

4. $\frac{1}{7}$

5. **a.** China

   b. Dem. Rep. of Congo, Germany, and Sudan

   c. 6

   d. $9\frac{1}{2}$

   e. 9

Use with Lesson 11.8.

Examples of Rates

Look for examples of rates in newspapers, in magazines, and on labels.

Study the two examples below, and then list some of the examples you find. If possible, bring your samples to class.

Example <u>Label on a can of corn</u>

Nutrition Facts
Serving Size 110 g
Serving Per Container 3 1/2

<u>says "Servings Per Container 3½"</u>

Example <u>Light bulbs come in cardboard holders that</u>
<u>have 4 bulbs. The holder doesn't say so, but there are</u>
<u>always 4 bulbs in each holder.</u>

Example _____

_____

_____

_____

_____

Example _____

_____

_____

_____

_____

_____

Example _____

_____

_____

_____

_____

Rates

SRB
149 150

Solve the problems.

1. Hotels R Us charges $45 a night for a single room.
   At that rate, how much does a single room cost *per week*? $_____

2. The Harrison family spends about $84 a week for
   food. On average, how much do they spend *per day*? $_____

3. Sharon practices playing the piano the same amount
   of time each day. She practiced a total of 4 hours
   on Monday and Tuesday. At that rate, how many hours
   would she practice *in a week*?   _____ hours

Hours							
Days	1	2	3	4	5	6	7

Challenge

4. People in the United States spend an average of 6 hours and 4 minutes
   each week reading newspapers.

   a. That's how many minutes *per week*?   _____ minutes per week

   b. At that rate, how much time does an average
      person spend reading newspapers in a *3-day period*?   _____ minutes

Minutes							
Days	1	2	3	4	5	6	7

Use with Lesson 12.2.

Water Usage

According to the American Waterworks Association, Americans each use an average of 123 gallons of water a day for their personal needs. This seems like a large amount, but you may be surprised at how much water is used for even the shortest activities. For example, people use an average of 1 to 2 gallons of water just to brush their teeth. They use about 20 gallons of water when doing dishes by hand. They may use as much as 30 gallons when taking a shower.

For each problem, complete the rate table and answer the question.

1. If you use an average of 20 gallons of water when taking a shower and you take one shower a day, about how many gallons of water do you use in 1 year?

Gallons	20			
Days	1	7 (1 week)	30 (1 month)	365 (12 months)

Answer: About _____ gallons per year

2. The average American household uses about 2,100 gallons of water a week. About how many gallons of water does it use in 1 year?

Gallons		2,100		
Days	1	7 (1 week)	30 (1 month)	365 (12 months)

Answer: About _____ gallons per year

3. Madison uses about $1\frac{1}{2}$ gallons of water each time she brushes her teeth. She brushes her teeth twice a day. About how many gallons of water does she use in 1 month for brushing teeth?

Gallons	3			
Days	1	7 (1 week)	30 (1 month)	365 (12 months)

Answer: About _____ gallons per month

4. About 39,000 gallons of water are used in making 1 new car. About how many gallons of water are used to make 5 new cars?   About _____ gallons

Supermarket Ads

Look in newspapers for supermarket ads. Choose some of the items in the ads.
Use the table below to record the price and quantity of each item.

Do not write anything in the Unit Price column.

Item	Quantity	Price	Unit Price
Golden Sun Raisins	24 ounces	$2.99	

Unit Pricing

1. A package of 3 rolls of paper towels costs $1.89.
   What is the price *per roll*?   _____

2. A 5-pound bag of rice costs $1.85.
   What is the price *per pound*?   _____

3. Chewy worms are sold at $2.40 per pound.
   What is the price *per ounce*?   _____

4. A 6-pack of bagels costs 90 cents.
   What is the price *per bagel*?   _____

5. A 2-pound bag of frozen corn costs $1.88.
   What is the price *per pound*?   _____

6. A store sells yogurt in two sizes: the 8-ounce cup costs 72 cents, and the
   6-ounce cup costs 60 cents. Which is the better buy? Explain your answer.

   _____

   _____

   _____

   _____

7. Make up your own "better buy" problem. Then solve it.

   _____

   _____

   _____

   _____

Country Statistics

SRB
149 150

1. China has the longest border in the world—13,759 miles. Russia has the second longest border in the world—12,514 miles. How much shorter is Russia's border than China's border? _____ miles

2. The area of Russia is about 1,818,629 square miles. The area of Spain, including offshore islands, is about 194,897 square miles. About how many times larger is Russia than Spain?   About _____ times larger

3. Students in China attend school about 251 days per year. Students in the United States attend school about 180 days per year.

   a. About what percent of the year do Chinese students spend in school?   About _____%

   b. About what percent of the year do American students spend in school?   About _____%

4. English is officially spoken in 54 countries. Portuguese is officially spoken in 8 countries. Portuguese is spoken in about what fraction of the number of English-speaking countries?   About _____

5. The table to the right shows the countries in the world with the most neighboring countries.

Country	Number of Neighbors
Brazil	10
China	15
Dem. Rep. of Congo	9
Germany	9
Russia	14
Sudan	9

Use the data in the table to answer the following questions.

a. Which country has the maximum number of neighbors? _____

b. Which countries have the minimum number of neighbors? _____

_____

c. What is the range? _____   d. What is the median? _____

e. What is the mode? _____

Family Letter

Congratulations!

By completing *Fourth Grade Everyday Mathematics*, your child has accomplished a great deal. Thank you for all of your support.

This Family Letter is here for you to use as a resource throughout your child's vacation. It includes an extended list of Do-Anytime Activities, directions for games that can be played at home, a list of mathematics-related books to check out over vacation, and a sneak preview of what your child will be learning in *Fifth Grade Everyday Mathematics.* Enjoy your vacation!

Do-Anytime Activities

Mathematics means more when it is rooted in real-life situations. To help your child review many of the concepts he or she has learned in fourth grade, we suggest the following activities for you and your child to do together over vacation. These activities will help your child build on the skills he or she has learned this year and help prepare him or her for *Fifth Grade Everyday Mathematics.*

1 Have your child practice any multiplication and division facts that he or she has not yet mastered. Include some quick drills.

2 Provide items for your child to measure. Have your child use personal references, as well as U.S. customary and metric measuring tools.

3 Use newspapers and magazines as sources of numbers, graphs, and tables that your child may read and discuss.

4 Have your child practice multidigit multiplication and division, using the algorithms that he or she is most comfortable with.

5 Ask your child to look at advertisements and find the sale prices of items using the original prices and rates of discount; or find rates of discount using original prices and sale prices. Have your child use a calculator and calculate unit prices to determine best or better buys.

6 Continue the World Tour by reading about other countries.

Building Skills through Games

The following section lists rules for games that can be played at home. You will need a deck of number cards, which can be made from index cards or by modifying a regular deck of cards, as follows:

A regular deck of playing cards includes 54 cards (52 regular cards, plus 2 jokers). Use a permanent marker to mark some of the cards:

• Mark each of the four aces with the number 1.

• Mark each of the four queens with the number 0.

• Mark the four jacks and four kings with the numbers 11 through 18.

• Mark the two jokers with the numbers 19 and 20.

Beat the Calculator

Multiplication Facts

Materials   number cards 1–10 (4 of each); calculator

Players   3

Directions

1. One player is the "Caller," one is the "Calculator," and one is the "Brain."

2. Shuffle the deck of cards and place it facedown.

3. The Caller draws two cards from the number deck and asks for their product.

4. The Calculator solves the problem with a calculator. The Brain solves it without a calculator. The Caller decides who got the answer first.

5. The Caller continues to draw two cards at a time from the number deck and asks for their product.

6. Players trade roles every 10 turns or so.

Example The Caller draws a 10 and 7 and calls out "10 times 7." The Brain and the Calculator solve the problem.

The Caller decides who got the answer first.

Variation 1: To practice extended multiplication facts, have the Caller draw two cards from the number deck and attach a 0 to either one of the factors or to both factors, before asking for the product.

Example If the Caller turns over a 4 and a 6, he or she may make up any one of the following problems:

4 * 60   40 * 6   40 * 60

Variation 2: Use a full set of number cards: 4 each of the numbers 1–10, and 1 each of the numbers 11–20.

Use with Lesson 12.7.

Building Skills through Games (cont.)

Name That Number

Materials 1 complete deck of number cards

Players 2 or 3

Object of the game To collect the most cards

Directions

1. Shuffle the cards and deal five cards to each player. Place the remaining cards number-side down. Turn over the top card and place it beside the deck. This is the **target number** for the round.

2. Players try to match the target number by adding, subtracting, multiplying, or dividing the numbers on as many of their cards as possible. A card may only be used once.

3. Players write their solutions on a sheet of paper or a slate. When players have written their best solutions:

   • They set aside the cards they used to name the target number.

   • Replace them by drawing new cards from the top of the deck.

   • Put the old target number on the bottom of the deck.

   • Turn over a new target number, and play another hand.

4. Play continues until there are not enough cards left to replace all of the players' cards. The player who sets aside more cards wins the game.

Example Target number: 16 A player's cards: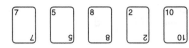

Some possible solutions:

  $10 + 8 - 2 = 16$ *(three cards used)*

  $7 * 2 + 10 - 8 = 16$ *(four cards used)*

  $8 / 2 + 10 + 7 - 5 = 16$ *(all five cards used)*

The player sets aside the cards used to make a solution and draws the same number of cards from the top of the deck.

Vacation Reading with a Mathematical Twist

Books can contribute to children's learning by presenting mathematics in a combination of real-world and imaginary contexts. The titles listed below were recommended by teachers who use *Everyday Mathematics* in their classrooms. They are organized by mathematical topic. Visit your local library and check out these mathematics–related books with your child.

Geometry

The Boy with Square Eyes by Juliet Snape

A Cloak for the Dreamer by Aileen Friedman

The Greedy Triangle by Marilyn Burns

Measurement

The Magic School Bus Inside the Earth by Joanna Cole

Anno's Flea Market by Mitsumasa Anno

The Hundred Penny Box by Sharon Bell Mathis

Numeration

Alexander, Who Used to be Rich Last Sunday by Judith Viorst

If You Made a Million by David M. Schwartz

Fraction Action by Loreen Leedy

How Much Is a Million? by David M. Schwartz

Operations

Anno's Mysterious Multiplying Jar by Masaichiro Anno

Bunches and Bunches of Bunnies by Louise Mathews

The King's Chessboard by David Birch

One Hundred Hungry Ants by Elinor J. Pinczes

A Remainder of One by Elinor J. Pinczes

Patterns, Functions, and Sequences

Eight Hands Round by Ann Whitford Paul

Visual Magic by David Thomas

Reference Frames

The Magic School Bus: Inside the Human Body by Joanna Cole

Pigs on a Blanket by Amy Axelrod

Looking Ahead: Fifth Grade Everyday Mathematics

Next year your child will ...

- Develop skills with decimals and percents
- Continue to practice multiplication and division skills, including operations with decimals
- Investigate methods for solving problems using mathematics in everyday situations
- Work with number lines, times, dates, and rates
- Collect, organize, describe, and interpret numerical data
- Further explore the properties, relationships, and measurment of 2- and 3-dimensional objects
- Read, write, and use whole numbers, fractions, decimals, percents, negative numbers, and exponential notation
- Explore scientific notation

Again, thank you for all of your support this year. Have fun continuing your child's mathematical experiences throughout the vacation!

Use with Lesson 12.7.

Unit 1 Checking Progress

1. Part of each polygon below is hidden. One of the 3 polygons is a
   parallelogram, another is a **trapezoid,** and another is a regular **hexagon.**
   Write the correct name of each polygon on the line.

_____   _____   _____

2.

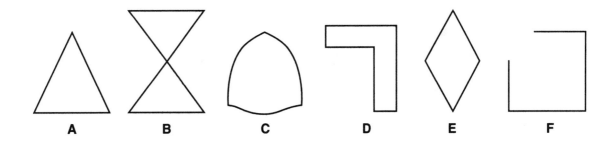

  A   B   C   D   E   F

  a. Which of the above shapes are not polygons? _____

  b. Choose one of the shapes that is not a polygon. Tell why it is not a polygon.

_____

_____

_____

_____

_____

3. I am a quadrangle.
I have 4 right angles.
I am not a square.

   a. What am I? _____

   b. Draw a picture of me in the space at the right.

   c. Use the letters *A, B, C,* and *D* to label the
vertices of the quadrangle you drew.

   d. Name the quadrangle in four different ways.

    _____   _____

    _____   _____

4. Draw $\overline{AB}$ parallel to $\overrightarrow{CD}$. Draw line *EF* so that it intersects line segment *AB*
and ray *CD*.

For Problems 5–8, fill in the ovals below to show your answers. There is more
than one correct answer for some items, so you may need to fill in more than
one oval.

5. ◯ $\overline{OP}$

   ◯ $\overleftrightarrow{OP}$

   ◯ $\overrightarrow{PO}$

6. ◯ $\overline{LA}$

   ◯ $\overrightarrow{AL}$

   ◯ $\overrightarrow{LA}$

7. ◯ quadrangle

   ◯ polygon

   ◯ parallelogram

8. ◯ square

   ◯ rhombus

   ◯ trapezoid

Unit 1 Checking Progress (cont.)

9. a. Sketch each figure in the third column of the table.

Label	Geometric Figure	Sketch
A	rhombus	
B	parallel line segments	
C	right angle	
D	trapezoid	
E	hexagon	
F	triangle	

b. Use your Geometry Template and straightedge to draw one picture of yourself doing something you like to do. Include as many geometric figures listed in the table as you can. Label each figure in your picture with its letter from the table. Draw your picture in the space below or on the back of this page.

Unit 2 Checking Progress

1. Su Lin wanted to show the number 27 on her calculator.
   The 7-key on her calculator was broken, so this is what she did:

   3 ⊗ 8 ⊕ 3 ⏎ 27

   Find two other ways to show 27 without using the 7-key.
   Try to use different numbers and operations.

   a. _____

   b. _____

Add or subtract.

2. $129 + 462 =$ _____

3. $507 + 1{,}829 =$ _____

4. _____ $= 4{,}326 + 2{,}974$

5. $208 - 72 =$ _____

6. _____ $= 924 - 648$

7. _____ $= 4{,}361 - 2{,}493$

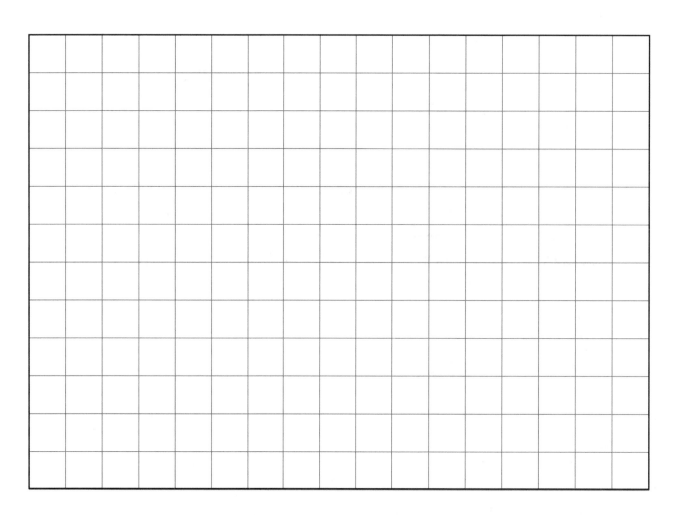

Use with Lesson 2.10.

Unit 2 Checking Progress (cont.)

Ivan asked his classmates to estimate the number of cans of soda they drink each week. He recorded the information on the tally chart below. Use Ivan's tally chart to answer the following questions:

8. What is the maximum number of cans?

_____

9. What is the minimum number of cans?

_____

10. What is the range of the number of cans?

_____

11. What is the mode of the number of cans?

_____

12. What is the median number of cans?

_____

Number of Cans of Soda	Number of Students
0	////
1	//
2	##/
3	##/ /
4	///
5	//
6	
7	/
8	/

13. Explain how you found the median.

_____

_____

14. Make a bar graph of the data.

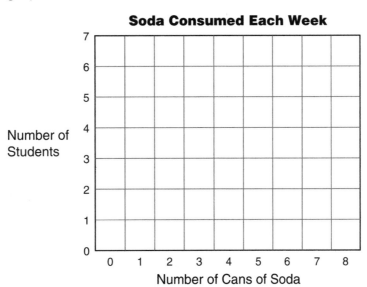

Soda Consumed Each Week

Unit 3 Checking Progress

Fill in the missing number in each Fact Triangle.

1.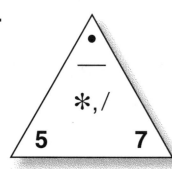

2.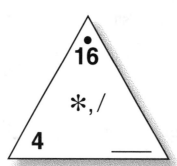

3.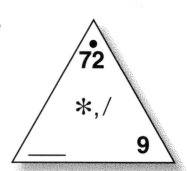

Next to each of the following, write "T" if it is true, "F" if it is false, or "?" if you can't tell.

4. 6 * 8 = 48 _____

5. 9 * 6 _____

6. 3 * 3 = 45 / 5 _____

7. 4 * 6 < 30 _____

8. 3 * (4 + 5) = 17 _____

9. (7 * 4) / 2 > 3 * 7 _____

Make a true sentence by filling in the missing number.

10. _____ = (8 * 9) + 13

11. _____ = (12 − 5) * 5

12. (14 − 6) + (32 / 8) = _____

13. (12 / 4) * (24 / 4) = _____

Make a true sentence by inserting parentheses.

14. 30 − 15 + 2 = 13

15. 56 / 8 + 48 = 1

16. 26 − 3 + 13 = 10

17. 6 * 4 + 57 = 81

Find the solution of each open sentence.

18. 19 = 12 + x   Solution: _____

19. 4 * n = 16   Solution: _____

20. z / 3 = 6   Solution: _____

21. x / 6 = 5   Solution: _____

22. 17 − x = 8   Solution: _____

23. 4 * 5 = 30 − t   Solution: _____

Use with Lesson 3.12.

Unit 3 Checking Progress (cont.)

Solve the following addition and subtraction number stories:

24. The Golden Gate Bridge was completed in 1937.
The length of its main span is 4,200 feet. The San
Francisco Bay Bridge was completed in 1936. The
length of its main span is 2,310 feet. How much
longer is the Golden Gate Bridge than the San
Francisco Bay Bridge?   _____ feet

25. A European eel can live up to 88 years. A giant
tortoise can live about 62 years longer. How long
can a giant tortoise live?   About _____ years

26. India is the top movie-producing country in the world.
In one year it produced 754 movies. That year, the
United States came in second with 685 movies. In
all, how many movies did these two countries
produce that year?   _____ movies

27. a. The largest book store chain in the United States
has 950 stores. Suppose they add 65 new stores.
How many stores will they have then?   _____ stores

    b. Suppose that instead of opening stores, they close
85 stores. How many stores will they have then?   _____ stores

Unit 3 Checking Progress (cont.)

Use the map and map scale to answer the following questions:

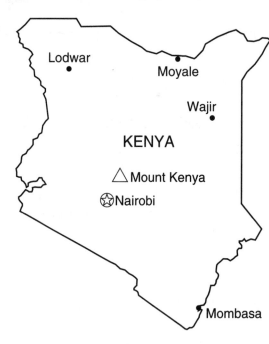

Lodwar

Moyale

Wajir

KENYA

△ Mount Kenya

⭐Nairobi

Mombasa

0   100   200 mi

1 inch represents 200 miles

28. The distance between Mombasa and Wajir is about _____ inches

on the map. That is about _____ miles.

29. The distance between Nairobi and Lodwar is about _____ inches

on the map. That is about _____ miles.

Unit 4 Checking Progress

1. Write 2 numbers between 0 and 1. Use decimals. _____

2. Write 2 numbers between 2 and 3. Use decimals. _____

Circle the best answer.

3. The length of my foot is about   1.85 cm   18.5 cm   185 cm

4. A child's height is about   1.25 m   12.5 m   125 m

5. The cost of 12 pieces of gum at a nickel a piece is $0.06 $0.60 $6.00

6. The number for the point marked X on the number line is   0.05   0.5   1.5

7. Use your ruler to measure the line segment below to the nearest centimeter.

   _____

   _____ cm

Use your ruler to measure the line segments below to the nearest millimeter.
Record your measurements in millimeters and centimeters.

8. A _____ B _____ mm   _____ cm

9. C _____ D _____ mm   _____ cm

10. Draw a line segment that is 12.5 centimeters long.

11. Draw a line segment that is 45 millimeters long.

Unit 4 Checking Progress (cont.)

Write < or > to make a true number sentence.

12. 5.46 _____ 5.9

13. 7.003 _____ 3.7

14. 4.8 + 6.9 _____ 3.4 + 7.7

15. 3.85 − 3.46 _____ 9.1 − 6.2

16. Write the following set of numbers in order from smallest to largest.

0.001, 4.3, 4.05, 0.6, 0.06, 0.1 _____

Complete.

17. 2 m = _____ cm

18. _____ m = 146 cm

19. 36 mm = _____ cm

20. _____ mm = 12 cm

21. The winner of the women's 400-meter run in the 1972 Olympics ran the race in about 51.08 seconds. The winning time in the 1996 Olympics was 48.25 seconds—an Olympic record. How much faster was the winning time in 1996 than in 1972?

Answer: _____ seconds

Number model: _____

22. Mrs. Austin had $98.37 in her savings account. She withdrew $42.50. A week later, she deposited $38.25. What is the new balance in her savings account?

Answer: _____

Write what you did to find the answer.

_____

_____

_____

_____

_____

_____

© 2002 Everyday Learning Corporation

Use with Lesson 4.11.

Unit 5 Checking Progress

1. Which of the following is closest to the sum of 486 and 732?

800   1,000   1,200   1,400

2. Which of the following is closest to the product of 58 and 34?

180   1,800   18,000   180,000

An average of about 10,000 babies are born in the United States each day.

3. About how many babies are born in a week? _____

4. About how many babies are born in a month? _____

5. Are there more or less than a million babies born in the U.S. in a year? _____

According to the 1990 U.S. Census, the population of Texas was 16,986,510.

6. Round this number to the nearest million. _____

7. Round it to the nearest thousand. _____

8. In Texas, there are about 700 registered motor vehicles for every 1,000 people. Which of the following is the best estimate for the number of registered motor vehicles in Texas?

12 million   11,891,000   11,890,557

Explain why you chose this answer.

_____

_____

_____

Write > or <.

9. 10,000,000 _____ 7,508,976   **10.** 368,972 _____ 364,986

11. 9 trillion _____ 54,000,000,000   **12.** 746,390,299 _____ 10^6

Unit 5 Checking Progress (cont.)

Multiply.

13. 8 * 6 = _____

80 * 6 = _____

8 * 600 = _____

14. 3 * 7 = _____

30 * 70 = _____

300 * 70 = _____

Multiply. Show your work.

15. 8 * 67 = _____

16. 43 * 6 = _____

17. 74 * 53 = _____

18. 23 * 19 = _____

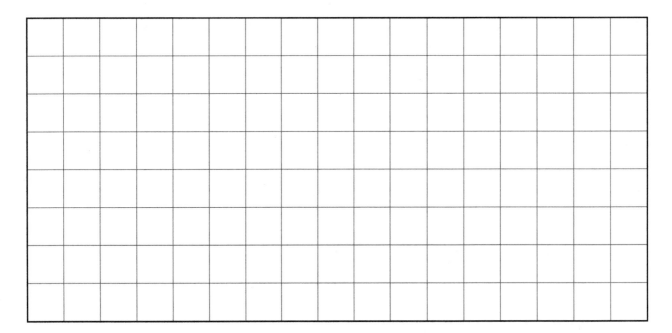

19. Mrs. Green wants to buy a washing machine and pay for it in 1 year. L-Mart offers two plans and she wants to choose the cheaper one.

   Plan A: $7 each week; a total of 52 payments.

   Plan B: $27 each month; a total of 12 payments.

Which plan should Mrs. Green choose? _____

Explain how you made your choice.

_____

_____

Use with Lesson 5.12.

Unit 6 Checking Progress

Measure each angle below as accurately as you can. For each angle, circle the type: acute, right, obtuse, straight, or reflex.

1. ∠ *BCA:* _____ °

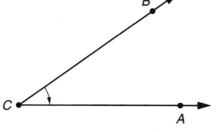

angle type: acute   right   obtuse   straight   reflex

2. ∠ *EDF:* _____ °

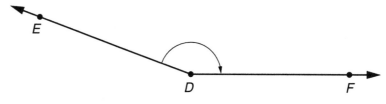

angle type: acute   right   obtuse   straight   reflex

3. ∠ *HGI:* _____ °

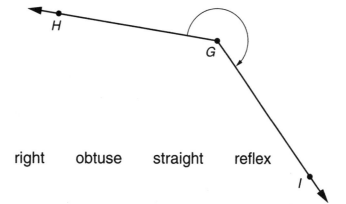

angle type: acute   right   obtuse   straight   reflex

Draw the following angles.

4. ∠ *ZYX:* 265°   **5.** ∠ *LMN:* 125°   **6.** ∠ *RTS:* 50°

Unit 6 Checking Progress (cont.)

7. At 3 o'clock, the minute hand and the hour hand
form a 90° angle.

Draw a minute hand and an hour hand on the clock
face at the right so that they form an obtuse angle.

Write the time that you drew on the clock face.

_____ : _____

Solve. If there is a remainder, write the answer as a mixed number.

8. 5)‾84‾   **Answer:** _____

9. 168 ÷ 8   **Answer:** _____

10. 314 / 12   **Answer:** _____

11. The ordered pairs in the table below give the locations of points of interest
on the map of Lookout Bluff. Put a dot at each location. Then write the
letter for the point of interest next to the dot.

Point of Interest	A Old House	B Turtle Creek	C Haunted Cave	D Pine Forest	E Lookout Point	F Catfish Pond
Location	(5,2)	(3,2)	(1,1)	(1,2)	(3,5)	(6,3½)

Lookout Bluff

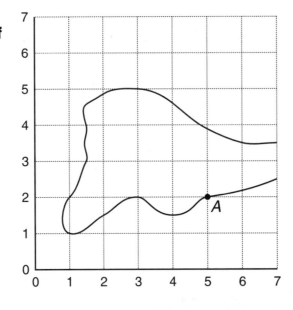

Unit 6 Checking Progress (cont.)

Solve these multiplication and division number stories.

12. A jumbo box of Ginger Man Cookies contains 38 cookies. Tina and
her two sisters decide to share them equally. How many whole
cookies will each girl get?   _____ cookies

13. When it snows, DeShawn charges $2 for every sidewalk he shovels
and $3 for every driveway he shovels. If he shovels 6 sidewalks and
3 driveways, how much does he earn? $_____

14. Grace baked 76 muffins for the fourth grade breakfast party and
put them on plates. Each plate holds 8 muffins. How many plates
were needed to hold all of the muffins?   _____ plates

15. Dugan and his 3 friends went to the video store. They rented several
movies and bought snacks to eat while watching them. The total cost
was $21.00. The friends split the bill evenly. How much did each
person pay? $_____

16. Jennifer is saving up for basketball camp. If she puts $20 in the bank
each week, how much will she have saved after 20 weeks? $_____

Unit 7 Checking Progress

For each fraction, write two equivalent fractions.

1. $\frac{1}{2}$ _____ _____

2. $\frac{1}{3}$ _____ _____

3. $\frac{2}{5}$ _____ _____

4. $\frac{6}{8}$ _____ _____

Write $>$, $<$, or $=$ between each pair of fractions.

5. $\frac{5}{6}$ _____ $\frac{5}{8}$

6. $\frac{11}{12}$ _____ $\frac{5}{12}$

7. $\frac{2}{3}$ _____ $\frac{8}{12}$

8. $\frac{2}{7}$ _____ $\frac{9}{10}$

Write each set of fractions in order from smallest to largest.

9. $\frac{1}{7}, \frac{1}{2}, \frac{1}{5}, \frac{1}{10}, \frac{1}{3}$ _____ _____ _____ _____ _____

10. $\frac{2}{10}, \frac{9}{10}, \frac{7}{10}, \frac{1}{10}, \frac{5}{10}$ _____ _____ _____ _____ _____

Use your pattern blocks to help you solve Problems 11 and 12.

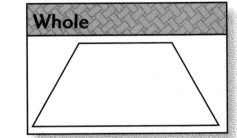

11. Look at the "whole" box to the right.

    a. If the red trapezoid is the whole, what fraction of the whole is

        1 green triangle? _____   1 blue rhombus? _____

    b. What fraction of the red trapezoid do
        1 green triangle and 1 blue rhombus cover? _____

12. Suppose the green triangle is $\frac{1}{2}$ of the whole. Which pattern block is

    a. 1 whole? _____   **b.** $1\frac{1}{2}$ wholes? _____

13. Liam had 9 quarters. He spent $\frac{2}{3}$ of them on video games.

    a. How many quarters did he spend? _____ quarters

    b. How much money does he have left? _____

Unit 7 Checking Progress (cont.)

14. Make a spinner.

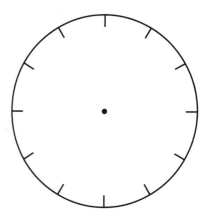

   a. Color it so that the paper clip will land on red about $\frac{1}{2}$ of the time and on blue about $\frac{1}{3}$ of the time. Color the remaining parts yellow. Try to make an interesting design.

   b. About what fraction of the time do you think the paper clip will land on yellow? _____

15. Use a paper clip and a pencil. Spin the paper clip 30 times on your new spinner.

   a. Record the results in the table below.

Color	Number of Times Clip Landed There	Fraction of Times Clip Landed There
red		
blue		
yellow		

   b. Were the results what you expected? _____ Explain.

_____

16. Queen Esther wants to divide her kingdom so that her oldest daughter gets $\frac{1}{2}$ of it and her two youngest children each get $\frac{1}{3}$.

   a. Can she do it? _____

   b. Explain your answer. Use your pattern blocks to help you answer the question.

_____

_____

   c. Can you think of a better way to divide the kingdom? Explain.

_____

_____

Use with Lesson 7.13.

Unit 8 Checking Progress

1. If you wanted to build a fence around your backyard, would you find the

backyard's perimeter or its area? _____

2. What is the area of the polygon at
the right?

Area = _____ square centimeters

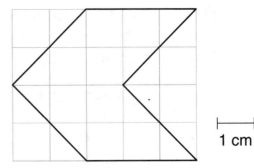

1 cm

Formulas		
Rectangle Area = base ∗ height	Parallelogram Area = base ∗ height	Triangle Area = $\frac{1}{2}$ ∗ (base ∗ height)

Complete the following. Measure each polygon with a centimeter ruler.

3. base = _____ cm

    height = _____ cm

    perimeter = _____ cm

    Area = _____ cm^2

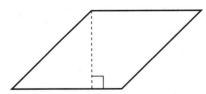

4. base = _____ cm

    height = _____ cm

    perimeter = _____ cm

    Area = _____ cm^2

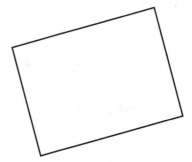

5. base = _____ cm

    height = _____ cm

    perimeter = _____ cm

    Area = _____ cm^2

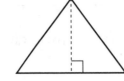

         Use with Lesson 8.9.

Unit 8 Checking Progress (cont.)

6. Mrs. Lopez wants to tile her dining room floor. The room is 12 feet wide and 21 feet long. How many 1-square-foot tiles does she need to cover the floor?

   Answer: _____ tiles

7. Suppose Mrs. Lopez chooses tiles that are 6 inches on each side. How many 6-inch tiles would she need in order to cover her dining room floor?

   6 in.

   Answer: _____ tiles

   Explain how you got your answer.

   _____

   _____

   _____

Below is a scale drawing of a very large forest. A river runs along the northwest border of the forest. Use the scale to answer the following questions:

8. What is the length of the river along the northwest border?

   About _____ miles

9. What is the perimeter of the boundary of the forest?

   About _____ miles

10. How many square miles does each little square in the scale drawing represent?

    About _____ square miles

11. What is the area of the forest?

    About _____ square miles

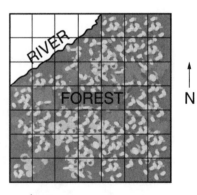

Scale: $\frac{1}{4}$ inch represents 10 miles

Use with Lesson 8.9.

Unit 9 Checking Progress

1. Gloria made 15 out of 20 shots in the school basketball free-throw contest.

    a. What fraction of the shots did she make? _____

    b. What percent of the shots did she make? _____

    c. At this rate, how many shots would she make if she took 100 shots? _____ shots

2. Jimmy set a goal of jogging a total of 100 miles over the summer. He filled in the square at the right to keep track of the miles he ran. During the first two weeks of June, he jogged 20 miles.

    a. What fraction of 100 miles did he jog in 2 weeks? _____

    b. What percent of 100 miles did he jog? _____

    c. At this rate, how many weeks will it take him to jog 100 miles? _____ weeks

3. Fill in the table of equivalent fractions, decimals, and percents.

Fraction	Decimal	Percent
$\frac{3}{10}$		
$\frac{1}{2}$		
		25%
$\frac{3}{4}$		
	0.80	
$\frac{5}{5}$		

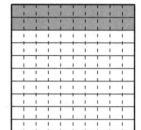

Use with Lesson 9.10.

Unit 9 Checking Progress (cont.)

4. Use a calculator to rename each fraction as a decimal.

a. $\frac{7}{16}$ = _____   **b.** $\frac{3}{25}$ = _____   **c.** $\frac{6}{32}$ = _____

5. Use a calculator to rename each fraction as a percent.

a. $\frac{3}{8}$ = _____%   **b.** $\frac{15}{16}$ = _____%   **c.** $\frac{3}{96}$ = _____%

6. Shade 40% of the square at the right.

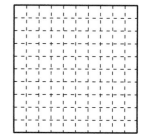

   a. What fraction of the square
      did you shade?   _____

   b. Write this fraction as a decimal.   _____

   c. What percent of the square
      is *not* shaded?   _____

7. Susan bought a coat that sold for $150. She had a coupon
for a 10% discount.

   a. How much money did she save
      with the discount?   _____

   b. How much did she pay for
      the coat?   _____

8. Randy is buying a color television. The television he wants costs $200 at
both L-Mart and Al's Department Store. After Christmas, L-Mart put it on
sale at a savings of $\frac{1}{4}$ off the regular price. Al's Department Store offered
a 30% discount on all items.

At which store should Randy buy the television?

_____

Why?

_____

_____

_____

Unit 9 Checking Progress (cont.)

Use an estimation strategy to multiply. Show your work.

9. $4.7 * 25 = $ _____

10. $0.98 * 63 = $ _____

11. _____ $= 205 * 3.5$

Use an estimation strategy to divide. Show your work.

12. $48.6 / 6 = $ _____

13. _____ $= 322.4 / 8$

14. _____ $= 5.25 / 7$

Use with Lesson 9.10.

Unit 10 Checking Progress

Use your Geometry Template to complete Problems 1–4.

1. Draw a shape that has no lines of symmetry.

2. Draw a shape that has exactly 1 line of symmetry.

3. Draw a shape that has exactly 2 lines of symmetry.

4. Draw a shape that has more than 2 lines of symmetry.

5. Which figure below is a reflection (flip) of the original figure? _____

  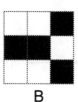

Original   A   B   C

6. Which figure below is a translation (slide) of the original figure? _____

Original   A   B   C

Unit 10 Checking Progress (cont.)

7. Which figure below shows the original figure rotated (turned) clockwise

$\frac{1}{4}$ turn? _____

   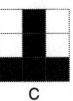

Original   A   B   C

8. Use a transparent mirror to draw the reflection of the preimage.

preimage   image

line of reflection

9. Use a transparent mirror to draw the other half of the figure across the line of symmetry.

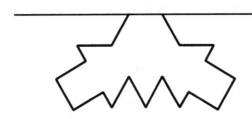

——————————————————— line of symmetry

10. Add.

a. $4 + 8 =$ _____

b. $5 + (-2) =$ _____

c. _____ $= -4 + (-6)$

d. _____ $= -9 + 3$

Use with Lesson 10.7.

Unit 11 Checking Progress

1. Each object below has the shape of a geometric solid. Name the geometric solid.

a.

b.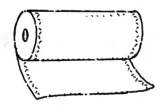

_____   _____

2. How many faces does the pentagonal pyramid have? _____ faces

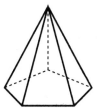

3. Mark Xs on the vertices of the triangular prism.

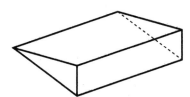

4. How many edges does the rectangular pyramid have? _____ edges

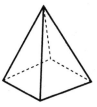

5. Name the shape of the base of the pyramid below. _____

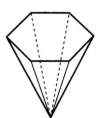

Unit 11 Checking Progress (cont.)

6. Find the volume of each stack of centimeter cubes.

a.

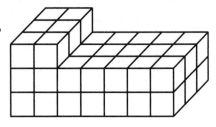

Volume = _____ cm³

b.

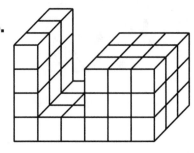

Volume = _____ cm³

7. Calculate the volume of each rectangular prism.

a.

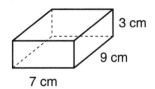

3 cm

9 cm

7 cm

Volume = _____ cm³

b.

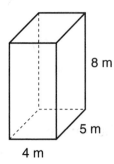

8 m

5 m

4 m

Volume = _____ m³

8. Add.

a. $14 + (-8) =$ _____

b. $(-20) + 9 =$ _____

c. _____ $= -5 + (-13)$

d. _____ $= 6 + (-6)$

9. Subtract.

a. $-10 - (-7) =$ _____

b. $-12 - (+7) =$ _____

c. _____ $= -6 - (-8)$

d. _____ $= 14 - (-3)$

10. Circle the most reasonable estimate for each weight.

a. A box of cereal might weigh about   1.8 oz   18 oz   180 oz

b. A pencil might weigh about   0.7 g   7 g   70 g

c. A female adult might weigh about   65 kg   650 kg   6,500 kg

Unit 12 Checking Progress

1. It was reported that on New Year's Day, 1907, Theodore Roosevelt shook hands with 8,513 people. Does this seem reasonable? Explain your answer.

_____

_____

_____

_____

2. Tina works 7 hours a day, 5 days a week. She earns $56.00 per day.

   a. How much does she earn per hour? _____

   b. How much does she earn per week? _____

3. The Davis family drove 280 miles to visit relatives. It took 5 hours. At that rate, how many miles had the Davises driven in 3 hours? _____ miles

   Fill in the rate table, if needed.

Hours			3		5
Miles					280

4. A store charges $1.49 for a 20-ounce box of Puff Flakes cereal and $1.72 for a 24-ounce box of the same cereal. Which is the better buy? _____

   Explain why.

   _____

   _____

   _____

Unit 12 Checking Progress (cont.)

5. Use the sign at the right to help you make good decisions. Solve the problems. Explain how you found your answers.

> 45 cents each
> 6 for $2.50
> $4.80 a dozen
>
> DOUGHNUTS

a. Joey goes to Doreen's Delicious Doughnuts to buy doughnuts for the class party. What is the least amount of money he will have to pay for 30 doughnuts?

_____

Explain.

_____

_____

_____

_____

b. Pretend that your mother sent you to buy 11 doughnuts. If you had enough money, would you buy a dozen doughnuts instead? Explain.

_____

_____

_____

_____

_____

6. Make up a rate number story. Then solve it.

_____

_____

_____

_____

Answer: _____
            (unit)

© 2002 Everyday Learning Corporation

Midyear Assessment

Add, subtract, or multiply.

1. Lisa's team had a cookie sale. During the first week of the sale, the girls sold 560 boxes of cookies. During the last week, they sold 138 boxes. How many boxes did they sell in all?

_____

2. A gallon of 2% milk costs $2.19 at the Gem supermarket and $2.45 at the 6-to-Midnight convenience store. How much more does a gallon of milk cost at the convenience store?

_____

Solve each problem. Show your work.

3. $653 - 289 =$ _____

4. _____ $= 551 + 279$

5. _____ $= 7 * 128$

6. $49 * 67 =$ _____

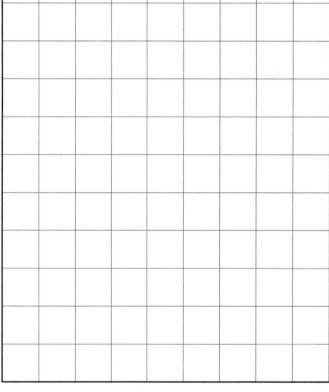

7. Make up a number story using the information below. Then solve the problem and write a number model.

- At Bloom's Flower Shop, roses cost 99 cents each.

- A dozen roses costs $10.00.

- Carnations cost 49 cents each or 3 for a dollar.

_____

_____

Answer: _____

_____

Number model:

_____

Midyear Assessment (cont.)

8. Write each number with digits.

   a. Twelve thousand, five hundred sixty-five _____

   b. Four million, six hundred thousand, twenty-seven _____

   c. Twelve and four tenths _____

   d. Five and sixteen hundredths _____

9. Each of the following names describes one of the geometric figures below.

   parallel lines   concentric circles   rectangle

   regular polygon   right angle   trapezoid

   Write the correct name below the picture.

   a.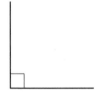

   _____

   b.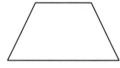

   _____

   c.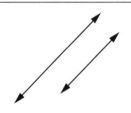

   _____

   d.

   _____

   e.

   _____

   f.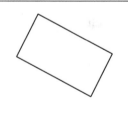

   _____

10. Draw $\overrightarrow{QR}$ parallel to $\overleftrightarrow{ST}$. Draw line segment *WX* so that it intersects ray *QR* and line *ST*.

Use with Lesson 6.11.

Midyear Assessment (cont.)

11. As part of her science project on sleep, Jeannie asked 13 students in her class how many hours they had slept the night before, to the nearest half-hour. Here are the results of her survey.

Number of hours of sleep: 7, 7.5, 8, 8, 8, 8, 8.5, 9, 9, 9.5, 10, 10, 10.5

a. What is the median number of hours the students slept? _____

b. What is the mode? _____

c. What is the minimum number of hours slept? _____

d. What is the maximum number of hours slept? _____

e. What is the range of hours they slept? _____

12. Circle the best estimate for each of the following measurements.

a. The width of my palm   8 mm   8 cm   8 m

b. The height of a doorway   2 m   20 m   200 m

c. The thickness of a penny   1 m   1 cm   1 mm

d. The length of a book   1 in.   1 ft   1 yd

13. Use your protractor. Measure each angle below to the nearest degree.

a.

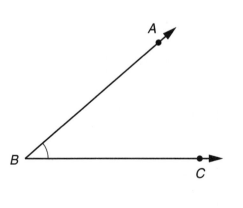

∠ABC measures _____°.

It is an (acute or obtuse) angle.

b.

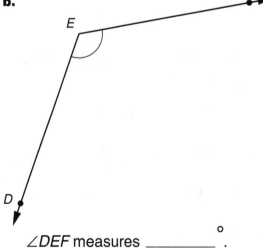

∠DEF measures _____°.

It is an (acute or obtuse) angle.

Midyear Assessment (cont.)

14. Measure the line segment to the nearest centimeter and to the nearest millimeter.

_____

a. _____ cm

b. _____ mm

15. Measure the line segment to the nearest inch.

_____

_____ in.

16. Measure the line segment to the nearest $\frac{1}{2}$ inch.

_____

_____ in.

17. Find the solution of each open sentence.

a. $53 = x + 25$

b. $7 * y = 42$

c. $m / 9 = 5$

Solution: _____

Solution: _____

Solution: _____

18. Divide. If there is a remainder, report it as a fraction. Show your work.

a. $385 \div 7 =$ _____

b. $6\overline{)572} =$ _____

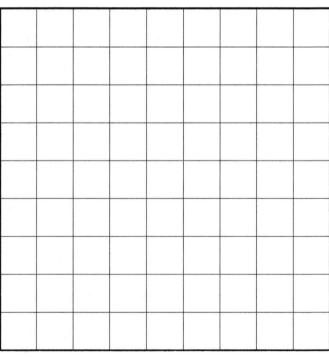

19. Tell whether each number sentence is true or false.

a. $(5 * 6) + 13 = 43$ _____

b. $(81 / 9) - (36 / 4) = 3$ _____

c. $(12 - 6) * 3^2 = 36$ _____

d. $30 - (4 * 7) = 2$ _____

Use with Lesson 6.11.

End-of-Year Assessment

Solve the problems. Don't forget to write the unit in your answer when it is needed.

1. Study the figure at the right. For each statement below, write true or false.

    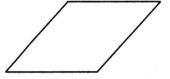

    a. This figure is a rectangle. _____

    b. This figure is a polygon. _____

    c. The opposite sides are parallel. _____

    d. All angles are right angles. _____

2. Joe and Shawna are setting up chairs for an assembly. They make 9 rows with 7 chairs in each row. How many chairs have they set up? _____

3. The Smiths are driving at about 50 miles per hour. At that rate,

    a. how far will they drive in half an hour? _____

    b. how far will they drive in 4 hours? _____

4. Find the solution of each open sentence.

    a. $8 * x = 32$

    Solution: _____

    b. $y - 27 = 55$

    Solution: _____

    c. $108 + r = 150$

    Solution: _____

5. Corrine left home at 10:40 A.M. to go to soccer practice. She got back from practice at 12:15 P.M. How long had she been gone? _____

End-of-Year Assessment (cont.)

6. Multiply. Show your work.

    a. $147 * 5 =$ _____

    b. $126 * 40 =$ _____

7. Divide. Report any remainders as fractions. Show your work.

    a. $438 / 6 =$ _____ .

    b. $5\overline{)329} =$ _____

8. According to the 1990 census, the population of Philadelphia was one million, five hundred eighty-five thousand, five hundred seventy-seven.

    a. Write this number with

         digits. _____

    b. Is the number more or less than 10^4?

         _____

    c. Round the number to the

         nearest thousand. _____

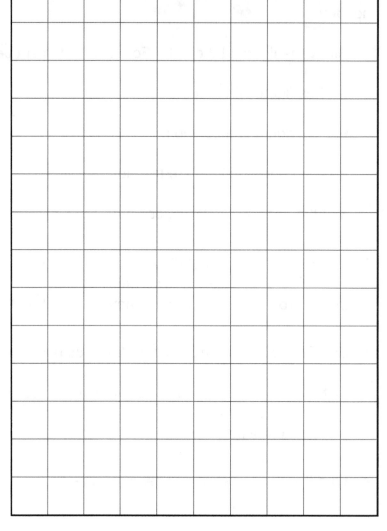

9. Use your centimeter ruler to measure the sides of the rectangle at the right to the nearest $\frac{1}{2}$ cm.

    a. Length = about _____

    b. Width = about _____

    c. Perimeter = about _____

    d. Area = about _____

width

length

Use with Lesson 12.7.

End-of-Year Assessment (cont.)

10. Bob kept a record for a week of how many hours the TV was on in his house. He showed this information in the following bar graph.

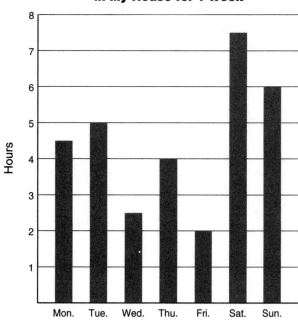

Number of Hours the TV Was on in My House for 1 Week

a. On Wednesday, how many hours was the TV on? _____

b. On what day was the TV on for the *maximum* number of hours? _____

c. On what day was the TV on for the *minimum* number of hours? _____

d. On what day was the TV on for the *median* number of hours? _____

11. a. Color $\frac{1}{4}$ of the spinner at the right.

b. What fraction of the spinner is *not* colored? _____

c. What *percent* of the spinner is colored? _____

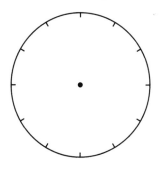

d. If you spin the spinner 100 times, about how many times would you expect it to land on the colored part? _____

e. If you spin the spinner 300 times, about how many times would you expect it to land on the colored part? _____

End-of-Year Assessment (cont.)

12. a. Circle $\frac{3}{4}$ of the stars.

    b. Write two fractions that are equivalent to $\frac{3}{4}$. _____

    c. Write the decimal that is equivalent to $\frac{3}{4}$. _____

    d. Write the percent that is equivalent to $\frac{3}{4}$. _____

13. Write <, >, or =.

    a. $\frac{3}{5}$ _____ $\frac{2}{5}$ **b.** $\frac{1}{4}$ _____ $\frac{1}{6}$

    c. $\frac{9}{10}$ _____ $\frac{2}{3}$ **d.** $\frac{3}{10}$ _____ 0.03

    e. $\frac{6}{10}$ _____ 0.6   **f.** $\frac{37}{100}$ _____ 0.2

    g. 1.2 _____ 1.096   **h.** 10^3 _____ 3 million

14. Circle the shapes that have exactly 1 line of symmetry.

End-of-Year Assessment (cont.)

15. The objects below have the shapes of geometric solids. Name the solids.

a.

_____

b.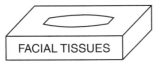

_____

16. Add or subtract.

a. _____ $= \frac{1}{5} + \frac{3}{5}$

b. _____ $= \frac{3}{4} + \frac{3}{4}$

c. $\frac{3}{4} - \frac{1}{4} =$ _____

d. $\frac{9}{10} - \frac{3}{10} =$ _____

17. Estimate. Is the sum or difference closest to 0, 1, or 2?

a. $\frac{1}{5} + \frac{1}{8}$ _____

b. $1\frac{2}{3} + \frac{1}{2}$ _____

c. $2\frac{1}{12} - \frac{9}{10}$ _____

d. $\frac{7}{8} - \frac{5}{6}$ _____

End-of-Year Assessment (cont.)

18. Add or subtract.

    a. $-5 + (-9) =$ _____   **b.** $-12 + 7 =$ _____

    c. $10 + (-4) =$ _____   **d.** $-8 + 8 =$ _____

    e. $-8 - (+7) =$ _____   **f.** $9 - (-3) =$ _____

    g. $-10 - (-2) =$ _____   **h.** $-7 - (-9) =$ _____

Use these formulas to calculate the areas of the figures below.

> Parallelogram:
>
> Area = base * height
>
> Triangle:
>
> Area = $\frac{1}{2}$ of (base * height)

19.

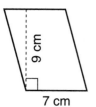

9 cm

7 cm

Area = _____

20.

4 in.

6 in.

Area = _____

21. What is the volume of the storage bin shown at the right?

    Volume = _____

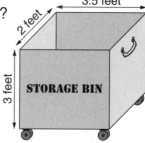

3.5 feet

2 feet

3 feet

STORAGE BIN

22. Which figure shows the original figure rotated counterclockwise $\frac{1}{4}$ turn?

_____

Original

A

B

C

End-of-Year Assessment (cont.)

23. Multiply. Show your work.

   a. 9 * 8.6 = _____   **b.** 0.37 * 5 = _____   **c.** _____ = 6.4 * 92

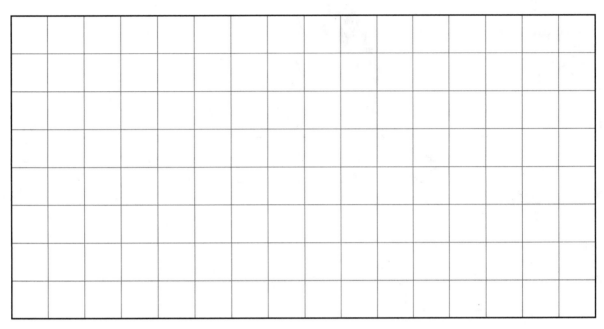

24. Divide. Show your work.

   a. 55.8 ÷ 6 = _____   **b.** 9.84 ÷ 8 = _____   **c.** _____ = 387.2 ÷ 4

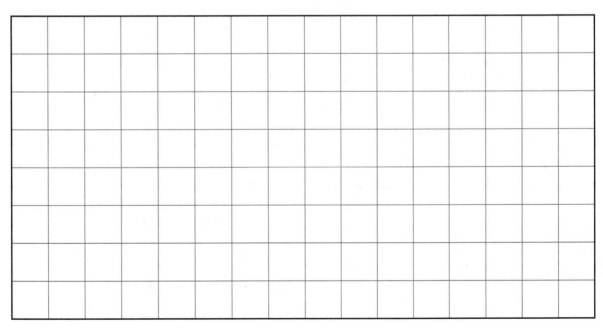

Class Checklist: Unit 1

Class _____

Dates _____

Learning Goals

1a Use a compass and straightedge to construct geometric figures.

1b Identify properties of polygons.

1c Classify quadrangles according to side and angle properties.

1d Name, draw and label line segments, lines, and rays.

1e Name, draw, and label angles, triangles, and quadrangles.

1f Identify and describe right angles, parallel lines, and line segments.

1g Solve addition and subtraction facts.

Students' Names	1a	1b	1c	1d	1e	1f	1g					
1.												
2.												
3.												
4.												
5.												
6.												
7.												
8.												
9.												
10.												
11.												
12.												
13.												
14.												
15.												
16.												
17.												
18.												
19.												
20.												
21.												
22.												
23.												
24.												
25.												
26.												
27.												
28.												
29.												
30.												

Use with Lesson 1.9.

Individual Profile of Progress: Unit 1

Check ✔				
B	**D**	**S**	**Learning Goals**	**Comments**
			1a Use a compass and straightedge to construct geometric figures.	
			1b Identify properties of polygons.	
			1c Classify quadrangles according to side and angle properties.	
			1d Name, draw, and label line segments, lines, and rays.	
			1e Name, draw, and label angles, triangles, and quadrangles.	
			1f Identify and describe right angles, parallel lines, and line segments.	
			1g Solve addition and subtraction facts.	

Notes to Parents

_____

_____

_____

_____

B = **B**eginning; **D** = **D**eveloping; **S** = **S**ecure

Class Checklist: Unit 2

Class _____

Dates _____

Learning Goals

Students' Names	2a Display data with a line plot, bar graph, or tally chart.	2b Use the statistical landmarks median, mode, and range.	2c Use the statistical landmarks maximum and minimum.	2d Have a successful strategy for subtracting multidigit numbers.	2e Have a successful strategy for adding multidigit numbers.	2f Read and write numerals to hundred-millions; give the value of the digits in numerals to hundred-millions.	2g Give equivalent names for numbers.					
1.												
2.												
3.												
4.												
5.												
6.												
7.												
8.												
9.												
10.												
11.												
12.												
13.												
14.												
15.												
16.												
17.												
18.												
19.												
20.												
21.												
22.												
23.												
24.												
25.												
26.												
27.												
28.												
29.												
30.												

Use with Lesson 2.10.

Individual Profile of Progress: Unit 2

Check ✔			Learning Goals	Comments
B	**D**	**S**		
			2a Display data with a line plot, bar graph, or tally chart.	
			2b Use the statistical landmarks median, mode, and range.	
			2c Use the statistical landmarks maximum and minimum.	
			2d Have a successful strategy for subtracting multidigit numbers.	
			2e Have a successful strategy for adding multidigit numbers.	
			2f Read and write numerals to hundred-millions; give the value of the digits in numerals to hundred-millions.	
			2g Give equivalent names for numbers.	

Notes to Parents

_____

_____

_____

_____

B = **B**eginning; **D** = **D**eveloping; **S** = **S**ecure

Class Checklist: Unit 3

Class _____

Dates _____

Students' Names	**Learning Goals**	3a Solve open sentences.	3b Insert parentheses to make true number sentences. Solve problems with parentheses.	3c Determine whether number sentences are true or false.	3d Use and explain strategies for solving addition and subtraction number stories.	3e Use a map scale to estimate distances.	3f Solve basic division facts.	3g Solve basic multiplication facts.	3h Understand the relationship between multiplication and division.				
1.													
2.													
3.													
4.													
5.													
6.													
7.													
8.													
9.													
10.													
11.													
12.													
13.													
14.													
15.													
16.													
17.													
18.													
19.													
20.													
21.													
22.													
23.													
24.													
25.													
26.													
27.													
28.													
29.													
30.													

Use with Lesson 3.12.

Individual Profile of Progress: Unit 3

Check ✔ B	D	S	Learning Goals	Comments
			3a Solve open sentences.	
			3b Insert parentheses to make true number sentences. Solve problems with parentheses.	
			3c Determine whether number sentences are true or false.	
			3d Use and explain strategies for solving addition and subtraction number stories.	
			3e Use a map scale to estimate distances.	
			3f Solve basic division facts.	
			3g Solve basic multiplication facts.	
			3h Understand the relationship between multiplication and division.	

Notes to Parents

_____

_____

_____

_____

B = **B**eginning; **D** = **D**eveloping; **S** = **S**ecure

Class Checklist: Unit 4

Class _____

Dates _____

Learning Goals

Students' Names	4a Express metric measures with decimals.	4b Convert between metric measures.	4c Read and write decimals to thousandths.	4d Compare and order decimals.	4e Draw and measure line segments to the nearest millimeter.	4f Use personal references to estimate lengths in metric units.	4g Solve 1- and 2-place decimal addition and subtraction problems and number stories.	4h Draw and measure line segments to the nearest centimeter.	4i Use dollars-and-cents notation.				
1.													
2.													
3.													
4.													
5.													
6.													
7.													
8.													
9.													
10.													
11.													
12.													
13.													
14.													
15.													
16.													
17.													
18.													
19.													
20.													
21.													
22.													
23.													
24.													
25.													
26.													
27.													
28.													
29.													
30.													

Use with Lesson 4.11.

Individual Profile of Progress: Unit 4

Check ✔			Learning Goals	Comments
B	**D**	**S**		
			4a Express metric measures with decimals.	
			4b Convert between metric measures.	
			4c Read and write decimals to thousandths.	
			4d Compare and order decimals.	
			4e Draw and measure line segments to the nearest millimeter.	
			4f Use personal references to estimate lengths in metric units.	
			4g Solve 1- and 2-place decimal addition and subtraction problems and number stories.	
			4h Draw and measure line segments to the nearest centimeter.	
			4i Use dollars-and-cents notation.	

Notes to Parents

_____

_____

_____

_____

B = **B**eginning; **D** = **D**eveloping; **S** = **S**ecure

Class Checklist: Unit 5

Class _____

Dates _____

Learning Goals

Students' Names	5a Use exponential notation to represent powers of 10.	5b Solve extended multiplication facts.	5c Make magnitude estimates for products of multidigit numbers.	5d Solve multidigit multiplication problems.	5e Round whole numbers to a given place.	5f Read and write numbers to billions; name the values of digits in numerals to billions.	5g Compare large numbers.	5h Estimate sums.			
1.											
2.											
3.											
4.											
5.											
6.											
7.											
8.											
9.											
10.											
11.											
12.											
13.											
14.											
15.											
16.											
17.											
18.											
19.											
20.											
21.											
22.											
23.											
24.											
25.											
26.											
27.											
28.											
29.											
30.											

Use with Lesson 5.12.

Individual Profile of Progress: Unit 5

Check ✔			Learning Goals	Comments
B	**D**	**S**		
			5a Use exponential notation to represent powers of 10.	
			5b Solve extended multiplication facts.	
			5c Make magnitude estimates for products of multidigit numbers.	
			5d Solve multidigit multiplication problems.	
			5e Round whole numbers to a given place.	
			5f Read and write numbers to billions; name the values of digits in numerals to billions.	
			5g Compare large numbers.	
			5h Estimate sums.	

Notes to Parents

_____

_____

_____

_____

B = **B**eginning; **D** = **D**eveloping; **S** = **S**ecure

Use with Lesson 5.12.   **435**

Class Checklist: Unit 6

Class _____

Dates _____

Learning Goals

6a Identify locations on Earth for which latitude and longitude are given; find latitude and longitude for given locations.

6b Have a successful strategy for solving whole-number division problems.

6c Express the remainder of a whole-number division problem as a fraction and the answer as a mixed number.

6d Interpret the remainder in division problems.

6e Name and locate points specified by ordered number pairs on a coordinate grid.

6f Identify acute, right, obtuse, straight, and reflex angles.

6g Make turns and fractions of turns; relate turns and angles.

6h Use a circular protractor and a half-circle protractor to measure and draw angles.

6i Use and explain strategies for solving multiplication and division number stories.

Students' Names	6a	6b	6c	6d	6e	6f	6g	6h	6i			
1.												
2.												
3.												
4.												
5.												
6.												
7.												
8.												
9.												
10.												
11.												
12.												
13.												
14.												
15.												
16.												
17.												
18.												
19.												
20.												
21.												
22.												
23.												
24.												
25.												
26.												
27.												
28.												
29.												
30.												

Use with Lesson 6.11.

Individual Profile of Progress: Unit 6

Check ✔			Learning Goals	Comments
B	**D**	**S**		
			6a Identify locations on Earth for which latitude and longitude are given; find latitude and longitude for given locations.	
			6b Have a successful strategy for solving whole-number division problems.	
			6c Express the remainder of a whole-number division problem as a fraction and the answer as a mixed number.	
			6d Interpret the remainder in division problems.	
			6e Name and locate points specified by ordered number pairs on a coordinate grid.	
			6f Identify acute, right, obtuse, straight, and reflex angles.	
			6g Make turns and fractions of turns; relate turns and angles.	
			6h Use a circular protractor and a half-circle protractor to measure and draw angles.	
			6i Use and explain strategies for solving multiplication and division number stories.	

Notes to Parents

_____

_____

_____

_____

B = **B**eginning; **D** = **D**eveloping; **S** = **S**ecure

Class Checklist: Unit 7

Class _____

Dates _____

Learning Goals

Students' Names	7a Add and subtract fractions.	7b Rename fractions with denominators of 10 and 100 as decimals.	7c Apply basic vocabulary and concepts associated with chance events.	7d Compare and order fractions.	7e Find fractions equivalent to a given fraction.	7f Identify the whole for fractions.	7g Identify fractional parts of a collection of objects.	7h Identify fractional parts of regions.				
1.												
2.												
3.												
4.												
5.												
6.												
7.												
8.												
9.												
10.												
11.												
12.												
13.												
14.												
15.												
16.												
17.												
18.												
19.												
20.												
21.												
22.												
23.												
24.												
25.												
26.												
27.												
28.												
29.												
30.												

Use with Lesson 7.13.

Individual Profile of Progress: Unit 7

Check ✔			Learning Goals	Comments
B	**D**	**S**		
▨			**7a** Add and subtract fractions.	
	▨		**7b** Rename fractions with denominators of 10 and 100 as decimals.	
	▨		**7c** Apply basic vocabulary and concepts associated with chance events.	
	▨		**7d** Compare and order fractions.	
	▨		**7e** Find fractions equivalent to a given fraction.	
		▨	**7f** Identify the whole for fractions.	
		▨	**7g** Identify fractional parts of a collection of objects.	
		▨	**7h** Identify fractional parts of regions.	

Notes to Parents

_____

_____

_____

_____

B = **B**eginning; **D** = **D**eveloping; **S** = **S**ecure

Class Checklist: Unit 8

Class _____

Dates _____

Students' Names	**Learning Goals**	8a Make and interpret scale drawings.	8b Use formulas to find areas of rectangles, parallelograms, and triangles.	8c Find the perimeter of a polygon.	8d Find the area of a figure by counting unit squares and fractions of unit squares inside the figure.								
1.													
2.													
3.													
4.													
5.													
6.													
7.													
8.													
9.													
10.													
11.													
12.													
13.													
14.													
15.													
16.													
17.													
18.													
19.													
20.													
21.													
22.													
23.													
24.													
25.													
26.													
27.													
28.													
29.													
30.													

Use with Lesson 8.9.

Individual Profile of Progress: Unit 8

| Check ✔ | | | | |
B	D	S	Learning Goals	Comments
			8a Make and interpret scale drawings.	
			8b Use formulas to find areas of rectangles, parallelograms, and triangles.	
			8c Find the perimeter of a polygon.	
			8d Find the area of a figure by counting unit squares and fractions of unit squares inside the figure.	

Notes to Parents

_____

_____

_____

_____

B = **B**eginning; **D** = **D**eveloping; **S** = **S**ecure

Class _____

Dates _____

Students' Names	**Learning Goals**	9a Use an estimation strategy to divide decimals by whole numbers.	9b Use an estimation strategy to multiply decimals by whole numbers.	9c Find a percent or a fraction of a number.	9d Give equivalencies between "easy" fractions (fourths, fifths, and tenths), decimals, and percents.	9e Give equivalencies between hundredths-fractions, decimals, and percents.	9f Use a calculator to rename any fraction as a decimal or percent.						
1.													
2.													
3.													
4.													
5.													
6.													
7.													
8.													
9.													
10.													
11.													
12.													
13.													
14.													
15.													
16.													
17.													
18.													
19.													
20.													
21.													
22.													
23.													
24.													
25.													
26.													
27.													
28.													
29.													
30.													

Use with Lesson 9.10.

Individual Profile of Progress: Unit 9

Check ✔			Learning Goals	Comments
B	**D**	**S**		
▨			**9a** Use an estimation strategy to divide decimals by whole numbers.	
▨			**9b** Use an estimation strategy to multiply decimals by whole numbers.	
	▨		**9c** Find a percent or a fraction of a number.	
	▨		**9d** Give equivalencies between "easy" fractions (fourths, fifths, and tenths), decimals, and percents.	
		▨	**9e** Give equivalencies between hundredths-fractions, decimals, and percents.	
		▨	**9f** Use a calculator to rename any fraction as a decimal or percent.	

Notes to Parents

_____

_____

_____

_____

B = **B**eginning; **D** = **D**eveloping; **S** = **S**ecure

Use with Lesson 9.10.

Class Checklist: Unit 10

Class _____

Dates _____

Students' Names	**Learning Goals**	10a Add integers.	10b Rotate figures.	10c Translate figures.	10d Use a transparent mirror to draw the reflection of a figure.	10e Identify lines of symmetry, lines of reflection, reflected figures, and figures with line symmetry.						
1.												
2.												
3.												
4.												
5.												
6.												
7.												
8.												
9.												
10.												
11.												
12.												
13.												
14.												
15.												
16.												
17.												
18.												
19.												
20.												
21.												
22.												
23.												
24.												
25.												
26.												
27.												
28.												
29.												
30.												

Use with Lesson 10.7.

Individual Profile of Progress: Unit 10

Check ✔			Learning Goals	Comments
B	**D**	**S**		
▨			**10a** Add integers.	
▨			**10b** Rotate figures.	
	▨		**10c** Translate figures.	
		▨	**10d** Use a transparent mirror to draw the reflection of a figure.	
		▨	**10e** Identify lines of symmetry, lines of reflection, reflected figures, and figures with line symmetry.	

Notes to Parents

_____

_____

_____

_____

B = **B**eginning; **D** = **D**eveloping; **S** = **S**ecure

Use with Lesson 10.7.

Class _____

Dates _____

Students' Names	**Learning Goals**	11a Use a formula to calculate volumes of rectangular prisms.	11b Subtract positive and negative integers.	11c Add positive and negative integers.	11d Estimate the weight of objects in ounces or grams; weigh objects in ounces or grams.	11e Solve cube-stacking volume problems.	11f Describe properties of geometric solids.						
1.													
2.													
3.													
4.													
5.													
6.													
7.													
8.													
9.													
10.													
11.													
12.													
13.													
14.													
15.													
16.													
17.													
18.													
19.													
20.													
21.													
22.													
23.													
24.													
25.													
26.													
27.													
28.													
29.													
30.													

Student's Name   Date

Check ✔				
B	**D**	**S**	**Learning Goals**	**Comments**
			11a Use a formula to calculate volumes of rectangular prisms.	
			11b Subtract positive and negative integers.	
			11c Add positive and negative integers.	
			11d Estimate the weight of objects in ounces or grams; weigh objects in ounces or grams.	
			11e Solve cube-stacking volume problems.	
			11f Describe properties of geometric solids.	

Notes to Parents

_____

_____

_____

_____

B = **B**eginning; **D** = **D**eveloping; **S** = **S**ecure

Use with Lesson 11.8.   **447**

Class _____

Dates _____

Learning Goals

12a Find unit rates.

12b Calculate unit prices to determine which product is the "better buy."

12c Evaluate reasonableness of rate data.

12d Collect and compare rate data.

12e Use rate tables, if necessary, to solve rate problems.

Students' Names

	12a	12b	12c	12d	12e						
1.											
2.											
3.											
4.											
5.											
6.											
7.											
8.											
9.											
10.											
11.											
12.											
13.											
14.											
15.											
16.											
17.											
18.											
19.											
20.											
21.											
22.											
23.											
24.											
25.											
26.											
27.											
28.											
29.											
30.											

Use with Lesson 12.7.

Individual Profile of Progress: Unit 12

Check ✔			Learning Goals	Comments
B	D	S		
			12a Find unit rates.	
			12b Calculate unit prices to determine which product is the "better buy."	
			12c Evaluate reasonableness of rate data.	
			12d Collect and compare rate data.	
			12e Use rate tables, if necessary, to solve rate problems.	

Notes to Parents

_____

_____

_____

_____

B = **B**eginning; **D** = **D**eveloping; **S** = **S**ecure

Use with Lesson 12.7 .

Class _____

Dates _____

Learning Goals

1. Solve addition and subtraction facts. (1g)
2. Have a successful strategy for subtracting multidigit numbers. (2d)
3. Have a successful strategy for adding multidigit numbers. (2e)
4. Read and write numerals to hundred-millions; give the value of the digits in numerals to hundred-millions. (2l)
5. Give equivalent names for numbers. (2g)
6. Solve open sentences. (3a)
7. Insert parentheses to make true number sentences. Solve problems with parentheses. (3b)
8. Determine whether number sentences are true or false. (3c)
9. Use and explain strategies for solving addition and subtraction number stories. (3d)
10. Solve basic division facts. (3f)
11. Solve basic multiplication facts. (3g)
12. Understand the relationship between multiplication and division. (3h)

Students' Names

	1.	2.	3.	4.	5.	6.	7.	8.	9.	10.	11.	12.
1.												
2.												
3.												
4.												
5.												
6.												
7.												
8.												
9.												
10.												
11.												
12.												
13.												
14.												
15.												
16.												
17.												
18.												
19.												
20.												
21.												
22.												
23.												
24.												
25.												
26.												
27.												
28.												
29.												
30.												

Class _____

Dates _____

Learning Goals

Students' Names	13. Name, draw, and label line segments, lines, and rays. **(1d)**	14. Name, draw, and label angles, triangles, and quadrangles. **(1e)**	15. Identify and label right angles, parallel lines, and line segments. **(1f)**	16. Identify properties of polygons. **(1b)**	17. Classify quadrangles according to side and angle properties. **(1c)**	18. Use a compass and straightedge to construct geometric figures. **(1a)**	19. Use a map scale to estimate distances. **(3e)**	20. Use the statistical landmarks maximum and minimum. **(2c)**	21. Display data with a line plot, bar graph, or tally chart. **(2a)**	22. Use the statistical landmarks median, mode, and range. **(2b)**		
1.												
2.												
3.												
4.												
5.												
6.												
7.												
8.												
9.												
10.												
11.												
12.												
13.												
14.												
15.												
16.												
17.												
18.												
19.												
20.												
21.												
22.												
23.												
24.												
25.												
26.												
27.												
28.												
29.												
30.												

Individual Profile of Progress: 1st Quarter

Check ✔			Learning Goals	Comments
B	**D**	**S**		
			1. Solve addition and subtraction facts. **(1g)**	
			2. Have a successful strategy for subtracting multidigit numbers. **(2d)**	
			3. Have a successful strategy for adding multidigit numbers. **(2e)**	
			4. Read and write numerals to hundred-millions; give the value of the digits in numerals to hundred-millions. **(2f)**	
			5. Give equivalent names for numbers. **(2g)**	
			6. Solve open sentences. **(3a)**	
			7. Insert parentheses to make true number sentences. Solve problems with parentheses. **(3b)**	
			8. Determine whether number sentences are true or false. **(3c)**	
			9. Use and explain strategies for solving addition and subtraction number stories. **(3d)**	
			10. Solve basic division facts. **(3f)**	
			11. Solve basic multiplication facts. **(3g)**	
			12. Understand the relationship between multiplication and division. **(3h)**	
			13. Name, draw, and label line segments, lines, and rays. **(1d)**	
			14. Name, draw, and label angles, triangles, and quadrangles. **(1e)**	
			15. Identify and describe right angles, parallel lines, and line segments. **(1f)**	
			16. Identify properties of polygons. **(1b)**	
			17. Classify quadrangles according to side and angle properties. **(1c)**	
			18. Use a compass and straightedge to construct geometric figures. **(1a)**	

B = **B**eginning; **D** = **D**eveloping; **S** = **S**ecure

Individual Profile of Progress: 1st Quarter

Check ✔			Learning Goals	Comments
B	**D**	**S**		
			19. Use a map scale to estimate distances. **(3e)**	
			20. Use the statistical landmarks maximum and minimum. **(2c)**	
			21. Display data with a line plot, bar graph, or tally chart. **(2a)**	
			22. Use the statistical landmarks median, mode, and range. **(2b)**	

Notes to Parents

_____

_____

_____

_____

B = **B**eginning; **D** = **D**eveloping; **S** = **S**ecure

Class _____

Dates _____

Learning Goals

1. Use dollars-and-cents notation. **(4i)**
2. Compare large numbers. **(5g)**
3. Estimate sums. **(5h)**
4. Read and write decimals to thousandths. **(4c)**
5. Compare and order decimals. **(4d)**
6. Solve 1- and 2-place decimal addition and subtraction problems and number stories. **(4g)**
7. Solve extended multiplication facts. **(5b)**
8. Make magnitude estimates for products of multidigit numbers. **(5c)**
9. Solve multidigit multiplication problems. **(5d)**
10. Round whole numbers to a given place. **(5e)**
11. Read and write numbers to billions; name the values of digits in numerals to billions. **(5f)**
12. Have a successful strategy for solving whole-number division problems. **(6b)**
13. Express the remainder of a whole-number division problem as a fraction and the answer as a mixed number. **(6c)**
14. Interpret the remainder in division problems. **(6d)**

Students' Names

	1.	2.	3.	4.	5.	6.	7.	8.	9.	10.	11.	12.	13.	14.
1.														
2.														
3.														
4.														
5.														
6.														
7.														
8.														
9.														
10.														
11.														
12.														
13.														
14.														
15.														
16.														
17.														
18.														
19.														
20.														
21.														
22.														
23.														
24.														
25.														
26.														
27.														
28.														
29.														
30.														

Use with Lesson 6.11.

Class _____

Dates _____

Students' Names	**Learning Goals**	15. Use and explain strategies for solving multiplication and division number stories. **(6i)**	16. Use exponential notation to represent powers of 10. **(5a)**	17. Draw and measure line segments to the nearest centimeter. **(4h)**	18. Express metric measures with decimals. **(4a)**	19. Convert between metric measures. **(4b)**	20. Draw and measure line segments to the nearest millimeter. **(4e)**	21. Use personal references to estimate lengths in metric units. **(4f)**	22. Identify locations on Earth for which latitude and longitude are given; find latitude and longitude for given locations. **(6a)**	23. Name and locate points specified by ordered number pairs on a coordinate grid. **(6e)**	24. Identify acute, right, obtuse, straight, and reflex angles. **(6i)**	25. Make turns and fractions of turns; relate turns and angles. **(6g)**	26. Use a circular protractor and a half-circle protractor to measure and draw angles. **(6h)**	
1.														
2.														
3.														
4.														
5.														
6.														
7.														
8.														
9.														
10.														
11.														
12.														
13.														
14.														
15.														
16.														
17.														
18.														
19.														
20.														
21.														
22.														
23.														
24.														
25.														
26.														
27.														
28.														
29.														
30.														

Individual Profile of Progress: 2nd Quarter

Check ✔				
B	**D**	**S**	**Learning Goals**	**Comments**
			1. Use dollars-and-cents notation. **(4i)**	
			2. Compare large numbers. **(5g)**	
			3. Estimate sums. **(5h)**	
			4. Read and write decimals to thousandths. **(4c)**	
			5. Compare and order decimals. **(4d)**	
			6. Solve 1- and 2-place decimal addition and subtraction problems and number stories. **(4g)**	
			7. Solve extended multiplication facts. **(5b)**	
			8. Make magnitude estimates for products of multidigit numbers. **(5c)**	
			9. Solve multidigit multiplication problems. **(5d)**	
			10. Round whole numbers to a given place. **(5e)**	
			11. Read and write numbers to billions; name the values of digits in numerals to billions. **(5f)**	
			12. Have a successful strategy for solving whole-number division problems. **(6b)**	
			13. Express the remainder of a whole-number division problem as a fraction and the answer as a mixed number. **(6c)**	
			14. Interpret the remainder in division problems. **(6d)**	
			15. Use and explain strategies for solving multiplication and division number stories. **(6i)**	
			16. Use exponential notation to represent powers of 10. **(5a)**	
			17. Draw and measure line segments to the nearest centimeter. **(4h)**	
			18. Express metric measures with decimals. **(4a)**	

B = **B**eginning; **D** = **D**eveloping; **S** = **S**ecure

Use with Lesson 6.11.

Individual Profile of Progress: 2nd Quarter

Check ✔			Learning Goals	Comments
B	**D**	**S**		
			19. Convert between metric measures. **(4b)**	
			20. Draw and measure line segments to the nearest millimeter. **(4e)**	
			21. Use personal references to estimate lengths in metric units. **(4f)**	
			22. Identify locations on Earth for which latitude and longitude are given; find latitude and longitude for given locations. **(6a)**	
			23. Name and locate points specified by ordered number pairs on a coordinate grid. **(6e)**	
			24. Identify acute, right, obtuse, straight, and reflex angles. **(6f)**	
			25. Make turns and fractions of turns; relate turns and angles. **(6g)**	
			26. Use a circular protractor and a half-circle protractor to measure and draw angles. **(6h)**	

Notes to Parents

_____

_____

_____

_____

B = **B**eginning; **D** = **D**eveloping; **S** = **S**ecure

Class _____

Dates _____

Students' Names	**Learning Goals**	1. Identify the whole for fractions. **(7f)**	2. Identify fractional parts of a collection of objects. **(7g)**	3. Identify fractional parts of regions. **(7h)**	4. Give equivalencies between hundredths-fractions, decimals, and percents. **(9e)**	5. Use a calculator to rename any fraction as a decimal or percent. **(9f)**	6. Rename fractions with denominators of 10 and 100 as decimals. **(7b)**	7. Compare and order fractions. **(7d)**	8. Find fractions equivalent to a given fraction. **(7e)**	9. Find a percent or a fraction of a number. **(9c)**	10. Give equivalencies between "easy" fractions (fourths, fifths, and tenths) decimals, and percents. **(9d)**	11. Add and subtract fractions. **(7a)**	
1.													
2.													
3.													
4.													
5.													
6.													
7.													
8.													
9.													
10.													
11.													
12.													
13.													
14.													
15.													
16.													
17.													
18.													
19.													
20.													
21.													
22.													
23.													
24.													
25.													
26.													
27.													
28.													
29.													
30.													

Use with Lesson 9.10.

Class _____

Dates _____

Learning Goals

12. Use an estimation strategy to divide decimals by whole numbers. **(9a)**
13. Use an estimation strategy to multiply decimals by whole numbers. **(9b)**
14. Apply basic vocabulary and concepts associated with chance events. **(7c)**
15. Use formulas to find areas of rectangles, parallelograms, and triangles. **(8b)**
16. Find the perimeter of a polygon. **(8c)**
17. Find the area of a figure by counting unit squares and fractions of unit squares inside the figure. **(8d)**
18. Make and interpret scale drawings. **(8a)**

Students' Names

	12.	13.	14.	15.	16.	17.	18.					
1.												
2.												
3.												
4.												
5.												
6.												
7.												
8.												
9.												
10.												
11.												
12.												
13.												
14.												
15.												
16.												
17.												
18.												
19.												
20.												
21.												
22.												
23.												
24.												
25.												
26.												
27.												
28.												
29.												
30.												

Use with Lesson 9.10.

Individual Profile of Progress: 3rd Quarter

Check ✔			Learning Goals	Comments
B	**D**	**S**		
			1. Identify the whole for fractions. **(7f)**	
			2. Identify fractional parts of a collection of objects. **(7g)**	
			3. Identify fractional parts of regions. **(7h)**	
			4. Give equivalencies between hundredths-fractions, decimals, and percents. **(9e)**	
			5. Use a calculator to rename any fraction as a decimal or percent. **(9f)**	
			6. Rename fractions with denominators of 10 and 100 as decimals. **(7b)**	
			7. Compare and order fractions. **(7d)**	
			8. Find fractions equivalent to a given fraction. **(7e)**	
			9. Find a percent or a fraction of a number. **(9c)**	
			10. Give equivalencies between "easy" fractions (fourths, fifths, and tenths), decimals, and percents. **(9d)**	
			11. Add and subtract fractions. **(7a)**	
			12. Use an estimation strategy to divide decimals by whole numbers. **(9a)**	
			13. Use an estimation strategy to multiply decimals by whole numbers. **(9b)**	
			14. Apply basic vocabulary and concepts associated with chance events. **(7c)**	
			15. Use formulas to find areas of rectangles, parallelograms, and triangles. **(8b)**	
			16. Find the perimeter of a polygon. **(8c)**	
			17. Find the area of a figure by counting unit squares and fractions of unit squares inside the figure. **(8d)**	
			18. Make and interpret scale drawings. **(8a)**	

B = **B**eginning; **D** = **D**eveloping; **S** = **S**ecure

Use with Lesson 9.10.

Class _____

Dates _____

Learning Goals

1. Add positive and negative integers. **(10a and 11c)**
2. Subtract positive and negative integers. **(11b)**
3. Use rate tables, if necessary, to solve rate problems. **(12e)**
4. Find unit rates. **(12a)**
5. Calculate unit prices to determine which product is the "better buy." **(12b)**
6. Evaluate reasonableness of rate data. **(12c)**
7. Collect and compare rate data. **(12d)**
8. Use a transparent mirror to draw the reflection of a figure. **(10d)**
9. Identify lines of symmetry, lines of reflection, reflected figures, and figures with line symmetry. **(10e)**
10. Translate figures. **(10c)**
11. Describe properties of geometric solids. **(11f)**

Students' Names	1.	2.	3.	4.	5.	6.	7.	8.	9.	10.	11.
1.											
2.											
3.											
4.											
5.											
6.											
7.											
8.											
9.											
10.											
11.											
12.											
13.											
14.											
15.											
16.											
17.											
18.											
19.											
20.											
21.											
22.											
23.											
24.											
25.											
26.											
27.											
28.											
29.											
30.											

Use with Lesson 12.7.

Class _____

Dates _____

Students' Names	Learning Goals	12. Rotate figures. (10b)	13. Estimate the weight of objects in ounces or grams; weigh objects in ounces or grams. (11d)	14. Solve cube-stacking volume problems. (11e)	15. Use a formula to calculate volumes of rectangular prisms. (11a)									
1.														
2.														
3.														
4.														
5.														
6.														
7.														
8.														
9.														
10.														
11.														
12.														
13.														
14.														
15.														
16.														
17.														
18.														
19.														
20.														
21.														
22.														
23.														
24.														
25.														
26.														
27.														
28.														
29.														
30.														

Use with Lesson 12.7.

Individual Profile of Progress: 4th Quarter

Check ✔				
B	**D**	**S**	**Learning Goals**	**Comments**
			1. Add positive and negative integers. **(10a and 11c)**	
			2. Subtract positive and negative integers. **(11b)**	
			3. Use rate tables, if necessary, to solve rate problems. **(12e)**	
			4. Find unit rates. **(12a)**	
			5. Calculate unit prices to determine which product is the "better buy." **(12b)**	
			6. Evaluate reasonableness of rate data. **(12c)**	
			7. Collect and compare rate data. **(12d)**	
			8. Use a transparent mirror to draw the reflection of a figure. **(10d)**	
			9. Identify lines of symmetry, lines of reflection, reflected figures, and figures with line symmetry. **(10e)**	
			10. Translate figures. **(10c)**	
			11. Describe properties of geometric solids. **(11f)**	
			12. Rotate figures. **(10b)**	
			13. Estimate the weight of objects in ounces or grams; weigh objects in ounces or grams. **(11d)**	
			14. Solve cube-stacking volume problems. **(11e)**	
			15. Use a formula to calculate volumes of rectangular prisms. **(11a)**	

Notes to Parents

_____

_____

_____

B = **B**eginning; **D** = **D**eveloping; **S** = **S**ecure

Ongoing Assessment

_____

_____

_____

_____

Product Assessment

_____

_____

_____

_____

Periodic Assessment

_____

_____

_____

_____

Outside Tests

_____

_____

_____

_____

Other

_____

_____

_____

_____

Use as needed.

Student's Name   Date

Individual Profile of Progress

| Check ✔ | | | | |
B	D	S	Learning Goals	Comments
			1.	
			2.	
			3.	
			4.	
			5.	
			6.	
			7.	
			8.	
			9.	
			10.	

Notes to Parents

_____

_____

_____

_____

_____

_____

_____

_____

© 2002 Everyday Learning Corporation

B = **B**eginning; **D** = **D**eveloping; **S** = **S**ecure

Use as needed.   **465**

Class Checklist

Class _____

Dates _____

Learning Goals

Students' Names

1.											
2.											
3.											
4.											
5.											
6.											
7.											
8.											
9.											
10.											
11.											
12.											
13.											
14.											
15.											
16.											
17.											
18.											
19.											
20.											
21.											
22.											
23.											
24.											
25.											
26.											
27.											
28.											
29.											
30.											

Use as needed.

Mathematical Topic Being Assessed: _____

	BEGINNING	DEVELOPING OR DEVELOPING+	SECURE OR SECURE+
First Assessment After Lesson: _____ Dates included: _____ to _____			
Second Assessment After Lesson: _____ Dates included: _____ to _____			
Third Assessment After Lesson: _____ Dates included: _____ to _____			

Notes

_____

_____

_____

_____

Use as needed.

Evaluating My Math Class

Interest Inventory

Dislike a Lot	Dislike	Neither Like nor Dislike	Like	Like a Lot
1	2	3	4	5

Use the scale above to describe how you feel about:

1. your math class. _____

2. working with a partner or in a group. _____

3. working by yourself. _____

4. solving problems. _____

5. making up problems for others to solve. _____

6. finding new ways to solve problems. _____

7. challenges in math class. _____

8. playing mathematical games. _____

9. working on Study Links. _____

10. working on projects that take
more than a day to complete. _____

11. Which math lesson has been your favorite so far? Why?

_____

_____

_____

_____

_____

_____

_____

Use as needed.

My Math Class

Interest Inventory

1. In math class, I am good at _____

_____

_____

_____ .

2. One thing I like about math is _____

_____

_____

_____ .

3. One thing I find difficult in mathematics class is _____

_____

_____

_____ .

4. The most interesting thing I have learned in math so far this year is _____

_____

_____

_____ .

5. Outside school, I used mathematics when I _____

_____

_____

_____ .

6. I would like to know more about _____

_____

_____

_____ .

Use as needed.

Weekly Math Log

1. What did you study in math this week?

_____

_____

_____

_____

_____

_____

_____

2. Many ideas in math are related to other ideas within math. Think about how the topic(s) you studied in class this week relate to other topics you learned before.

Your reflection can include what you learned in previous years.

_____

_____

_____

_____

_____

_____

_____

_____

_____

_____

Math Log

Number-Story Math Log

1. Write an easy number story that uses mathematical
ideas that you have studied recently. Solve the problem.

Number Story _____

_____

_____

_____

Solution _____

_____

_____

_____

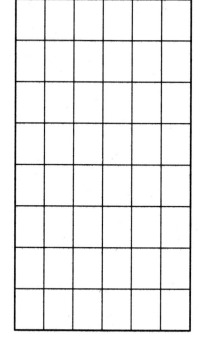

2. Write a difficult number story that uses mathematical
ideas that you have studied recently. If you can, solve
the number story. If you are not able to solve it,
explain what you need to know to solve it.

Number Story _____

_____

_____

_____

Solution _____

_____

_____

_____

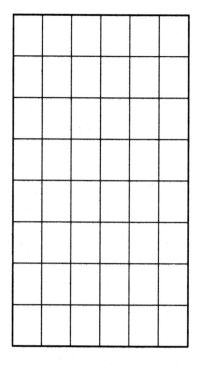

Use as needed.

Sample Math Work

Self-Assessment

Attach a sample of your work to this form.

1. This work is an example of:

_____

_____

_____

_____

_____

_____

2. This work shows that I can:

_____

_____

_____

_____

_____

_____

_____

OPTIONAL

3. This work shows that I still need to improve:

_____

_____

_____

_____

_____

_____

_____

Discussion of My Math Work

Self-Assessment

Attach a sample of your work to this page. Tell what you think is important about your sample.

_____

_____

_____

_____

_____

_____

_____

_____

_____

_____

_____

_____

_____

_____

_____

_____

_____

_____

Use as needed.

Name   Date   Time

Exit Slip

Name   Date   Time

Exit Slip

Use as needed.

Arithmetic Training: Auto Mode

Solving Problems that the Calculator Gives You

Pressing ◉ puts your calculator into Arithmetic Training: Auto Mode. In Auto mode, the calculator displays a problem for you to solve. The calculator tells you if you are correct and gives hints (> or <) if you are wrong. You have up to three tries for each problem.

After every five problems, the calculator shows a scoreboard with the number of problems you have solved correctly and incorrectly. You can see your scoreboard at any time by pressing (Mode) once. Press (Mode) again to return to the problems. To exit from arithmetic-training mode, press ◉.

1. Press ◉ to enter arithmetic-training mode. Practice 10 basic addition facts. Press ◉ to leave arithmetic-training mode.

2. Complete the following scoreboard for the for the 10 basic addition facts you solved:

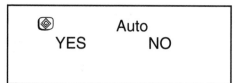

Changing the Kind of Problem that the Calculator Gives You

The calculator has menus for changing the kind of problems it gives you. In each menu, the current choice is underlined. Use ⬅ and ➡ to go to a different choice. Then press (Enter) to make your new choice active. (If you don't press (Enter), then the old menu choice will still be active.) Press (Mode) to go back to the problems.

The following table shows how to control the kind of problems the calculator gives you:

Key Sequence	Menu	Function
◉ (Mode) (pause)	◆ Auto **AUTO** MAN	**Choose the mode.** In AUTO mode, the calculator makes up the problems. In MAN mode, you make up the problems. Press ➡ (Enter) to change from AUTO to MAN. Press ⬅ (Enter) to change from MAN to AUTO.
⬇	◆ Auto 1̲ 2 3 ... ▥ ▦	**Choose the level of difficulty.** Level 1 problems are the easiest; level 3 the hardest. Press ➡, ⬅, and (Enter) to change levels.
⬇	◆ Auto ±̲ − × ÷ ?	**Choose the operation.** Press ➡, ⬅, and (Enter) to change operations. If you choose ?, the calculator will give you problems with missing operations.

Arithmetic Training: Auto Mode (cont.)

The following example shows you how to set the calculator for multiplication problems at the medium level of difficulty:

Example

Key Sequence	Display
◎ (Mode) (pause) ⬇ ⮕ (Enter)	◆ Auto 1 2̲ 3 ... ꠸ ꠸꠸
⬇ ⮕ ⮕ (Enter)	◆ Auto + − ×̲ ÷ ?
(Mode)	◆ Auto 9 X ? = 720

3. Solve 10 subtraction problems at the medium level of difficulty. Use only the AUTO mode. (You will learn how to use the MAN mode on *Math Masters,* page 478.)

   a. Press ◎ (Mode) to be sure the calculator is in AUTO mode.

   b. Press ⬇ ⮕ (Enter) to select 2, the medium level of difficulty.

   c. Press ⬇ ⮕ (Enter) to select −, subtraction.

   d. Press (Mode). Solve 10 extended subtraction fact problems.

   e. Press ◎ to leave arithmetic-training mode.

4. Complete the following scoreboard for the 10 subtraction problems you solved:

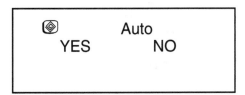

5. Set the calculator for problems that would be good practice for you. Refer to the table on *Math Masters,* page 476 to remind you which keys to press.

   a. Be sure the calculator is in AUTO mode.

   b. Choose the problem difficulty.

   c. Choose the operation.

Arithmetic Training: Manual Mode

Making Up Your Own Problems to Solve

In Arithmetic Training: Manual Mode, you make up your own problems to solve.
Use ⟨?⟩ for a missing number or operation. The calculator tells you how many solutions
your problem has. (Only whole numbers are allowed.) To exit from arithmetic-training
mode, press ⟨◈⟩.

Example

Key Sequence	Display
⟨◈⟩ ⟨Mode⟩ (pause) ⟨⇨⟩ ⟨Enter⟩	◆ AUTO MAN
⟨Mode⟩ 84 − ⟨?⟩ ⟨Enter⟩ 76 ⟨Enter⟩	◆ 84 − ? = 76 1 SOL
	◆ 84 − ? = 76
8 ⟨Enter⟩	◆ 84 − 8 = 76 YES

Set your calculator for MAN-mode arithmetic training.

1. Enter the following problems and then solve them:

    a. 123 × 2 = ?   **b.** 7 × ? = 42   **c.** 140 ? 5 = 28

Testing whether Inequalities Are True or False

In Manual mode, you can use ⟨◇⟩ to test whether an inequality is true or not. You can
use decimals in inequalities in Manual mode. Press ⟨◇⟩ to get <. Press ⟨◇⟩ ⟨◇⟩ to get >.

Example

Key Sequence	Display
⟨◈⟩ ⟨Mode⟩ (pause) ⟨⇨⟩ ⟨Enter⟩	◆ AUTO MAN
⟨Mode⟩ 1 ⟨·⟩ 75 ⟨◇⟩ 1 ⟨Enter⟩	◆ 1.75 < 1 NO

2. Use the calculator to test the following inequalities:

    a. 15 < 15.00   **b.** 2.1 < 2.01   **c.** 3.04 > 30.4

Place Value

Using the Manual Mode to Practice Place Value

When the calculator is in MAN-mode of arithmetic training, you can use ▦ to practice place value. You enter a number, press ▦, and then press one of the red place-value keys (1000, 100, and so on). The calculator will tell how many units of that value are in the number. Press Clear to enter another number. To exit from place-value mode, press Clear. To exit from arithmetic-training mode, press ◈.

Example

Key Sequence	Display	Explanation
◈ Mode (pause) ⇨ Enter	◈ AUTO MAN	
Mode 123 ⊡ 456 ▦	◈ ▦. 123.456	
10.	◈ ▦. 123.456 12_.___	There are 12 tens in the number 123.456.

Using the Manual Mode to Find Place Value

You can set the calculator so that it will tell the place value of a digit in a number and also what digit is in a given place in a number.

Example

Key Sequence	Display	Explanation
◈ Mode (pause) ⇨ Enter	◈ AUTO MAN	
⬇ ⇨ Enter	◈ ‖‖-. -|-. ▦ ۱ .	
Mode 123 ⊡ 456 ▦	◈ ▦. 123.456	
0.01	◈ ▦. 123.456 ___._5_	The digit 5 is in the hundredths place.
4	◈ ▦. 123.456 ___.4__	The digit 4 is in the tenths place.
	◈ ▦. 123.456 4→0.1	There are 4 tenths in the number 123.456.

1. Enter 987.654. What digit is in the 10s place? _____

2. In the number 987.654, what is the place value of the digit 5? _____

Seega Game Mat

Player 1

Player 2

Sz'kwa Game Mat

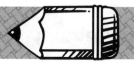

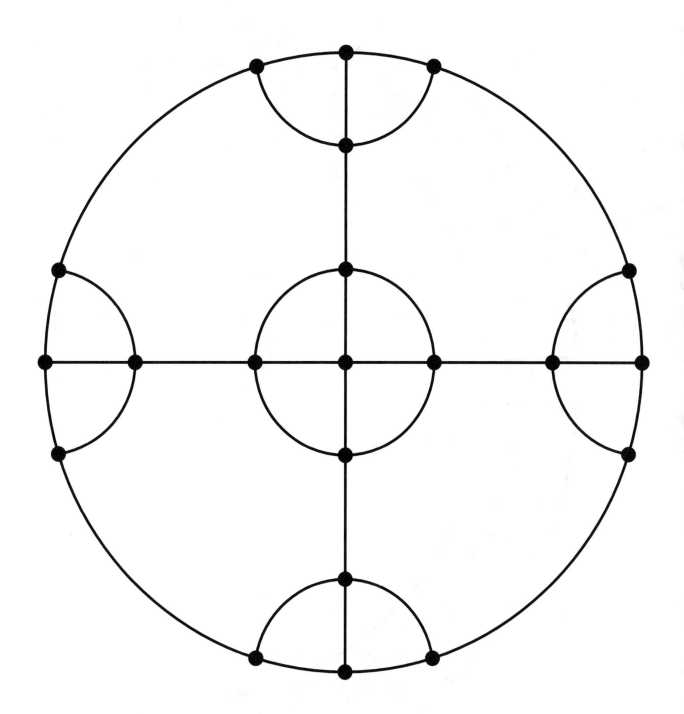

Alleyway Game Mat

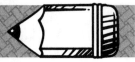

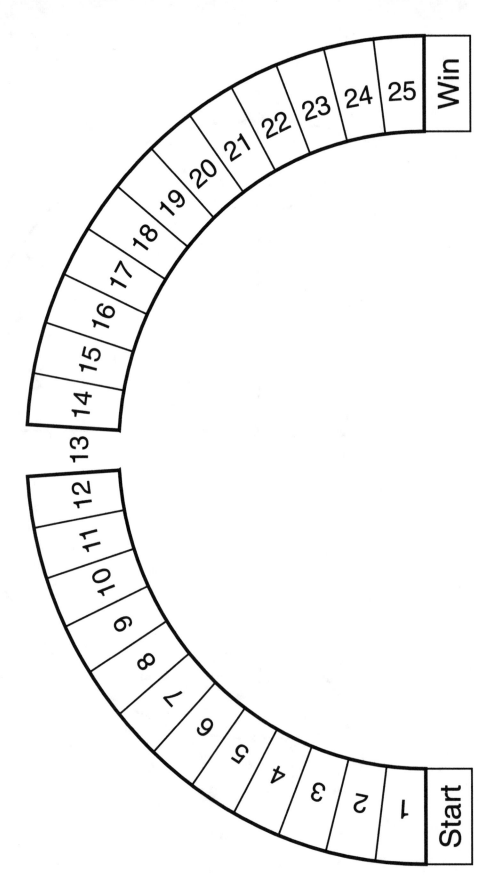

© 2002 Everyday Learning Corporation

Patolli Game Mat

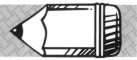

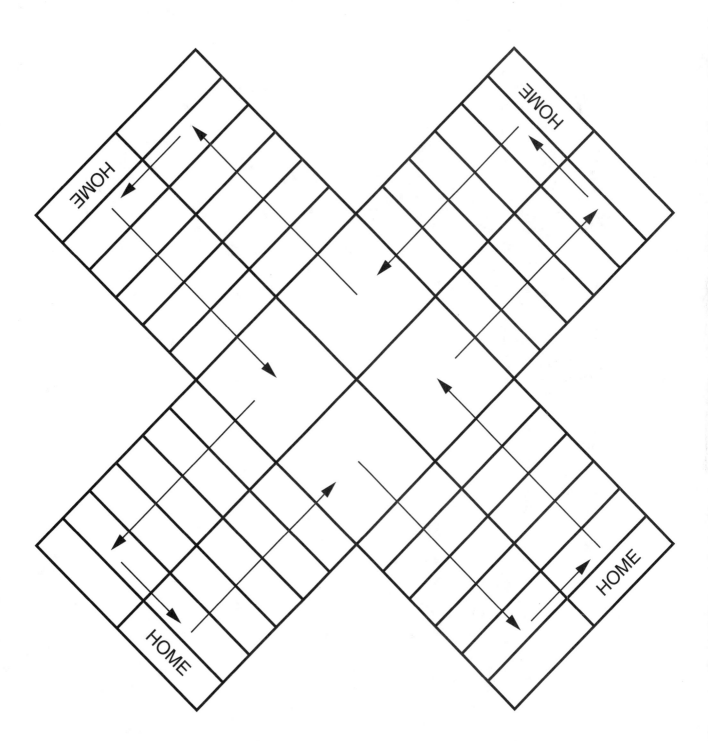